OUTLOOK 2003 PERSONAL TRAINER

CustomGuide, Inc.

O'REILLY®

Beijing • Cambridge • Farnham • Köln • Paris • Sebastopol • Taipei • Tokyo

Outlook 2003 Personal Trainer

by CustomGuide, Inc.

Published by O'Reilly Media, Inc., 1005 Gravenstein Highway
North, Sebastopol, CA 95472.

O'Reilly books may be purchased for educational, business, or
sales promotional use. Online editions are also available for
most titles (*safari.oreilly.com*). For more information, contact
our corporate/institutional sales department: (800) 998-9938
or *corporate@oreilly.com*.

Editor	Michele Filshie
Production Editor	Mary Brady
Art Director	Michele Wetherbee
Cover Designer	Emma Colby
Cover Illustrator	Lou Brooks
Interior Designer	Melanie Wang

Printing History

February 2005:	First Edition.

RepKover™ This book uses RepKover™, a durable and flexible lay-flat binding.

ISBN: 0-596-00935-6

[C]

CONTENTS

Contents

Contents

About CustomGuide, Inc.

CustomGuide, Inc. (*http://www.customguide.com*) is a leading provider of training materials and e-learning for organizations; their client list includes Harvard, Yale, and Oxford universities. CustomGuide was founded by a small group of instructors who were dissatisfied by the dry and technical nature of computer training materials available to trainers and educators. They decided to write their own series of courseware that would be fun and user-friendly; and best of all, they would license it in electronic format so instructors could print only the topics they needed for a class or training session. Later, they found themselves unhappy with the e-learning industry and decided to create a new series of online, interactive training that matched their courseware. Today employees, students, and instructors at more than 2,000 organizations worldwide use CustomGuide courseware to help teach and learn about computers.

CustomGuide, Inc. Staff and Contributors

Jonathan High	President	Jeremy Weaver	Senior Programmer
Daniel High	Vice President of Sales and Marketing	Luke Davidson	Programmer
		Lisa Price	Director of Business Development
Melissa Peterson	Senior Writer/Editor	Soda Rajsombath	Office Manager and Sales Representative
Kitty Rogers	Writer/Editor		
Stephen Meinz	Writer/Editor	Megan Diemand	Sales Representative
Stan Keathly	Senior Developer	Hallie Stork	Sales Representative
Jeffrey High	Developer	Sarah Saeger	Sales Support
Chris Kannenman	Developer	Julie Geisler	Narrator

INTRODUCTION

About the Personal Trainer Series

Most software manuals are as hard to navigate as the programs they describe. They assume that you're going to read all 500 pages from start to finish, and that you can gain intimate familiarity with the program simply by reading about it. Some books give you sample files to practice on, but when you're finding your way around a new set of skills, it's all too easy to mess up program settings or delete data files and not know how to recover. Even if William Shakespeare and Bill Gates teamed up to write a book about Microsoft Outlook, their book would be frustrating to read because most people learn by doing the task.

While we don't claim to be rivals to either Bill, we think we have a winning formula in the Personal Trainer series. We've created a set of workouts that reflect the tasks you really want to do, whether as simple as resizing or as complex as integrating multimedia components. Each workout breaks a task into a series of simple steps, showing you exactly what to do to accomplish the task.

And instead of leaving you hanging, the interactive CD in the back of this book recreates the application for you to experiment in. In our unique simulator, there's no worry about permanently damaging your preferences, turning all your documents purple, losing data, or any of the other things that can go wrong when you're testing your new skills in the unforgiving world of the real application. It's fully interactive, giving you feedback and guidance as you work through the exercises—just like a real trainer!

Our friendly guides will help you buff up your skills in record time. You'll learn the secrets of the professionals in a safe environment, with exercises and homework for those of you who really want to break the pain barrier. You'll have your Outlook 2003 skills in shape in no time!

About This Book

We've aimed this book at Outlook 2003. Some features may look different or simply not exist if you're using another version of the program. If our simulator doesn't match your application, check the version number to make sure you're using the right version.

Since this is a hands-on course, each lesson contains an exercise with step-by-step instructions for you to follow.

To make learning easier, every exercise follows certain conventions:

- This book never assumes you know where (or what) something is. The first time you're told to click something, a picture of what you're supposed to click appears in the illustrations in the lesson.
- When you see a keyboard instruction like "press Ctrl + B," you should press and hold the first key ("Ctrl" in this example) while you press the second key ("B" in this example). Then, after you've pressed both keys, you can release them.

Our exclusive Quick Reference box appears at the end of every lesson. You can use it to review the skills you've learned in the lesson and as a handy reference—when you need to know how to do something fast and don't need to step through the sample exercises.

Conventions Used in This Book

The following is a list of typographical conventions used in this book:

Italic

Shows important terms the first time they are presented.

`Constant Width`

Shows anything you're actually supposed to type.

Color

Shows anything you're supposed to click, drag, or press.

 ⁞ NOTE ⁞   *Warns you of pitfalls that you could encounter if you're not careful.*

TIP   *Indicates a suggestion or supplementary information to the topic at hand.*

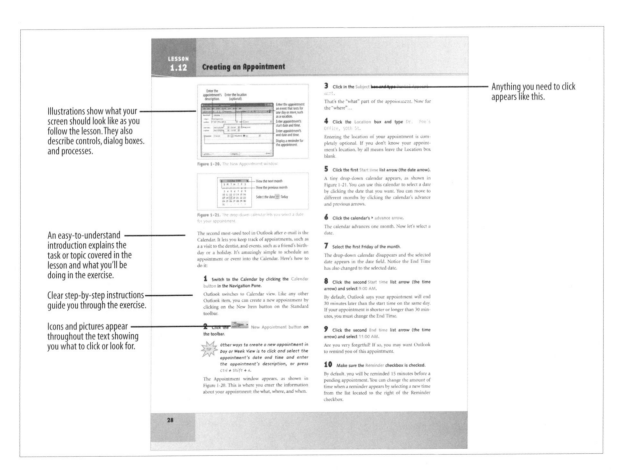

Illustrations show what your screen should look like as you follow the lesson. They also describe controls, dialog boxes, and processes.

An easy-to-understand introduction explains the task or topic covered in the lesson and what you'll be doing in the exercise.

Clear step-by-step instructions guide you through the exercise.

Icons and pictures appear throughout the text showing you what to click or look for.

Anything you need to click appears like this.

Using the Interactive Environment

Minimum Specs

- Windows 98 or better
- 64 MB RAM
- 150 MB Disk Space

Installation Instructions

Insert disc into CD-ROM drive. Click the Install button at the prompt. The installer will give you the option of installing the Interactive Content and the Practice Files. These are both installed by default. Practice files are also included on the CD in a directory called "Practice Files," which can be accessed without installing anything. If you select the installation item, the installer will then create a shortcut in your Start menu under the title "Personal Trainer," which you can use to access your installation selections.

Use of Interactive Content

Once you've installed the interactive content, placing the disc in your drive will cause the program to launch automatically. Then, once it has launched, just make your lesson selections and learn away!

How to Contact Us

We have tested and verified the information in this book to the best of our ability, but you might find that features have changed (or even that we have made mistakes!). As a reader of this book, you can help us to improve future editions by sending us your feedback. Please let us know about any errors, inaccuracies, bugs, misleading or confusing statements, and typos that you find anywhere in this book.

Please also let us know what we can do to make this book more useful to you. We take your comments seriously and will try to incorporate reasonable suggestions into future editions. You can write to us at:

O'Reilly Media, Inc.
1005 Gravenstein Highway North
Sebastopol, CA 95472
(800) 998-9938 (in the U.S. or Canada)
(707) 829-0515 (international or local)
(707) 829-0104 (fax)

To ask technical questions or to comment on the book, send e-mail to:

> *bookquestions@oreilly.com*

The web site for *Outlook 2003 Personal Trainer* lists examples, errata, and plans for future editions. You can find this page at:

> *http://www.oreilly.com/catalog/outlookpt/*

For more information about this book and others, see the O'Reilly web site at:

> *http://www.oreilly.com*

CHAPTER 1
THE FUNDAMENTALS

CHAPTER OBJECTIVES:

Start Microsoft Outlook: Lesson 1.2

Understand the Outlook program screen: Lesson 1.3

Give commands to Outlook: Lessons 1.4 through 1.8

Compose, send, and receive an e-mail message: Lessons 1.9 and 1.10

Cut, copy, and paste text: Lesson 1.11

Create and reschedule an appointment: Lessons 1.12 through 1.14

Use the Contacts list: Lessons 1.15 and 1.16

Use the Tasks list: Lesson 1.17

Use Notes: Lesson 1.18

Understand and work with Outlook Today: Lesson 1.19

Use the Help feature: Lessons 1.20 and 1.21

Print an item: Lesson 1.22

Exit Microsoft Excel: Lesson 1.23

CHAPTER TASK: LEARN THE MOST COMMON OUTLOOK TASKS

Prerequisites

- A computer with Windows 2000 or XP and Outlook 2003 installed.
- An understanding of basic computer functions (how to use the mouse and keyboard).

Welcome to your first chapter of Microsoft Outlook 2003! Microsoft Outlook is a messaging and personal information manager, or PIM. Outlook lets you send and receive e-mail messages, schedule appointments, and organize your contacts and addresses. It also reminds you of tasks you need to complete. For many people, Outlook is often the least-used Microsoft Office application—unless you're part of a large organization, in which case Outlook may be your most frequently used application.

The different tools included with Outlook work together seamlessly. For example, you can select several names from Outlook's Contacts list and send those people an e-mail message in a few clicks. This chapter introduces the Outlook basics. You will learn what the different Outlook tools are and how they can make you more productive and organized. You will learn how to compose and send an e-mail message, schedule an appointment, and add an address to the Contacts list. Ready? Then let's get started!

What's New in Outlook 2003?

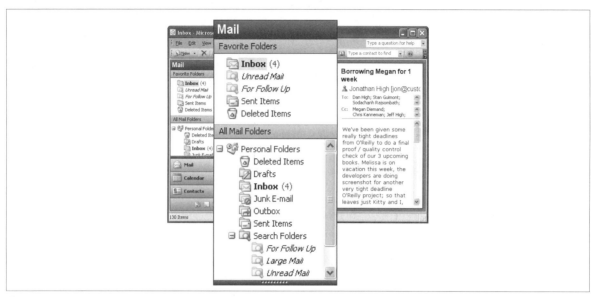

Figure 1-1. New design features like the Navigation Pane make working with e-mail and folders more efficient.

Figure 1-2. Use Search Folders to find items related to your specified search criteria.

In many ways, Outlook 2003 is almost completely different from previous versions so it might take a while to get used to. Table 1-1 lists a few of the biggest changes in Outlook 2003:

Table 1-1. What's New

New Feature	Description
Streamlined User Interface (new in 2003)	Outlook 2003 has a new look and feel that makes working with e-mail more efficient and user-friendly. This is due to a new window layout, designed to optimize your screen size so you can see more information on the screen at a time.
Navigation Pane (new in 2003)	The Navigation Pane, shown in Figure 1-1, is a combination of the Folder List and Outlook Bar from previous versions and is designed to help you find information quickly and easily. For example, in Mail, you can see more folders and even add your favorite folders at the top of the list. In Calendar, you can view other people's calendars alongside your own.
Junk E-mail Filter (new in 2003)	An improved Junk E-mail Filter uses advanced criteria when it looks at the content of messages to evaluate whether the message should be treated as junk e-mail. Junk e-mail is then moved to the Junk E-mail folder where you can later retrieve it, if you want.
Rules and Alerts (new in 2003)	Rules are not new in Outlook 2003, but the new mail message alert is. When a new message arrives in the Inbox, a phantom window appears on your screen displaying the sender of the message and the first line of text. This lets you know if the message needs to be attended to immediately, or if it can wait.
Search Folders (new in 2003)	Search Folders, shown in Figure 1-2, don't contain actual e-mail messages; they contain the results of searches that are constantly updated. For example, the Unread Mail Search Folder shows all messages that have not yet been read. You can also create Search Folders to match your own criteria.
Reading Pane (new in 2003)	The Reading Pane is a vast improvement on the Preview Pane from previous versions of Outlook. It lies vertically in the Outlook window so you can see nearly twice as much of an e-mail message at a time, and it's easier to read.
Arrange by Conversation (new in 2003)	This new view shows messages in a conversation-oriented view, so that all messages with related content are grouped together under the same heading. Just expand the group to show all the messages in the conversation.
Quick Flags (new in 2003)	If you don't have time to respond to a message immediately, you can use a quick flag to remind you later on.
Side-by-Side Calendars (new in 2003)	View multiple calendars side-by-side in the Outlook Calendar window. All calendars can be used with this feature, including other user's calendars and SharePoint Services events lists.
Smart Tags (new in 2002)	Perhaps the biggest new feature in Outlook 2003 is context-sensitive Smart Tags. These are a set of buttons that provide speedy access to relevant information by alerting you to important actions, such as formatting options for pasted information, formula error correction, and more.
Task Pane (new in 2002)	The Task Pane appears on the right side of the screen and lets you quickly perform searches, open or start a new workbook, and view the contents of the clipboard.
Word is the default editor; HTML is the default message format (new in 2002)	Now you can take advantage of the powerful text editing capabilities of Microsoft Word from within Outlook. Enhance your messages with tables, graphics, themes, and other Microsoft Word features.
Color Appointments (new in 2002)	You can color individual and recurring appointments with one of 10 predefined colors. Each color has an associated label, so you can organize your appointments according to the labels.
Internet and Exchange Account (new in 2002)	Microsoft Outlook no longer has separate Internet and Exchange modes. With the new E-mail Accounts Wizard, you can create several e-mail account types (Microsoft Exchange, POP3, IMAP, HTTP) in one profile.

Table 1-1. What's New (Continued)

New Feature	Description
Hotmail Support (new in 2002)	You can now add your Hotmail account to Outlook and use all the features that Outlook offers for viewing and managing your information.
Speech (new in 2002)	Office XP increases user productivity with voice commands. Users can dictate text, make direct formatting changes, and navigate menus using speech and voice commands.
Multiple Cut, Copy, and Paste Clipboard	The Office 2003 clipboard lets you copy up to 24 pieces of information from all the Office applications or the web and store them in the Office Clipboard Task Pane. The Task Pane gives you a visual representation of the copied data and a sample of the text, so you can easily distinguish clipboard items as they transfer to other documents.

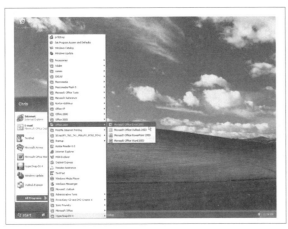

Figure 1-3. Programs located under the Windows Start button.

Figure 1-4. The Microsoft Outlook program screen.

Before starting Microsoft Outlook, you have to make sure your computer is on—if it's not, turn it on! You start Outlook the same as any other Windows program—with the Start button. Because every computer is set up differently (some people like to rearrange and reorder their Programs menu), the procedure for starting Outlook on your computer may be slightly different from the one listed here.

1 Make sure your computer is on and the Windows desktop is open.

2 Click the **start** Start button, located on the lefthand side of the Windows taskbar at the bottom of the screen.

The Windows Start menu pops up.

3 Move your mouse until the cursor points to All Programs.

A menu similar to the one shown in Figure 1-3 shoots out to the right side of the Start menu. The programs and menus listed will depend on the programs installed on your computer, so your menu will probably look somewhat different from the illustration.

4 Select Microsoft Office 2003 from the menu.

5 Click Microsoft Office Outlook 2003.

Depending on how many programs are installed on your computer and how they are organized, launching the program might be a little different. Once you click the Microsoft Outlook program icon, your computer's hard drive will whir for a moment while it loads Outlook. After a few seconds, the Outlook program screen appears, as shown in Figure 1-4.

That's it! You are ready to start using Microsoft Outlook. In the next lesson, you will learn what all those strange looking buttons, bars, and menus are used for.

QUICK REFERENCE

TO START MICROSOFT OUTLOOK:

1. CLICK THE WINDOWS START BUTTON.

2. SELECT ALL PROGRAMS → MICROSOFT OFFICE OUTLOOK 2003.

Understanding the Outlook Screen

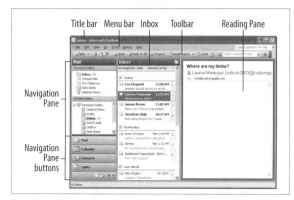

Figure 1-5. Parts of the Outlook 2003 program screen.

The Outlook 2003 program screen may seem confusing and overwhelming the first time you see it. What are all those buttons, icons, menus, and arrows for? This lesson will help you become familiar with the Outlook program screen.

The Mail pane opens as the default pane in Outlook. All the Mail folders that handle your e-mail messages are shown in the Navigation Pane. The Inbox is shown in the middle column of the window. Because e-mail is the most commonly used tool in Outlook, the Mail pane is a good pane to have open.

Now look at your screen, look at Figure 1-5, and then look at Table 1-2 to see what everything is. And, most of all, relax! This lesson is only meant to help you get acquainted with the Outlook screen; you don't have to memorize anything.

Table 1-2. Parts of the Outlook 2003 program screen

Object	Description
Title bar	Displays the name of the program you are currently using (Microsoft Outlook, of course) and the name of the document you are working on. The title bar appears at the top of all Windows programs.
Menu bar	Displays a list of menus that you use to give commands to Outlook. Clicking a menu name displays a list of commands—for example, clicking the Edit menu name displays different editing commands.
Standard toolbar	Toolbars are shortcuts—they contain buttons for the most common commands (instead of wading through several menus). The Standard toolbar contains buttons for the Outlook commands you use the most, such as creating new items, printing items, and getting help. The buttons on the Standard toolbar change depending on the view or folder you are using.
Navigation Pane	Contains shortcut icons you can click to move among Outlook's tools and folders.
Navigation Pane buttons	Click a button to see the folders and tools for a certain category—i.e., Mail, Calendar, Contacts, etc.
Favorite Folders	At the top of the Navigation Pane, displays the folders and views you're likely to use the most.
All Mail Folders	In the Navigation Pane, displays all your mail folders, including the Inbox, Outbox, Junk E-mail, Drafts, and Sent Items folders.
Inbox	Displays your incoming e-mail messages.
Reading Pane	Displays the selected message.

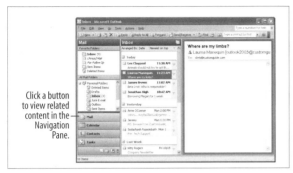

Click a button to view related content in the Navigation Pane.

Figure 1-6. Click a button in the Navigation Pane to open its corresponding folder.

With Microsoft Word, Microsoft Outlook, and many other computer applications, you have to memorize the application window along with all of the different buttons and features that appear on it. With Microsoft Outlook 2003, this task is a little more difficult because there are several different screens.

Outlook is a program made up of several tools, and each tool has its own separate and unique screen. Each of these tools is listed in the Navigation Pane, and you can learn more about them in Table 1-3. This lesson will give you a brief tour of all the Outlook tools and what they have to offer.

1 Click the Mail button **in the Navigation Pane.**

This is normally what you see when you open Outlook. The Mail pane contains all of the folders you use to manage your e-mail messages.Here, you can compose, send, and receive e-mail messages.

Notice that the Inbox is the folder currently shown in the middle column of the window (see Figure 1-6). To view the contents of another mail folder, click the folder in the Navigation Pane.

2 Click the Deleted Items folder **in the Navigation Pane.**

The view changes to show all your deleted items.

Now try viewing another pane.

3 Click the Calendar button **in the Navigation Pane.**

Outlook's Calendar is great for keeping track of your schedule and appointments. You can view the Calendar in Today, One-Day, Work Week, Week, and Month Views.

4 Click the Contacts button **in the Navigation Pane.**

Outlook's Contacts list is an electronic address book where you can store people's names, phone numbers, addresses, and of course, the ever-important e-mail address.

5 Click the Tasks button **in the Navigation Pane.**

The Tasks list, also known as a to-do list, keeps track of your tasks, making them easier to remember and manage. You can assign priorities to your tasks so that you know which tasks are more important, start dates to remind yourself when to start working on a task, and due dates when the task needs to be completed.

6 Click the Notes button **in the Navigation Pane.**

Outlook's Notes are the electronic equivalent of Post-it® Notes and are a great tool to jot down small bits of information, such as driving directions.

Table 1-3. The Navigation Pane

Folder or button	Folder name	Description?
Mail	Mail	Compose, manage, organize, send, and receive messages.
	Inbox	Contains all your recent incoming messages and e-mails.
	Unread Mail	Contains all your unread messages.
	For Follow Up	Contains those messages that you have flagged for follow up.
	Sent Items	Stores copies of messages you have sent.

Table 1-3. The Navigation Pane (Continued)

Folder or button	Folder name	Description?
	Mailbox	(Previously Outlook Today) Provides a preview of your day; summarizes appointments, tasks, and new e-mail messages.
	Deleted Items	Works like the Windows Recycle Bin; where you can find deleted Outlook items.
	Drafts	Stores draft messages that you haven't completed yet.
	Junk E-mail	Contains messages that Outlook considers spam. You should check this folder periodically to check for incorrectly flagged messages and to delete its contents.
	Outbox	Temporarily stores any messages that you've composed that have not been sent.
	Search Folders	Provides quick access to your flagged messages, unread messages, and messages with large attachments.
Calendar	Calendar	Enables you to view and schedule appointments, events, and meetings.
Contacts	Contacts	Use to keep track of addresses, numbers, and e-mail addresses.
Tasks	Tasks	Use to manage and organize to-do lists.
	Notes	Use like electronic Post-It® Notes to jot down information.
	Folder List	Displays all the folders in Microsoft Outlook.
	Shortcuts	Contains shortcuts to other folders, such as the My Documents folder. You can also add your own shortcuts here.
	Configure buttons	Add or remove buttons from the Navigation Pane.
	Journal	Records information about items that you send or receive and files that you create with Microsoft Office (not shown by default).

QUICK REFERENCE

TO SWITCH BETWEEN THE VARIOUS OUTLOOK PANES:

- CLICK THE CORRESPONDING BUTTON IN THE NAVIGATION PANE.

OR...

- SELECT GO FROM THE MENU BAR AND SELECT THE PANE YOU WANT TO VIEW.

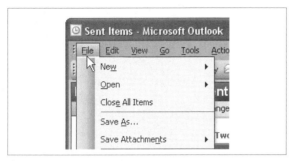

Figure 1-7. The File menu.

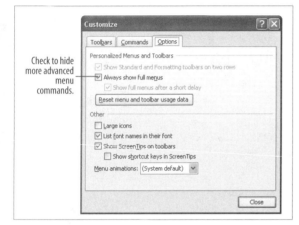

Check to hide more advanced menu commands.

Figure 1-8. The Customize dialog box.

This lesson explains one of the most popular ways to give commands to Outlook—by using the menus. Menus for all Windows programs can be found at the top of a window, just beneath the program's title bar. Notice the words File, Edit, View, Go, Tools, Actions, and Help. The next steps will show you why they're there.

1 **Click the word** File **on the menu bar.**

A menu drops down from the word File, as shown in Figure 1-7.

The File menu contains a list of file-related commands—such as New, which creates a new item; Open, which opens an item; and Close All items, which closes all open items. Menu items with ▸ arrows are actually submenus. You open submenus simply by clicking on the arrow.

2 **Point to the word** New **in the File menu.**

The File submenu appears. Now let's try selecting a command from the New submenu.

3 **Point to and click the word** Mail Message **in the New submenu.**

An Untitled – Message window appears, ready for you to enter a new e-mail message. We'll learn about creating messages later on, so you can close this window for now.

4 **Close the Untitled – Message window by clicking its** Close button.

The Untitled – Message window closes.

Notice that each of the menus has an underlined letter somewhere in it. For example, the letter F in the File menu is underlined. Holding down the Alt key and pressing the underlined letter in a menu does the same thing as clicking it. Thus, pressing the Alt key and then the F key would open the File menu.

The menus in Outlook 2003 work quite a bit differently than menus in other Windows programs—even previous versions of Outlook! Microsoft Outlook 2003 displays its menu commands on the screen in three different ways:

• By displaying every command possible.

• By hiding the commands you don't use as frequently (the more advanced commands).

• By allowing you to display the hidden commands by clicking the downward-pointing double arrows at the bottom of the menu or after waiting a couple seconds.

5 **Click the word** Tools **in the menu bar.**

The most common menu commands appear in the Tools menu. Some people feel intimidated by being confronted with so many menu options, so the menus in Outlook 2003 don't display the more advanced commands at first. To display a menu's advanced commands, either click the downward-pointing double arrow at the bottom of the menu or keep the menu open a few seconds.

6 **Click the** downward-pointing double arrow **at the bottom of the Tools menu.**

The more advanced commands appear shaded on the Tools menu.

If you're accustomed to working with earlier versions of Microsoft Office, you may find that hiding the more advanced commands is disconcerting. If so, you can easily change how the menus work. Here's how:

7 Select View → Toolbars → Customize **from the menu and click the** Options **tab.**

The Customize dialog box appears, as shown in Figure 1-8. This is where you can change how Outlook's menus work. There are two checkboxes here that are important:

- **Always show full menus:** Clear this checkbox if you want to show all the commands on the menus, instead of hiding the advanced commands.

- **Show full menus after a short delay:** If checked, this option waits a few seconds before displaying the more advanced commands on a menu.

8 Click Close.

One more important note: Outlook's menus and toolbars change depending on which pane is open. For example, when the Inbox folder is open, Outlook displays message-related menus and buttons. Switch to the Calendar folder, and Outlook displays appointment-related menus and buttons. See Table 1-4 for a description of Outlook's amazing, ever-changing menus.

Table 1-4. Menus found in Microsoft Outlook

Menu	Description
File	File-related commands to open, save, close, print, and create new messages, contacts, tasks, and appointments.
Edit	Commands to copy, cut, paste, find, and replace text.
View	Commands to change how information is displayed on the screen.
Go	Go to a pane or folder in Outlook. This is the menu version of the Navigation Pane.
Tools	Lists tools such as the Address Book and Organize. You can also change the default options for Outlook here. spellchecker
Actions	More advanced commands to do such things as create a recurring appointment or create a message in a different format.
Help	Click to get help on using Microsoft Outlook.

QUICK REFERENCE

TO OPEN A MENU:

- CLICK THE MENU NAME WITH THE MOUSE.

  OR...

- PRESS ALT AND THEN THE UNDERLINED LETTER IN THE MENU NAME.

TO DISPLAY A MENU'S HIDDEN COMMANDS:

- CLICK THE DOWNWARD-POINTING DOUBLE ARROW AT THE BOTTOM OF THE MENU.

  OR...

- OPEN THE MENU AND WAIT A FEW SECONDS.

TO CHANGE HOW MENUS WORK:

1. SELECT VIEW → TOOLBARS → CUSTOMIZE FROM THE MENU AND CLICK THE OPTIONS TAB.

2. CHECK OR CLEAR EITHER THE ALWAYS SHOW FULL MENUS OR SHOW FULL MENUS AFTER A SHORT DELAY OPTION, THEN CLICK CLOSE.

Using Toolbars

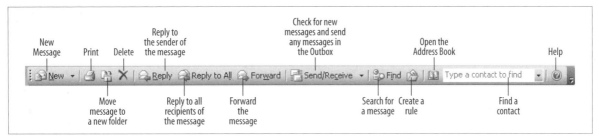

Figure 1-9. The Standard toolbar in the Inbox folder.

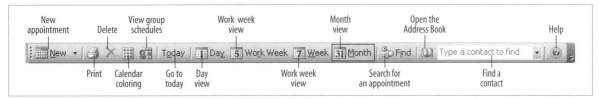

Figure 1-10. The Standard toolbar in the Calendar folder.

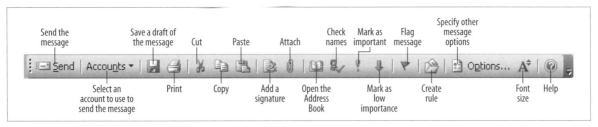

Figure 1-11. The Standard toolbar in a new e-mail message window.

In this lesson we move on to another very common way of giving commands to Outlook—using the toolbar. Toolbars are shortcuts—they contain buttons for the most often used commands. Instead of wading through several menus to access a command, you can click a single button on a toolbar.

Outlook's menus and toolbar buttons change depending on which folder is open. For example, when the Inbox folder is open, Outlook displays message-related menus and buttons. Switch to the Calendar folder and Outlook displays appointment-related menus and buttons. See Figures 1-9, 1-10, and 1-11 for examples of Outlook's amazing, ever-changing toolbar.

This lesson explains how to use Outlook's toolbar.

1 Click the Mail button in the Navigation Pane.

Now we want to create a new mail message.

2 Point to the New New Mail Message button on the toolbar (but don't click the mouse yet).

A Screen Tip that briefly identifies the button appears—in this case, "New Mail Message." If you don't know what a button on a toolbar does, simply move the pointer over it, wait a second, and a Screen-Tip will appear and tell you what the button does.

3 Click the New Mail Message button on the toolbar.

The Untitled – Message window appears.

4 Close the Untitled – Message window by clicking its Close button.

That's it! You've learned the extraordinarily difficult task of using toolbars!

QUICK REFERENCE

TO DISPLAY A TOOLBAR BUTTON'S DESCRIPTION:

- POSITION THE POINTER OVER THE TOOLBAR BUTTON AND WAIT A SECOND. A SCREENTIP WILL APPEAR, TELLING YOU WHAT THE BUTTON DOES.

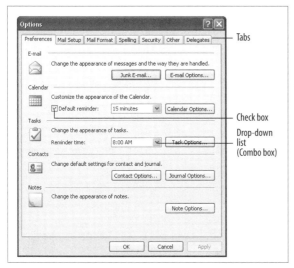

Figure 1-12. The Options dialog box.

Some commands are more complicated than others. Creating a message is a simple process—simply select File → New → Mail Message from the menu or click the New Mail Message button on the toolbar. Other commands are more complex, such as changing the default options for Outlook. Whenever you want to do something relatively complicated, you must fill out a dialog box. If you have worked with Windows at all, you have undoubtedly filled out hundreds of dialog boxes. Dialog boxes usually contain several types of controls, including:

- Text boxes
- List boxes
- Checkboxes
- Drop-down lists (also called Combo boxes)

It is important that you know the names of these controls because this book will refer to them in many lessons. This lesson will give you a tour of a dialog box and explain each of these controls to you so that you will know what they are and how to use them.

1 Click the word Tools **from the menu bar.**

The Tools menu appears. Notice the Options menu in the Tools menu is followed by ellipses (…). The ellipses indicate that there is an Options dialog box.

2 Select Options **from the Tools menu.**

The Options dialog box appears, as shown in Figure 1-12. Some dialog boxes have so many options

that they are organized and grouped on separate sheets. Such dialog boxes have several sheet tabs near the top of the dialog box. To view a sheet, simply click its sheet tab.

3 Click the Mail Setup **tab.**

The Mail Setup tab appears in front of the dialog box. The Mail Setup tab contains several different types of components that you can fill out.

Remember: the purpose of this lesson is to learn about dialog boxes—not how to change the default options for Outlook (we'll get to that later). The next destination on our dialog box tour is the text box.

4 Click the Send/Receive button.

There is one text box within the Send/Receive box, labeled "Schedule an automatic send/receive every 10 minutes". Text boxes are the most common dialog box components and are nothing more than the fill-in-the-blank you're familiar with if you've filled out any type of paper form.

To use a text box, select it by clicking it or pressing the Tab key until the insertion point appears in the text box. Then enter the text into the text box.

5 Click the Schedule an automatic send/receive every 10 minutes **text box and replace the number with** 20**.**

You've just filled out the text box—nothing to it. We need to switch to another tab in order to find some more types of controls.

6 Click the Close button **and select the** Preferences **tab.**

The next stop in our dialog box tour is the *drop-down list*, or *combo box*. There's a drop-down list located in the Calendar section of the Preferences tab. A drop-down list displays several (or many) options in a small box. You must first click a drop-down list's downward pointing arrow to display its options. Sometimes a drop-down list will contain so many options that they can't all be displayed at once, and you must use the *scroll bar* to move up or down the list.

7 Click the Default reminder **list arrow.**

A list of time options appears.

8 Select 30 minutes **from the list.**

Sometimes you need to select items from a dialog box—in such cases, use the *checkbox* control when you're presented with one or more choices.

9 **In the Calendar section, click the** Default reminder **checkbox to de-select it.**

The last item on our dialog box tour is the *button*. Buttons are found in every dialog box and are used to execute or cancel commands. The two buttons you'll see the most are:

- **OK:** Applies and saves any changes you have made and then closes this dialog box. Pressing the Enter key usually does the same thing as clicking the OK button.
- **Cancel:** Closes the dialog box without applying and saving any changes. Pressing the Esc key usually does the same thing as clicking the cancel button.

10 **Click the** Cancel button **to cancel the changes you made.**

The Options dialog box closes.

QUICK REFERENCE

TO USE A TEXT BOX:

- SIMPLY TYPE THE INFORMATION DIRECTLY INTO THE TEXT BOX.

TO USE A DROP-DOWN LIST:

- CLICK THE LIST ARROW TO VIEW ALL AVAILABLE OPTIONS IN THE DROP-DOWN LIST. CLICK AN OPTION FROM THE LIST TO SELECT IT.

TO CHECK OR UNCHECK A CHECKBOX:

- CLICK THE CHECKBOX.

TO VIEW A DIALOG BOX TAB:

- CLICK THE TAB YOU WANT TO VIEW.

TO SAVE YOUR CHANGES AND CLOSE A DIALOG BOX:

- CLICK THE OK BUTTON OR PRESS ENTER.

TO CLOSE A DIALOG BOX WITHOUT SAVING YOUR CHANGES:

- CLICK THE CANCEL BUTTON OR PRESS ESC.

Keystroke and Right Mouse Button Shortcuts

Figure 1-13. Right-click any object to display a list of things that you can do to the object.

Figure 1-14. Hold down the Ctrl key and press another key to execute a keystroke shortcut.

You are probably starting to realize that there are several methods to do the same thing in Outlook. For example, to open an e-mail message, you can use the menu (select File → Open) or the toolbar (click the Open button). This lesson introduces you to two more methods of executing commands: right mouse button shortcut menus and keystroke shortcuts.

You know that the left mouse button is the primary mouse button, used for clicking and double-clicking—and it's the mouse button that you will use over 95% of the time. So what's the right mouse button for? Whenever you right-click something, it brings up a shortcut menu that lists everything you can do to the object. Whenever you're unsure or curious about what you can do with an object, right-click it. A shortcut menu will appear with a list of commands related to the object or area you right-clicked.

Right mouse button shortcut menus are an especially effective way to give commands in Outlook, because you don't have to wade through several levels of menus to do something.

1 Click the Inbox folder in the Navigation Pane.

In this lesson, assume you have received a new e-mail message.

2 Position the pointer over a message and click the right mouse button.

A shortcut menu appears where you clicked the mouse, as shown in Figure 1-13. Notice one of the items listed on the shortcut menu is Print. This is the same Print command that you can select from the menu by clicking File → Print.

If you open a shortcut menu and then change your mind, you can close it without selecting anything. Here's how:

3 Move the mouse anywhere outside the shortcut menu and click the left mouse button to close the shortcut menu.

Remember that the options listed in the shortcut menu will differ, depending on what or where you right-clicked.

4 Position the pointer over the toolbar and click the right mouse button.

> NOTE *Right-click an object to open a shortcut menu that lists the most common things you can do to the object.*

5 Move the mouse anywhere outside the shortcut menu and click the left mouse button to close the shortcut menu.

On to keystroke shortcuts. Without a doubt, keystroke shortcuts are the fastest way to give commands to Outlook, even if they are a little hard to remember. They're great time-savers for issuing frequently used commands. To issue a keystroke shortcut, press and hold down the Ctrl key, press the shortcut key, and release both buttons (see Figure 1-14).

6 Press Ctrl + N (at the same time.).

This is the keystroke shortcut to create a new message and thus an Untitled – Message window appears, ready for you to enter a new message.

7 Close the Untitled – Message window by clicking its Close button.

The Untitled – Message window closes.

Table 1-5 lists the shortcut keystrokes you're likely to use the most in Outlook.

Table 1-5. Common keystroke shortcuts

Keystroke	Description
Ctrl + S	Save Item
Ctrl + P	Print
Ctrl + Z	Undo
Ctrl + X	Cut
Ctrl + C	Copy
Ctrl + V	Paste
F7	Check Spelling
Ctrl + M or F9	Check for New Mail
Alt + S	Save, Close, and Send
Ctrl + R	Reply
Ctrl + Shift + R	Reply to All
Ctrl + Shift + B	Address Book
F1	Help
Alt + Tab	Switch Between Applications
Ctrl + N	New Item
Ctrl + Shift + M	New Message
Ctrl + Shift + A	New Appointment
Ctrl + Shift + C	New Contact
Ctrl + Shift + N	New Note
Ctrl + Shift + K	New Task

QUICK REFERENCE

TO OPEN A CONTEXT-SENSITIVE SHORTCUT MENU:

• RIGHT-CLICK THE OBJECT.

TO USE A KEYSTROKE SHORTCUT:

• PRESS CTRL + THE LETTER OF THE KEYSTROKE SHORTCUT YOU WANT TO EXECUTE.

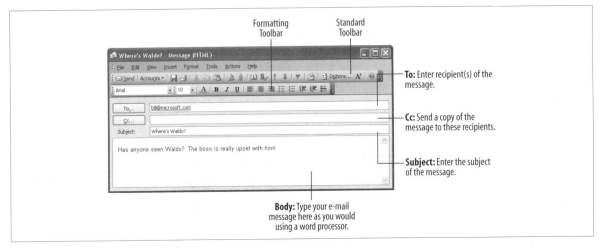

Figure 1-15. The New Message window.

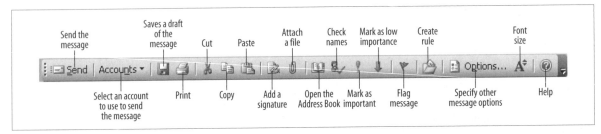

Figure 1-16. The Standard toolbar for a new message.

For most people, e-mail is by far the most important feature of Outlook, so it's best if you start learning how to use it right away. This lesson offers a quick explanation on how to compose and send an e-mail message. Figure 1-15 shows an example of the New Message Window, and Figure 1-16 shows an example of a new message's Standard toolbar.

1 **If necessary, click the** Mail button **in the Navigation Pane.**

The contents of the Inbox folder appear.

2 **Click the** 🖃New ▾ New Mail Message button **on the toolbar.**

An Untitled – Message form appears ready for you to enter a new message. First, you need to specify the recipient's e-mail address in the To: field. There are two ways of doing this:

- If you know the e-mail address, you can type it into the To: box.

- If you don't know the address, you can click the To: button and select the address from your list of contacts.

In this exercise, we will send the same message to two people, using both methods. First let's enter a name directly into the To: box.

3 **Type your e-mail address into the** To: **box.**

If you need to send a message to more than one person, simply place a semicolon (;) between the recipients' e-mail addresses—for example: JohnH@acme.com; BettyT@yahoo.com. Let's send this message to another person, this time using the address book to address the message.

4 **Click the** To button.

The Select Names dialog box appears.

5 **Click the** ☑ Show Names from the **list arrow and select** Contacts, **if necessary.**

This will display the names and addresses in the Contacts folder.

6 Click the name of the recipient in the Name list, then click the To button.

Repeat this step to add the other recipients.

When you're finished adding recipients, move on to the next step.

7 Click OK.

The Select Recipients dialog box closes and the recipient(s) appear in the To: field.

8 (Optional) To send a copy of a message to someone, click the Cc: or Bcc: button and repeat Steps 4–7 to enter e-mail addresses.

Table 1-6 describes Carbon Copies (Cc) and Blind Carbon Copies (Bcc) of messages.

Next, enter the subject of the message so your recipient(s) will know what your message is about.

9 Click the Subject field and type Where's Waldo?

Now you can type an actual e-mail message.

10 Click the pointer in the body of the message, and type Has anyone seen Waldo? The boss is really upset with him!

Type the message as you would in a word processor. All the Windows editing commands—such as cutting, copying, and pasting text—work the same in Outlook.

11 (Optional) To check the spelling of your message, select Tools → Spelling from the menu.

Outlook checks the spelling in your message, flags each word it can't find in its dictionary, and suggests an alternate word.

To replace an unknown word with a suggestion, select the suggestion in the Change To list and click the Change button. To ignore a word the spell checker doesn't recognize, such as the name of a city, click on Ignore All. When you receive a message saying "The spelling check is complete" click OK and proceed to the next step.

12 When you're finished, click the Send button on the toolbar.

 Another way to send an e-mail is to press Ctrl + S.

The message is moved to the Outbox folder, and will be sent the next time you click the Send/Receive button. Or, to send the message immediately…

13 Click the Send/Receive button on the toolbar.

Press Ctrl + M.

Table 1-6. Ways to address an e-mail message

Address	Description
To	Sends the message to the recipient you specify (required).
Carbon Copy (Cc)	Sends a copy of the message to a recipient who is not directly involved, but who might be interested in the message.
Blind Carbon Copy (Bcc)	Sends a copy of the message to a recipient without anyone else knowing that she received the message. You need to select View → Bcc Field from the menu to use the Bcc Field.

QUICK REFERENCE

TO COMPOSE A MESSAGE:

1. CLICK THE INBOX FOLDER IN THE NAVIGATION PANE.

2. CLICK THE NEW MAIL MESSAGE BUTTON ON THE TOOLBAR.

3. TYPE THE RECIPIENT'S ADDRESS IN THE TO: FIELD.

   OR...

   CLICK THE TO BUTTON TO THE LEFT OF THE TO: BOX, CLICK THE NAME OF THE RECIPIENT IN THE NAME LIST, THEN CLICK THE TO BUTTON. CLICK OK WHEN YOU'RE FINISHED.

4. CLICK THE SUBJECT BOX AND ENTER THE MESSAGE'S SUBJECT.

5. CLICK THE POINTER IN THE LOWER PANE AND TYPE THE MESSAGE.

6. CLICK THE SEND BUTTON ON THE TOOLBAR OR PRESS ALT + S TO SEND THE MESSAGE.

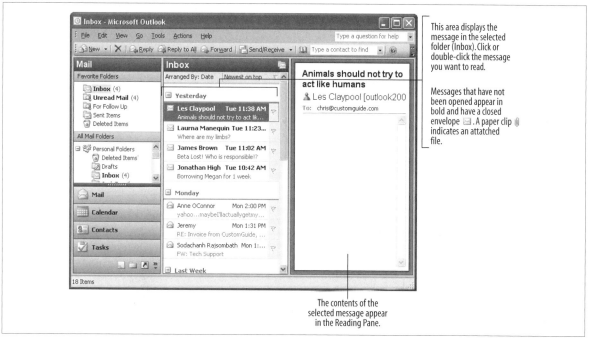

Figure 1-17. The Inbox.

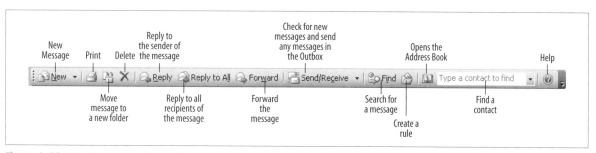

Figure 1-18. The Standard toolbar in the Mail pane.

This lesson explains how to receive and read your e-mail messages in Outlook—and then what you can do to your messages after reading them. You'll find it's a lot easier to retrieve and read e-mail messages than it is to sort through and read postal mail—no envelopes to tear open, and no scribbled handwriting to decipher. Let's get started! For your reference, Figure 1-17 displays the Outlook Inbox, and Figure 1-18 shows the Mail pane's Standard toolbar.

1 Click the Mail button in the Navigation Pane.

When you receive e-mail messages, they appear in the Inbox. Normally, Outlook automatically checks your mail server for new messages every 10 minutes (although you can change this setting). If Outlook finds any new messages on your mail server, it downloads them and saves them to your computer. You can force Outlook to check for new messages by clicking the Send/Receive button on the toolbar.

Let's see if you have any new e-mail.

2 Click the 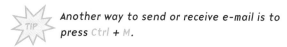 Send/Receive button on the toolbar.

Another way to send or receive e-mail is to press Ctrl + M.

You should receive at least one message (the message you sent yourself in the previous lesson). Any new, unread messages appear in **bold** and have a closed envelope icon (✉) next to them. Here's how to open and read a message:

3 Click the Where's Waldo? **message.**

The contents of the message appear in the Reading Pane, located on the right-hand side of the Outlook window. You can also open a message in its own window by double-clicking the message.

4 Double-click the Where's Waldo? **message in the Inbox Pane.**

The message appears in its own window. You can close the message window when you're finished reading it by clicking the window's close button.

5 Close the Message window by clicking its Close button.

Once you have received a message, there are several things that you can do with it. You can select the message and do one or more of following:

• **Reply to the Message:** When you reply to a message, Outlook opens a Message form that contains the e-mail address, subject, and body of the message to which you are responding. To reply to a message, click the Reply button on the toolbar.

• **Forward the Message:** When you forward a message to another recipient, Outlook opens a Message form that contains the subject and body of the message you are forwarding. You must specify to whom you want to forward the message in the To box. To forward a message, click the Forward button on the toolbar.

• **View or Download any Attachments:** Messages with the 📎 icon have one or more files attached to them. To view and/or download these files, click the 📎 icon on the message header and select the files you want to open or view from the list that appears.

• **Print the Message:** To print a message, click the Print button on the toolbar.

• **Delete the Message:** To delete a message, press the Delete key.

• **Move the Message to a Different Folder:** If you're the type of person who has your desk and filing cabinets neatly organized, you can create your own set of folders and move important messages that you want to save to those folders. We will discuss creating and working with your own folders later.

• **Ignore the Message:** Most people don't do anything with their messages and let them fill their inbox like a stack of unpaid bills. Having hundreds of old e-mail messages in your Inbox doesn't hurt any-thing—it only makes it more difficult to find important messages.

Remember that this lesson is only an introduction to e-mail—we will discuss each of the preceding items in depth a little later.

All messages have one or more icons to indicate their status, importance, and contents. Table 1-7 lists these icons.

Table 1-7. Message icons

Icon	Icon name	Description
✉	Unopened Message	This message has not yet been read or opened.
📭	Opened Message	This message has been read (or at least opened).
📬	Reply	This is an e-mail message to which you have replied.
📪	Forward	This is a forwarded e-mail message.
📎	Attachment	This message has one or more files attached to it.
❗	Urgent	This message is marked as urgent—you better look at it soon!
⚑	Flagged	This message has been flagged to remind you about something.
🗓	Scheduled Appointment	This message is a scheduled meeting request sent to you by another user.
✉	Undeliverable Mail	This message could not be delivered.

QUICK REFERENCE

TO RECEIVE AND READ E-MAIL MESSAGES:

1. CLICK THE MAIL BUTTON IN THE NAVIGATION PANE.

2. CLICK THE SEND AND RECEIVE BUTTON ON THE TOOLBAR.

3. CLICK OR DOUBLE-CLICK THE MESSAGE YOU WANT TO READ.

THINGS YOU CAN DO WITH AN E-MAIL MESSAGE:

• REPLY TO THE MESSAGE

• FORWARD THE MESSAGE

• VIEW OR DOWNLOAD ANY ATTACHMENTS

• PRINT THE MESSAGE

• DELETE THE MESSAGE

• MOVE THE MESSAGE TO A DIFFERENT FOLDER

• IGNORE THE MESSAGE

Cutting, Copying, and Pasting Text

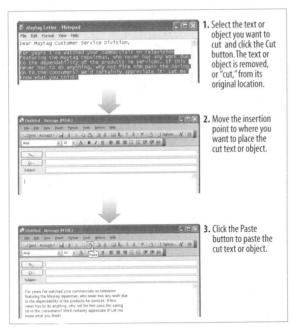

1. Select the text or object you want to cut and click the Cut button. The text or object is removed, or "cut," from its original location.

2. Move the insertion point to where you want to place the cut text or object.

3. Click the Paste button to paste the cut text or object.

Figure 1-19. The steps involved in cutting and pasting text.

Cutting, copying, and pasting text is a common computer task that comes in very handy when you are composing and replying to e-mail messages. Instead of having to retype text, you can copy text from a message or document and paste it into your new e-mail message—or any Outlook item. Anything you cut or copy is placed in a temporary storage area called the Windows Clipboard. The Clipboard is available to any Windows program, so you can cut, copy, and paste text between Microsoft Outlook and other programs.

In this lesson, you will copy text from the Notepad application and paste it into a new e-mail message.

1 Start the Notepad program by clicking the Windows Start button and selecting All Programs → Accessories → Notepad from the menu.

The Notepad program appears. Notepad is a mini word processor that comes with Windows.

Next, you need to open the document that contains the text you want to copy.

2 Select File → Open on the toolbar, navigate to your Practice folder, then find and double-click the Maytag Letter file.

You want to copy some of the text in this letter and paste it into an e-mail message. First, you need to select the text you want to copy.

3 Select the last paragraph of the letter.

You can select text by pointing to the beginning or end of the text you want to select, clicking and holding the left mouse button, dragging the cursor across the text, and then releasing the mouse button.

Now you can copy the selected text to the Windows clipboard.

4 Select Edit → Copy from the menu.

The selected text is copied from Notepad and placed in the Windows Clipboard, ready to be moved to a new location.

> **TIP** *Another way to copy is to press Ctrl + C. The Windows Clipboard can only hold one piece of information at a time. Every time you cut or copy something to the Clipboard, it replaces the previous information.*

You don't need the Notepad program anymore, so it's time to end this lesson.

5 Close the Notepad program.

You should be back in Microsoft Outlook—if you're not, click the Outlook icon on the Windows taskbar. Next, you need to create a new e-mail message.

6 Click the New Mail Message button on the toolbar.

An Untitled – Message form appears, ready for you to enter a new message. You want to paste the text you copied from the Notepad program into the body of the new e-mail message.

7 Click the pointer in the body of the message, in the lower pane, and click the Paste button on the toolbar.

> **TIP** *Another way to paste is to press Ctrl + V.*

Poof! The copied text appears at the insertion point.

Since we really don't want to send another e-mail message, you can close the message form without sending the message.

8 **Click the** Close button **for the Untitled – Message form.**

Outlook will ask you if you want to save your changes to the message.

9 **Click** No.

Outlook closes the Untitled – Message form without saving a draft of the e-mail message.

Copying information is very similar to cutting information. Both commands put your selected information in the Clipboard where you can then paste it to a new location. The only difference between the two commands is that the Cut command deletes selected information when it copies it to the clipboard, while the Copy command copies the selected information to the clipboard without deleting it.

QUICK REFERENCE

TO CUT SOMETHING:

1. SELECT THE TEXT OR OBJECT YOU WANT TO CUT.

2. CLICK THE CUT BUTTON ON THE STANDARD TOOLBAR.

   OR...

   SELECT EDIT → CUT FROM THE MENU.

   OR...

   PRESS CTRL + X.

TO COPY SOMETHING:

1. SELECT THE TEXT OR OBJECT YOU WANT TO COPY.

2. CLICK THE COPY BUTTON ON THE STANDARD TOOLBAR.

   OR...

   SELECT EDIT → COPY FROM THE MENU.

   OR...

   PRESS CTRL + C.

TO PASTE A CUT OR COPIED OBJECT:

1. PLACE THE INSERTION POINT WHERE YOU WANT TO PASTE THE TEXT OR OBJECT.

2. CLICK THE PASTE BUTTON ON THE STANDARD TOOLBAR.

   OR...

   SELECT EDIT → PASTE FROM THE MENU.

   OR...

   PRESS CTRL + V.

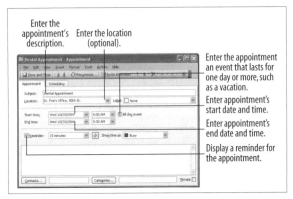

Enter the
appointment's
description.

Enter the location
(optional).

Enter the appointment
an event that lasts for
one day or more, such
as a vacation.

Enter appointment's
start date and time.

Enter appointment's
end date and time.

Display a reminder for
the appointment.

Figure 1-20. The New Appointment window.

View the next month

View the previous month

Select the date 19 : Today

Figure 1-21. The drop-down calendar lets you select a date
for your appointment.

The second most-used tool in Outlook after e-mail is the
Calendar. It lets you keep track of appointments, such as
a a visit to the dentist, and events, such as a friend's birthday or a holiday. It's amazingly simple to schedule an
appointment or event into the Calendar. Here's how to
do it:

1 Switch to the Calendar by clicking the Calendar
button in the Navigation Pane.

Outlook switches to Calendar view. Like any other
Outlook item, you can create a new appointment by
clicking on the New Item button on the Standard
toolbar.

2 Click the [New ▾] New Appointment button on
the toolbar.

 *Other ways to create a new appointment in
Day or Week View are to click and select the
appointment's date and time and enter
the appointment's description, or press
Ctrl + Shift + A.*

The Appointment window appears, as shown in
Figure 1-20. This is where you enter the information
about your appointment: the what, where, and when.

3 Click in the Subject box and type Dental Appointment.

That's the "what" part of the appointment. Now for
the "where"…

4 Click the Location box and type Dr. Poe's
Office, 50th St.

Entering the location of your appointment is completely optional. If you don't know your appointment's location, by all means leave the Location box
blank.

5 Click the first Start time list arrow (the date arrow).

A tiny drop-down calendar appears, as shown in
Figure 1-21. You can use this calendar to select a date
by clicking the date that you want. You can move to
different months by clicking the calendar's advance
and previous arrows.

6 Click the calendar's ▸ advance arrow.

The calendar advances one month. Now let's select a
date.

7 Select the first Friday of the month.

The drop-down calendar disappears and the selected
date appears in the date field. Notice the End Time
has also changed to the selected date.

8 Click the second Start time list arrow (the time
arrow) and select 9:00 AM.

By default, Outlook says your appointment will end
30 minutes later than the start time on the same day.
If your appointment is shorter or longer than 30 minutes, you must change the End Time.

9 Click the second End time list arrow (the time
arrow) and select 11:00 AM.

Are you very forgetful? If so, you may want Outlook
to remind you of this appointment.

10 Make sure the Reminder checkbox is checked.

By default, you will be reminded 15 minutes before a
pending appointment. You can change the amount of
time when a reminder appears by selecting a new time
from the list located to the right of the Reminder
checkbox.

≗ NOTE ≗   *Depending on your Outlook setup, Outlook may automatically add a reminder for new appointments. You can change this default setting by selecting Tools → Options from the main Outlook menu and changing the Default Reminder settings in the Calendar section of the Preferences tab.*

That's all the information we need for this particular appointment. Let's save it.

11   Click the Save and Close button on the Standard Toolbar.

TIP   *Another way to save and close is to press Alt + S.*

Outlook saves the new appointment—but where is it? We discuss this in the next lesson!

If you're in Day or Week View (we will cover these views in the next lesson), you can also enter a new appointment by selecting the appointment's date and time and entering the appointment's description—without having to open a single form!

QUICK REFERENCE

TO VIEW THE CALENDAR:

- CLICK THE CALENDAR BUTTON IN THE NAVIGATION PANE.

TO SCHEDULE AN APPOINTMENT:

- FROM DAY OR WEEK VIEW, SELECT THE APPOINTMENT'S DATE AND TIME AND ENTER THE APPOINTMENT'S DESCRIPTION.

OR...

1. CLICK THE NEW APPOINTMENT BUTTON OR PRESS CTRL + N.

2. ENTER THE APPOINTMENT AND ITS DATE AND TIME.

3. CLICK THE SAVE AND CLOSE BUTTON OR PRESS ALT + S WHEN YOU'RE FINISHED.

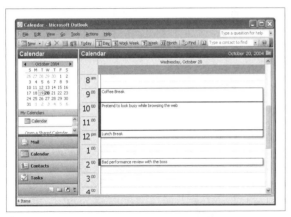

Figure 1-22. The Calendar in Day View.

Figure 1-23. The Calendar in Month View.

Figure 1-24. The Date Navigator is a small calendar that appears in Day, Work, and Week Views and lets you select the day or week you want to display.

When is your son's birthday? What day of the week does Easter fall on this year? When is your anniversary again? A monthly calendar is useful for displaying which days your appointments/special events fall on, but not at displaying all the details of your daily schedule. On the other hand, a daily schedule is helpful for planning the details of your day, but not at displaying the "big picture" of your upcoming appointments or events. Outlook's Calendar gives you the best of both worlds. Simply click one of the View buttons on the toolbar to display the following views:

- **Today** **Today View:** No matter where you are in the Calendar, click this button to view everything on your calendar for the current day in Day view.

- **1 Day** **Day View:** Displays one day at a time. You can easily see when your appointments start and end and when you have free time. You can only see appointments for the selected day, however.

- **5 Work Week** **Work Week View:** Displays a weekly calendar, without weekends. You can see when your appointments start and end and when you have free time. You can only see appointments for the selected five business days.

- **7 Week** **Week View:** Displays a weekly calendar, including weekends. You can only see appointments for the selected week, and it's not very easy to see your busy and free times.

- **31 Month** **Month View:** Displays a monthly calendar. Month View does not display much information about your appointments, such as how long they are and what time they are over. In Month View, you use the scroll bar to move from month to month.

In this lesson, you will learn to use each of these views and how to navigate through dates and months in the calendar. Let's get started!

1 **If necessary, click the** Calendar button **in the Navigation Pane.**

The calendar view always opens in the view that was used last. Let's change the view by clicking one of the View buttons on the toolbar.

2 **Click the** Day View button **on the toolbar.**

Day View is great for when you want to look over your daily appointments. Outlook displays your appointments' starting and ending times and when you have free time.

The Date Navigator, shown in Figure 1-22, is displayed in the upper-left of the calendar. The Date Navigator shows the current month, today's date, and the selected date. You can use the Date Navigator to move to different dates so that you view or add appointments on other days. Dates displayed in bold have at least one appointment.

Just below the Date Navigator is "My Calendars," which allows you to view different calendars, such as those you have created or shared calendars.

3 Click the Date Navigator's ▸ advance arrow.

The Date Navigator scrolls to the next month.

4 Click any date in the Date Navigator.

The Appointment area displays appointments for the selected day. Switch to Work Week View.

5 Click the Work Week View button on the toolbar.

Work Week View is similar to Day View, except instead of displaying a single day, Work Week View displays the five business days in the selected week.

6 Click the Week View button on the toolbar.

Week View displays a 7-day weekly calendar. Week View displays the start times for the appointments in the selected week, but not their durations.

7 Click the Month View button on the toolbar.

Month View, as shown in Figure 1-23, is just like the calendar you hang on your wall and lets you look at the "big picture." Month View doesn't have a lot of room to work with, so it displays appointments in a truncated format and does not display their durations or end times.

Before we leave the Calendar folder, let's try deleting the appointment we added in the previous lesson.

8 Use the Date Navigator to select the date of the dentist appointment you added in the previous lesson.

Find the appointment? Great!

 To delete an appointment, select it and press the Delete key.

Poof! The appointment vanishes from the calendar.

We're almost finished with our tour of the Calendar folder. In the next lesson, you will learn how to reschedule an appointment.

QUICK REFERENCE

TO SWITCH BETWEEN CALENDAR VIEWS:

CLICK ONE OF THE FOLLOWING BUTTONS ON THE TOOLBAR:

- TODAY VIEW DISPLAYS THE CURRENT DAY.
- DAY VIEW DISPLAYS ONE DAY AT A TIME.

- WORK WEEK VIEW DISPLAYS A WEEKLY CALENDAR WITHOUT WEEKENDS.
- WEEK VIEW DISPLAYS A WEEKLY CALENDAR INCLUDING WEEKENDS.
- MONTH VIEW DISPLAYS A MONTHLY CALENDAR.

Editing and Rescheduling Appointments

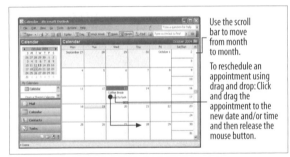

Use the scroll bar to move from month to month.

To reschedule an appointment using drag and drop: Click and drag the appointment to the new date and/or time and then release the mouse button.

Figure 1-25. Dragging and dropping is probably the fastest and easiest way to reschedule an appointment.

We don't live in a perfect world, so sometimes our appointments don't work out as planned. Coworkers cancel appointments at the last minute, meetings run longer than expected, and cable installation workers are famous for arriving late. Fortunately for us, rescheduling an appointment in Outlook is a very simple task.

There are two ways to reschedule an appointment in Outlook:

- **Dragging and Dropping the Appointment:** This is probably the most common way to reschedule an appointment (see Figure 1-25). You're probably already familiar with dragging and dropping if you have ever dragged a file to the Windows Recycle Bin or to another folder. To reschedule an appointment by dragging and dropping, switch Calendar Views, if necessary, select the appointment, and click and drag the appointment to the new date and time.
- **Opening and Editing the Appointment:** You can double-click any appointment to display its form. From there, you can change the date and/or time of the appointment and click the Save and Close button on the toolbar.

In this lesson, you will learn how to reschedule an appointment using these methods.

1 If necessary, click the Calendar button in the Navigation Pane.

First, we need to add a new appointment.

2 Click the New ▾ New Appointment button on the toolbar.

> *TIP* *Other ways to create a new appointment are to switch to Day or Week view, click and select the appointment's date and time, and enter the appointment's description; or press Ctrl + Shift + A.*

The Appointment window appears. You should already know the basic procedure for adding a new appointment.

3 Schedule an appointment using the following information:

Subject: Meet with Accountant
Start Time: 4:30 PM, April 15 2004
End Time: 5:00 PM, April 15 2004

Make sure that you click the Save and Close button when you're finished!

April 15, 2004 arrives. You're just about to have your taxes prepared when you notice the headlines of today's paper. Apparently, Congress has changed the tax-filing deadline from April 15 to April 30. Lucky you! There's no reason to do today what you can put off until tomorrow, so you decide to reschedule the appointment for April 30, 2004.

We'll reschedule this appointment using the drag-and-drop technique. First, you need to be able to see the original appointment and the destination date and/or time for when you want to reschedule the appointment. You will need to be in Month View to reschedule this particular appointment using drag and drop.

4 Click the Month View button on the toolbar and use the Vertical scroll bar to view April 2004.

You should be able to see the appointment you added in Step 3. Now let's reschedule the appointment.

5 Click the Meet with Accountant appointment in the April 15 box, drag it to the April 30 box, and release the mouse button.

The appointment has been rescheduled to 4:30 PM on April 30, 2004. Had you wanted to change the time as well, you would have needed to be in Day or Work Week View or else have used the Open and Edit method to reschedule the appointment.

Whoops! You must have misread the paper's headlines: what you thought was a new tax filing date was when the IRS will now begin garnishing the paychecks of those people who don't get their returns in on time. Better reschedule that appointment with your accountant.

This time we will use the Open and Edit method to reschedule the appointment.

6 Double-click the Meet with Accountant appointment.

The appointment appears in an appointment form. Rescheduling an appointment is not much different than creating a new appointment—all you have to do is select the new Start and End times and dates.

7 Click the first Start time list arrow (the date arrow) and select April 15, 2004 from the calendar.

Now all you have to do is save the rescheduled appointment.

8 Click the 🔲 Save and Close Save and Close button on the toolbar.

Another way to save and close is to press Alt + S.

Outlook saves the rescheduled appointment and closes the appointment form.

That's it! We've finished the Calendar portion of our Outlook tour. You've just learned the basics about adding, viewing, and rescheduling appointments.

QUICK REFERENCE

TO RESCHEDULE AN APPOINTMENT:

1. SWITCH TO A CALENDAR VIEW THAT DISPLAYS BOTH THE ORIGINAL DATE AND TIME AND THE NEW DATE AND TIME.

2. CLICK THE APPOINTMENT TO SELECT IT.

3. CLICK AND DRAG THE APPOINTMENT TO THE NEW DATE AND TIME.

OR...

1. DOUBLE-CLICK THE APPOINTMENT TO OPEN IT.

2. MODIFY THE APPOINTMENT'S START TIME AND END TIME.

3. CLICK THE SAVE AND CLOSE BUTTON, OR PRESS ALT + S WHEN YOU'RE FINISHED.

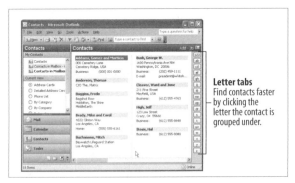

Figure 1-26. The Contacts view shows the information about all of your existing contacts at once.

Letter tabs
Find contacts faster by clicking the letter the contact is grouped under.

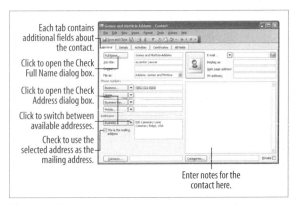

Each tab contains additional fields about the contact.

Click to open the Check Full Name dialog box.

Click to open the Check Address dialog box.

Click to switch between available addresses.

Check to use the selected address as the mailing address.

Enter notes for the contact here.

Figure 1-27. The Contact window is where you add information for a specific contact.

After you have received a business card or phone number from someone you want to remember, it's time to enter it into Outlook's Contacts list. The Contacts list has several major advantages over traditional "paper" planners. You can:

- Enter as much (or as little) information about your contacts as you want, such as their name, phone number, address—even their web address or birthday!

- Easily change a contact's information if he or she gets a new address or phone number.

- Use the Contacts list with other Outlook tools. For example, with a few clicks of the mouse, you can send an e-mail to a contact or schedule an appointment with him.

- Use the Contacts list with other programs. For example, you could store all your contacts on a Palm organizer (with the right software, of course!).

Actually, that's just the tip of the iceberg. Once you get used to using Outlook's Contacts list, you will wonder how you ever could have used a paper address book. This lesson will give you a quick tour of the Contacts list. You'll learn how to find your way around the Contacts list and how to add a new contact. Ready? Let's get started.

1 Click the Contacts button in the Navigation Pane.

TIP **Another way to create a new contact is to press** *Ctrl* **+** *Shift* **+** *C.*

Outlook switches to Contacts view, as shown in Figure 1-26.

2 Click the  New Contact button on the toolbar.

The new Contact form appears, as shown in Figure 1-27. It's up to you how much information you enter about each contact.

3 Click in the Full Name box and type Dr. Howard Smith.

Outlook is pretty smart about determining a person's first name, last name, title, and so on. Occasionally, an unusual or improperly entered name will confuse Outlook (hasn't a foreign name confused you at least once?), and the Check Full Name dialog box will appear, asking you to clarify which is the first name, last name, and title. You can summon the Check Full Name dialog box yourself by clicking the Full Name button—although you normally shouldn't need to do this.

4 Click the Full Name button.

The Full Name dialog box appears. Everything looks fine here.

5 Click OK to close the Full Name box.

Next, let's enter Dr. Smith's business phone number and e-mail address.

6 In the Phone numbers section, click in the first text box and type (612) 555-8080.

7 Click in the E-mail box, and type drsmith@the-hospital.com.

You can also use the Tab key to move between the fields in the contact form—press Tab to move to the next field and Shift + Tab to move to the previous field.

Move on to the next step and enter the address for this contact.

8 In the Address section, enter the following address:

500 Pine Street
Chaska, MN 55418

You may have noticed that a lot of text boxes in the Contacts form have arrow buttons next to them. These buttons are used if a contact has more than one phone number, e-mail account, or address. For example, clicking the arrow button next to the Address box would let you display a contact's home address.

9 Click the list arrow next to the Address box.

A list appears with the various addresses you can display. For this exercise, you only need to enter the business address.

10 Click anywhere outside the list to close the list without selecting any options.

Just like the Full Name box, the Address box has a special "Check Address" dialog box you can use to help you enter foreign or confusing addresses—just click the Address button to use it.

We've finished entering all the information for this contact, so you can save your changes and close the New Contact form.

 Another way to save and close is to press Alt + S.

The Contact form closes and Outlook adds the contact to the Contacts list.

QUICK REFERENCE

TO VIEW THE CONTACT LIST:
- CLICK THE CONTACTS BUTTON IN THE NAVIGATION PANE.

TO CREATE A NEW CONTACT:
1. CLICK THE NEW CONTACT BUTTON OR PRESS CTRL + N.
2. ENTER THE INFORMATION ABOUT THE CONTACT.
3. CLICK THE SAVE AND CLOSE BUTTON OR PRESS ALT + S WHEN YOU'RE FINISHED.

Figure 1-28. You can edit contact information directly in Contacts view...

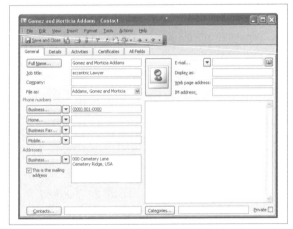

Figure 1-29. ...or by double-clicking a contact and editing it in the Contact window.

It's easy to change information about your contacts. You can edit contact information directly in Contacts view by clicking an entry and changing its text in place, or by double-clicking a contact to open it in the Contact form.

In this lesson, you will learn how to edit a contact using both methods and how to delete a contact that you no longer need.

1 Click the Contacts button in the Navigation Pane.

You can edit information about a contact directly in Contacts view (see Figure 1-28). Simply select the contact you wish to edit and then make the changes.

2 Click the Smith, Howard contact in the Contacts list.

Next, you need to select the text you want to change. For this lesson, we will change Dr. Howard's business number.

3 Select the business number for the Smith, Howard contact and replace it with the number (952) 555-8156.

You can also edit a contact by displaying the Contacts window. This may be necessary when the contact information that you want to edit isn't readily available from the Contacts list.

To open a contact in the Contacts window, simply double-click the contact.

4 Double-click the Smith, Howard contact.

The Howard Smith contact appears in the Contact window.

Notice that the Contact window is organized into several tabs: General, Details, Activities, Certificates, and All Fields (see Figure 1-29). Ninety-five percent of the time, you will find all the fields you need on the General tab. Sometimes you may want to enter additional information about a contact, such as their birthday, which department they work in, or the name of their spouse. When you want to enter more detailed information about a contact, you can click the Details tab.

5 Click the Details tab.

The Details tab appears.

6 Click in the Department box and type Radiology.

We're finished editing the Howard Smith contact.

7 Click the Save and Close button on the toolbar.

When you no longer need a contact, you can delete it from your Contacts list. The procedure for deleting a contact is no different than deleting any other Outlook item.

Another way to delete a contact is to select the contact and press the Delete key.

Outlook deletes the Howard Smith contact from the Contacts list and puts it in the Deleted Items folder.

Table 1-8 describes the contents and purpose of the tabs you'll find in the Contacts dialog box.

Table 1-8. The Contact window tabs

Contact tab	Description
General	Basic information: the contact's name, phone number(s), address(es), and e-mail.
Details	Detailed information: the contact's spouse, manager, birthday, etc.
Activities	Track your activities with the contact, such as calls and e-mails.
Certificates	Store digital ID's for the contact so that you can send them encrypted e-mail.
All Fields	Create and use your own custom fields for the contact.

QUICK REFERENCE

TO EDIT A CONTACT:

- IF THE INFORMATION YOU WANT TO MODIFY APPEARS IN THE CONTACT LIST, SELECT THE CONTACT AND MODIFY ITS INFORMATION IN PLACE.

OR...

1. DOUBLE-CLICK THE CONTACT YOU WANT TO EDIT.
2. MAKE THE NECESSARY CHANGES IN THE CONTACT WINDOW.
3. CLICK THE SAVE AND CLOSE BUTTON OR PRESS ALT + S WHEN YOU'RE FINISHED.

TO DELETE A CONTACT:

- SELECT THE CONTACT AND CLICK THE DELETE BUTTON ON THE TOOLBAR.

OR...

- SELECT THE CONTACT AND PRESS THE DELETE KEY.

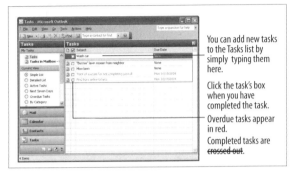

You can add new tasks to the Tasks list by simply typing them here.

Click the task's box when you have completed the task.

Overdue tasks appear in red.

Completed tasks are ~~crossed out~~.

Figure 1-30. The Tasks list helps you organize your daily tasks.

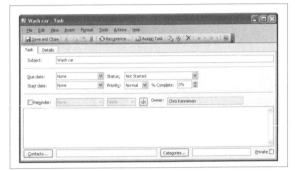

Figure 1-31. The Task window lets you enter more detailed information about a task.

Tasks are an unavoidable part of life. Often, writing down your tasks on a to-do list or task list makes them easier to remember and manage. To help you organize your tasks, Outlook comes with the Tasks list, as shown in Figure 1-30. As with most other Outlook items, you can make your tasks as simple or as detailed as needed. Here are a few more things to know about Outlook's tasks list:

- You can assign priorities to your tasks. For example, you could give a "Pay mortgage" task a higher priority than a "Wash the dog" task.

- You can assign start dates to your tasks for when they should appear as reminders in the Tasks list and due dates for when the task must be completed. For example, a "Pay mortgage" task might have a start date of January 25, 2004 and a due date of January 31, 2004.

- Tasks can be recurring. For example, you could create a "Take out the trash" task that appears in the Tasks list every Tuesday.

- Perhaps most satisfying of all, tasks in the Tasks list can be crossed off when you've finished them.

In this lesson, you will learn how to use Outlook's Tasks list to manage your to-do's.

1 Click the Tasks button in the Navigation Pane.

Outlook switches to the Tasks list, as shown in Figure 1-30. Although you can create a new task by clicking the New Task button on the toolbar, it's usually easier to create a new task by entering it directly in Task View.

2 Click in the Click here to add a new Task box and type Wash car, as shown in Figure 1-30.

> **TIP**
> Other ways to add a new task are to click the New Task button on the toolbar, or to press Ctrl + Shift + K.

You can also specify a due date for the task.

3 Click in the Due Date box to the right of the new task, click the arrow, and select a future date from the drop-down calendar.

You can edit a task directly in Task View or by double-clicking the task and editing it in the Task window.

4 Double-click the Wash car task.

The Wash car task appears in the Task window, as shown in Figure 1-31. The Task window lets you specify additional information about the task, such as the task's priority or the percentage of the task that is finished.

5 Click the Priority list arrow and select Low.

That's enough changes for now.

6 Click the Save and Close button on the toolbar.

Outlook saves the task and closes the Task window.

As you complete tasks, you will want to mark them as complete without deleting them from the Tasks folder in order to keep a record of what you've accomplished (something that is especially useful to keep on your computer screen when the boss passes by). Here's how to mark a task as complete:

7 Check the empty checkbox to the left of the Wash car task.

A check appears in the checkbox and a line appears through the task to indicate that it is complete. Eventually, you will want to delete some of your completed tasks. The procedure for deleting a task is no different than deleting any other Outlook item.

8 **Click the** Wash car **task, then press** Delete.

Outlook deletes the task from the Tasks list and puts it in the Deleted Items folder.

Table 1-9 describes the fields you'll see in the Task window.

Table 1-9. Fields in the Task window

Field	Description
Due Date	Specifies when the task must be completed.
Start Date	Specifies the date when the task will appear in the Tasks list as a reminder.
Status	Specifies the status of the task: Not Started, In Progress, Completed, Waiting on Someone Else, or Deferred.
Priority	Specifies the importance level of the task: High, Normal, or Low.
% Complete	Specifies the percentage of the task that is finished.
Reminder	Displays a reminder for the task.
Owner	Specifies the name of the person who created the task. If the task is sent to another person, that person becomes the owner of the task.

QUICK REFERENCE

TO VIEW THE TASKS LIST:

- CLICK THE TASKS BUTTON IN THE NAVIGATION PANE.

TO CREATE A NEW TASK:

- CLICK THE CLICK HERE TO ADD A NEW TASK BOX AND ENTER THE TASK AND ITS DUE DATE.

   OR...

1. CLICK THE NEW TASK BUTTON OR PRESS CTRL + N.
2. ENTER THE INFORMATION ABOUT THE TASK.
3. CLICK THE SAVE AND CLOSE BUTTON OR PRESS ALT + S WHEN YOU'RE FINISHED.

TO DELETE A TASK:

- SELECT THE TASK AND CLICK THE DELETE BUTTON ON THE TOOLBAR.

   OR...

- SELECT THE TASK AND PRESS THE DELETE KEY.

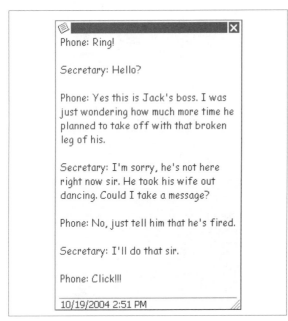

Figure 1-32. Outlook's notes.

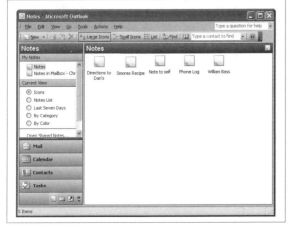

Figure 1-33. Outlook in Notes View.

Outlook's notes are the electronic equivalent of those sticky Post-It® Notes you use at home and in the office (see Figure 1-32). Use notes when you need to jot down a quick message or reminder to yourself. They are handy when you need to create a quick note, such as the directions to a meeting or a shipping address. Outlook's notes also don't clutter up your office the way Post-It® Notes seem to.

This lesson explains the quick and easy process of creating and deleting a note.

1 Click the Notes button **in the Navigation Pane.**

Outlook switches to Notes View, as shown in Figure 1-33. Here's how to create a note:

2 Click the New ▾ New Note button **on the tool-bar.**

> **TIP**
>
> *Another way to create a note is to press Ctrl + Shift + N.*

Outlook displays an empty note.

3 Type The combination to the safe is 24-17.

That's all there is to creating a note. Easy, isn't it?

4 Click the ☒ button **in the upper-right corner of the note.**

Outlook saves and closes the note. Modifying a note is just as easy.

5 Double-click the note you just created.

Outlook displays the note window.

6 Click after the 17 and type –58, **then close the note window.**

When you no longer need a note, you should probably delete it. Here's how:

7 Select the note you created and press Delete.

Outlook deletes the selected note.

QUICK REFERENCE

TO VIEW THE NOTES FOLDER:

- CLICK THE NOTES BUTTON IN THE NAVIGATION PANE.

TO CREATE A NEW NOTE:

- CLICK THE NEW NOTE BUTTON AND ENTER THE NOTE.

OR...

- PRESS CTRL + SHIFT + N, OR (FROM THE NOTES FOLDER) PRESS CTRL + N AND ENTER THE NOTE.

TO DELETE A NOTE:

- SELECT THE NOTE AND CLICK THE DELETE BUTTON.

OR...

- SELECT THE NOTE AND PRESS THE DELETE KEY.

Working with Outlook Today

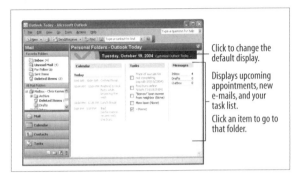

Figure 1-34. Outlook Today summarizes your appointments, tasks, and messages for the current day.

If you like seeing all your appointments, tasks, and upcoming events summarized in one place, then you'll love Outlook Today. Microsoft designed Outlook Today to look and work like a web page—just click any item to open it.

In this lesson, you will learn how to work with and customize Outlook Today.

1 Click the Mail button in the Navigation Pane. Click the Mailbox – Your Name folder at the top of the All Mail Folders list in the Navigation Pane.

The Outlook Today screen appears, as shown in Figure 1-34. Depending on your configuration, Outlook Today displays your appointments and tasks for the day and how many new e-mail messages you've received.

2 Click any item in the Outlook Today screen.

Whether you clicked an appointment, e-mail message, or task, Outlook opens that item in its appropriate folder so that you can view it in more detail or change it. Let's go back to the Outlook Today screen.

3 Close the item you just opened. Click the Mailbox – Your Name folder at the top of the All Mail Folders list.

You can easily customize Outlook Today and change the options for how e-mail messages, calendar items, and tasks are displayed. Here's how:

4 Click Customize Outlook Today.

The options are pretty much self-explanatory. You can specify whether or not you want to display the Outlook Today screen when you start Outlook, how many days to display in the Calendar, and how your tasks should be sorted.

5 Click Save Changes located in the upper righthand corner.

> **TIP**
>
> To Make Outlook Today the default page, click Customize Outlook Today on the Outlook Today page, select the When starting, go directly to Outlook Today checkbox, and click Save Changes.

QUICK REFERENCE

TO VIEW THE OUTLOOK TODAY SCREEN:

- IN THE MAIL PANE, CLICK THE MAILBOX-YOUR NAME FOLDER AT THE TOP OF THE ALL MAIL FOLDERS LIST IN THE NAVIGATION PANE.

TO CUSTOMIZE OUTLOOK TODAY:

1. CLICK CUSTOMIZE OUTLOOK TODAY.

2. MAKE THE DESIRED CHANGES.

3. CLICK SAVE CHANGES.

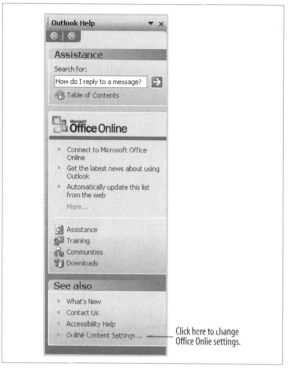

Figure 1-35. Asking a question in the Outlook Help task pane.

Figure 1-36. Possible topic answers for your question.

When you don't know how to do something in Windows or a Windows-based program, don't panic—just look up your question in the Outlook Help files. The Outlook

Help files can answer your questions, offer tips, and provide help for all of Outlook's features. Many Outlook users forget to use Help—which is unfortunate, because the Help files know more about Outlook than most Outlook reference books do!

You can make the Outlook Help files appear by pressing the F1 key. Then all you have to do is ask your question in normal English. This lesson will show you how you can get help using the Help files.

⸱ NOTE ⸱ *Microsoft has totally changed the way Help works in Office 2003 with Office Online. Instead of searching for help in the files already stored on your computer, Office Online searches the topic in their online database. The purpose of this feature is to provide current, up-to-date information on search topics. In their efforts to provide information on more advanced topics, however, they forgot the most basic and important ones—like replying to a message.*

1 Press the F1 key.

The Outlook Help task pane appears, as shown in Figure 1-35. You can ask Outlook Help questions in normal English, just as if you were asking a person instead of a computer. The program identifies key words and phrases in your questions such as "reply" and "message."

TIP *The F1 key is the help key for all Windows-based programs.*

2 Type How do I reply to a message? in the "Search for:" text box, as shown in Figure 1-35.

TIP *Another way to get help is to type your question in the Type a question for help box on the menu bar and press Enter. The results appear in the Outlook Help task pane. Alternatively, click the Table of Contents link in the Outlook Help task pane and search by topic.*

3 Click the Start searching button.

Office Online finds advanced results like "Remove comment marking from a message reply."

Let's try looking in the trusty old Offline Help files for help.

Fortunately, you can change your settings to perform Help searches without Office Online. Go to the See also section at the bottom of the Outlook Help task pane. Click the Online Content Settings option. Uncheck the Search online content when connected option and click OK. Office Online will automatically refer to Offline Help files if a connection to the Internet is not detected.

4 Click the Search list arrow in the Search area at the bottom of the task pane. Select Offline Help from the list and click the Start searching button.

The Offline Help search results appear, including a topic that actually helps us out.

5 Click the Reply to or forward a message help topic.

Another window appears with more subtopics.

6 Click the Reply to a message help topic.

Outlook displays information on how to reply to a message, as shown in Figure 1-36.

Notice that the Microsoft Office Outlook Help window has a toolbar that looks like some of the buttons you might have seen on a web browser. This lets you navigate through help topics just like you would while browsing the Web.

7 Click the Microsoft Office Outlook Help window's Close button and then click the Outlook Help task pane's Close button.

Both the Help window and task pane close.

Table 1-10 displays the Outlook Help buttons and describes what each does.

Table 1-10. Help buttons

Button	Description
	Tiles the Outlook program window and the Help window so you can see both at the same time.
⇐	Moves back to the previous help topic.
⇒	Moves forward to the next help topic.
🖨	Prints the current help topic.

QUICK REFERENCE

TO GET HELP:

1. PRESS THE F1 KEY.

2. TYPE YOUR QUESTION IN THE OUTLOOK HELP TASK BAR AND CLICK THE START SEARCHING BUTTON OR PRESS ENTER.

3. CLICK THE HELP TOPIC THAT BEST MATCHES WHAT YOU'RE LOOKING FOR. (REPEAT THIS STEP AS NECESSARY.)

TO TURN OFF OFFICE ONLINE:

1. CLICK THE ONLINE CONTENT SETTINGS OPTION IN THE OUTLOOK HELP TASK PANE.

2. UNCHECK THE SEARCH ONLINE CONTENT WHEN CONNECTED OPTION AND CLICK OK.

Changing the Office Assistant and Using the Help Button

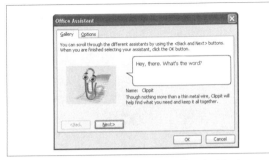

Figure 1-37. You can choose a new Office Assistant.

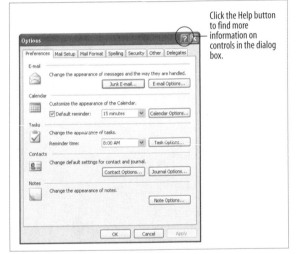

Click the Help button to find more information on controls in the dialog box.

Figure 1-38. Click the Help button to view a brief description of all the controls in a dialog box.

The Office Assistant is a cute animated character (a paper clip by default) that can answer your questions, offer tips, and provide help for all of Outlook's features. Many Outlook users don't use the Office Assistant, but it can be a very useful tool. If you like using the Office Assistant but want a change of pace from Clippit's antics, you can choose one of eight different Office Assistants to guide you through Outlook. Of course, if you really hate the Office Assistant, you can always shut it off.

The other topic covered in this lesson is how to use the Help button. During your journey with Outlook, you will undoubtedly come across a dialog box or two with a number of confusing controls and options. To help you find out what these are for, many dialog boxes contain a Help (?) button that explains the purpose of each of the dialog box's controls. This lesson will show you how

to use the Help button—but first, let's start taming the Office Assistant.

1 Select Help → Show the Office Assistant from the menu.

The Office Assistant appears.

2 Right-click the Office Assistant and select Choose Assistant from the shortcut menu.

The Office Assistant dialog box appears, as shown in Figure 1-37.

3 Click the Back or Next button to see the available Office Assistants.

The Office Assistant you select is completely up to you. They all work the same—they just look and act different.

4 Click OK when you find an Office Assistant that you like.

If you find the Office Assistant annoying (as many people do) and want to get rid of it altogether, here's how:

5 Right-click the Office Assistant.

A shortcut menu appears.

6 Select Hide from the shortcut menu.

You can always bring the Office Assistant back whenever you need its help.

Now, let's move on to how to use the Help button to discover the purpose of confusing dialog box controls.

7 Select Tools → Options from the menu and click the Preferences tab.

The Options dialog box appears, as shown in Figure 1-38. Notice the Help button located in the dialog box's title bar just to the left of the dialog box's close button.

8 Click the Help button (?).

A Microsoft Office Outlook Help window appears.

9 Click the Mail Setup tab link.

Links to more information about all the sections of the Mail Setup tab appear.

10 Click the Close button to close the Microsoft Office Outlook Help window. Click Cancel to close the Options dialog box.

QUICK REFERENCE

TO CHANGE OFFICE ASSISTANTS:

1. IF NECESSARY, SELECT HELP → SHOW THE OFFICE ASSISTANT FROM THE MENU.

2. RIGHT-CLICK THE OFFICE ASSISTANT AND SELECT CHOOSE ASSISTANT FROM THE SHORTCUT MENU.

3. CLICK THE NEXT OR BACK BUTTONS UNTIL YOU FIND AN OFFICE ASSISTANT YOU LIKE, THEN CLICK OK.

TO HIDE THE OFFICE ASSISTANT:

• RIGHT-CLICK THE OFFICE ASSISTANT AND SELECT HIDE FROM THE SHORTCUT MENU.

TO SEE WHAT A CONTROL IN A DIALOG BOX DOES:

1. CLICK THE DIALOG BOX HELP BUTTON (LOCATED RIGHT NEXT TO THE CLOSE BUTTON).

2. FIND THE CONTROL DESCRIPTION IN THE MICROSOFT OFFICE OUTLOOK HELP WINDOW.

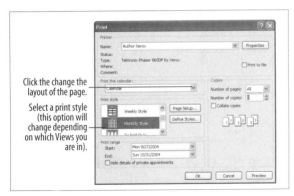

Click the change the layout of the page.

Select a print style (this option will change depending on which Views you are in).

Figure 1-39. The Print dialog box.

This lesson will show you how to send whatever you're working on to the printer. Printing is one of the easiest things you can do in Outlook. Here's how to print out a weekly schedule:

1 Click the Calendar button in the Navigation Pane.

Outlook switches to Calendar view.

2 Click the Print button on the toolbar.

The Print dialog box appears, as shown in Figure 1-39. The Print dialog box may differ depending on the current folder and the kind of printer you're connected to, but it should usually contain the options listed in Table 1-11.

> **TIP** Other ways to print are to press Ctrl + P or select File → Print from the menu. The options listed in the Print dialog box will change dramatically, depending on the View you are in.

3 Select Weekly Style from the Print style list and click OK.

Windows sends the item to the printer.

Table 1-11 describes the different Print dialog box options.

Table 1-11. Print dialog box options

Print option	Description
Name	Used to select which printer you want to send your files to (if you are connected to more than one printer). The currently selected printer is displayed.
Properties	Displays a dialog box with options available for your specific printer, such as the paper size you want to use, whether your document should be printed in color or black and white, etc.
Page range	Lets you specify what you want to print, such as a range of dates in the Calendar or selected items in the Contact list and Tasks list.
Number of copies	Specifies the number of copies you want to print.

QUICK REFERENCE

TO PRINT A VIEW:

1. CLICK THE PRINT BUTTON.

   OR...

   SELECT FILE → PRINT FROM THE MENU.

OR...

PRESS CTRL + P

2. SPECIFY THE DESIRED PRINT OPTIONS AND CLICK OK.

Exiting Microsoft Outlook

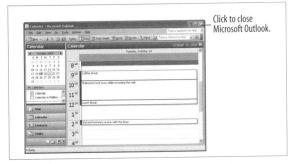

Click to close
Microsoft Outlook.

Figure 1-40. The Outlook program and its Close button.

Because the task covered in this lesson is so simple—exiting Microsoft Outlook—you're looking at what is undoubtedly the shortest and easiest lesson in this book.

Here then, is the long, technical, and complicated process of how to exit Microsoft Outlook.

1 **Click the** Close button **on the Microsoft Outlook Title Bar.**

The Outlook program window closes and you return back to the Windows desktop.

That's it! You've just completed your first chapter and are well on your way toward mastering Microsoft Outlook. You've already learned the Outlook basics: how to start Outlook and how to compose, send, and receive e-mail. You will use these skills often in your long and illustrious career with Microsoft Outlook.

QUICK REFERENCE

TO EXIT MICROSOFT OUTLOOK:

- CLICK THE OUTLOOK PROGRAM'S CLOSE BUTTON.

OR...

SELECT FILE → EXIT FROM THE MENU.

Chapter One Review

Lesson Summary

Starting Outlook

To Start Microsoft Outlook: Click the Windows Start button and select All Programs → Microsoft Office 2003 → Microsoft Office Outlook 2003.

Understanding the Outlook Screen

Be able to identify the major components of the Microsoft Outlook screen.

Using the Navigation Pane

To Switch between the Various Outlook Panes: Click the corresponding button in the Navigation Pane or select Go from the menu and select the pane you want to view.

Using Menus

To Open a Menu: Either click the menu with the mouse pointer or press the Alt key and the letter that is underlined in the menu name.

To Display a Menu's Hidden Commands: Click the downward-pointing arrow at the bottom of the menu or open the menu and wait a few seconds.

To Change How Menus Work: Select View → Toolbars → Customize from the menu and click the Options tab. Check or clear either the Always show full menus and/or Show Full Menus After a Short Delay options, then click Close.

Using Toolbars

To Use the Toolbars: Simply click the toolbar button you want to use.

To See a Description of a Toolbar Button: Position the pointer over the toolbar button and wait a second. A ScreenTip will appear and tell you what the button does.

Filling out Dialog Boxes

To Use a Text Box: Simply type the information directly into the text box.

To Use a Drop-Down List: Click the Down Arrow to list the drop-down list's options. Click an option from the list to select it.

To Check or Uncheck a Checkbox: Click the checkbox.

To View a Dialog Box Tab: Click the tab you want to view.

To Save Your Changes and Close a Dialog Box: Click the OK button or press Enter.

To Close a Dialog Box without Saving Your Changes: Click the Cancel button or press Esc.

Keystroke and Right Mouse Button Shortcuts

To Open a Context-Sensitive Shortcut Menu: Right-click the object.

To Use a Keystroke Shortcut: Press Ctrl + the letter of the keystroke shortcut you want to execute.

Composing and Sending E-mail

To Compose a Message: Click the Inbox folder in the Navigation Pane and click the New Mail Message on the toolbar. Type the recipient's address in the To: field or, click the To button to the left of the To box, click the name of the recipient in the Name list, then click the To button. Click the Subject box and enter the message's subject, click the pointer in the lower pane, and type the message. Click the Send button on the toolbar to send the message.

Receiving E-mail

To Receive and Read E-mail Messages: Click the Inbox folder in the Navigation Pane, click the Send/Receive button on the toolbar, and then click or double-click the message you want to read.

Things You Can Do with an E-mail Message: Reply to the message; forward the message; view or download any attachments; print the message; delete the message; move the message to a different folder; or ignore the message

Cutting, Copying, and Pasting Text

To Cut: Cut text or objects by selecting the text or object and using one of four methods to cut: Click the Cut button on the toolbar; select Edit → Cut from the menu; press Ctrl + X; or right-click and select Cut from the shortcut menu.

To Copy: Copy text or objects by selecting the text or object and using one of four methods to copy: click the Copy button on the toolbar; select Edit → Copy from the menu; press Ctrl + C; or right-click and select Copy from the shortcut menu.

To Paste: Paste text or objects by selecting the text or object and using one of four methods to paste the data: click the Paste button on the toolbar; select Edit → Paste from the menu; press Ctrl + V; or right-click and select Paste from the shortcut menu.

Creating an Appointment

To View the Calendar: Click the Calendar button in the Navigation Pane.

To Schedule an Appointment Directly on the Calendar: From Day or Week View, select the appointment's date and time and enter the appointment's description.

To Schedule an Appointment in a Form: Click the New button or press Ctrl + N. Enter the appointment and its date and time and click the Save and Close button, or press Alt + S when you're finished.

Viewing the Calendar

To Switch Between Calendar Views: Click one of the following buttons on the toolbar:

- Today View displays the current day.
- Day View displays one day at a time.
- Work Week View displays a weekly calendar without weekends.
- Week View displays a weekly calendar including weekends.
- Month View displays a monthly calendar.

Editing and Rescheduling Appointments

To Reschedule an Appointment (Using Drag and Drop): Switch to a Calendar view that displays both the original date and time and the new date and time. Click the appointment to select it, and then click and drag the appointment to the new date and time.

To Reschedule an Appointment (Using the Appointment Form): Double-click the appointment to open it. Modify the appointment's Start Time and End Time, and then click the Save and Close button or press Alt + S when you're finished.

Using the Contacts List

To View the Contacts List: Click the Contacts button in the Navigation Pane.

To Create a New Contact: Click the New button or press Ctrl + N. Enter the information about the contact, then click the Save and Close button or press Alt + S when you're finished.

Viewing, Editing, and Deleting Contacts

To Edit a Contact (In Place): If the information you want to modify appears in the Contact list, select the contact and modify its information in place.

To Edit a Contact (Using the Contact Form): Double-click the contact you want to edit, make the necessary changes, and then click the Save and Close button or press Alt + S when you're finished.

To Delete a Contact: Select the contact and click the Delete button on the toolbar or select the contact and press the Delete key.

Using the Tasks List

To View the Tasks List: Click the Tasks button in the Navigation Pane.

To Create a New Task (Directly in the Tasks List): Click the Click here to add a new Task box and enter the task.

To Create a New Task (Using the Task Form): Click the New Task button or press Ctrl + N, enter the information about task, and click the Save and Close button or press Alt + S when you're finished.

To Delete a Task: Select the task and click the Delete button on the toolbar or select the task and press the Delete key.

Using Notes

To View the Notes Folder: Click the Notes button in the Navigation Pane.

To Create a New Note: Click the New Note button and enter the note, or press Ctrl + Shift + N, or (from the Notes folder) press Ctrl + N and enter the note.

To Delete a Note: Select the note and click the Delete button or select the note and press the Delete key.

Working with Outlook Today

To View the Outlook Today Screen: In the Mail pane, click the Mailbox-Your Name folder at the top of the All Mail Folders list in the Navigation Pane.

To Customize Outlook Today: Click Customize Outlook Today, make the desired changes, and click Save Changes.

Getting Help

To Get Help: Press the F1 key. Type your question in the Outlook Help task bar and click the Start searching button or press Enter. Click the help topic that best matches what you're looking for. (Repeat this step as necessary.)

To Turn Off Office Online: Click the Online Content Settings option in the Outlook Help task pane. Uncheck the Search online content when connected option and click OK.

Changing the Office Assistant and Using the Help Button

To Change Office Assistants: If necessary, select Help → Show the Office Assistant from the menu. Right-click the Office Assistant and select Choose Assistant from the shortcut menu. Click the Next or Back buttons until you find an Office Assistant you like, then click OK.

To Hide the Office Assistant: Right-click the Office Assistant and select Hide from the shortcut menu.

To See what a Control in a Dialog Box Does: Click the Dialog box Help button (located right next to the close button) and find the control description in the Microsoft Office Outlook Help window.

Printing an Item

To Print a View: Click the Print button, select File → Print from the menu, or press Ctrl + P. Specify the desired print options and click OK.

Exiting Microsoft Outlook

To Exit Microsoft Outlook: Click the Outlook Program's Close button or select File → Exit from the menu.

Quiz

1. Right-clicking something in Outlook…
   A. Deletes the object.
   B. Opens a shortcut menu that lists everything you can do to the object.
   C. Selects the object.
   D. Nothing—the right mouse button is there for lefthanded people.

2. Which Outlook component do you use to quickly switch between Outlook tools?
   A. The Outlook Tools Wizard
   B. The Folder List
   C. The Navigation Pane
   D. The Tools List on the toolbar

3. You want to send a carbon copy of an e-mail to your boss. Where should you enter your boss's e-mail address?
   A. In the To: field
   B. In the Cc: field
   C. In the Bcc: field
   D. In the Address: field

4. Which of the following is *not* one of Outlook's built-in tools?
   A. E-mail
   B. Tasks list
   C. Expense Tracking
   D. Contact list

5. The Navigation Pane contains buttons that represent *every* folder in Microsoft Outlook. (True or False?)

6. You suspect that a foreign spy works at your company, and that at night she secretly uses your computer to send covert e-mail. How could you check Outlook for messages that have been sent?

    A. Click the Sent button in the Navigation Pane.

    B. You can't—Outlook doesn't save copies of sent messages.

    C. Open the Send Message Archive file, located in the My Documents folder.

    D. In the Mail pane, display the contents of the Sent Items folder.

7. When you receive an e-mail message, you can do the following: (Select all that apply.)

    A. Reply to the message.

    B. Forward the message to someone else.

    C. Return the message, unopened to the sender.

    D. View or download any files attached to the message.

8. Which of the following statements about the Calendar is NOT true?

    A. You can display the calendar in Today, Day, Work Week, Week, and Month Views.

    B. You can add a reminder to your appointments to prompt you of imminent appointments.

    C. You can schedule appointments by clicking and dragging them to the new desired day and/or time.

    D. Outlook can use Aztec, Babylonian, and Roman calendar systems in addition to the standard Gregorian calendar. You can also download calendars for the solar cycles of Mars and Venus from Microsoft's web site.

Homework

1. Start Microsoft Outlook.

2. Click the Mail button in the Navigation Pane.

3. Create a new e-mail message to yourself, using the following information:

    To: (Enter your e-mail address here)
    Subject: Hi (Enter your name)!
    Body: Hi (Enter your name), this is (Enter your name). How are you doing?Enjoying your Outlook class? Take care!

4. Click the Send button on the toolbar when you've finished writing the message.

5. Click the Send/Receive button on the toolbar to send and (hopefully) receive your message.

6. Click the Calendar button in the Navigation Pane.

7. Practice navigating through the calendar and switching between Day, Work Week, Week, and Month Views.

8. Create an appointment titled "My Birthday!" at 7:00 PM on your birthday.

9. Reschedule the "My Birthday!" appointment to 5:00 PM on the same day.

10. Click the Tasks button in the Navigation Pane.

11. Create a new task titled "Finish Outlook homework assignment."

12. Mark the "Finish Outlook homework assignment" as complete and exit Microsoft Outlook.

Quiz Answers

1. B. Right-clicking an object displays a shortcut menu for the object.

2. C. The Navigation Pane lets you switch between Outlook's tools.

3. B. Entering an e-mail address in the Cc: field sends that person a carbon copy of the message.

4. C. Outlook doesn't have an Expense Tracking tool—at least not in the current version!

5. False. The Navigation Pane contains buttons for the most common Outlook folders, such as the Inbox, Calendar, and Tasks list, but it doesn't include buttons for such folders as the Sent Items and Drafts folders.

6. D. The Sent Items folder contains copies of all the e-mail messages that you've sent—unless they've been deleted.

7. A, B, and D. All of these are things you can do to an e-mail message.

8. D. Though it's hard to believe, Outlook's calendar is available only in the standard Gregorian system, using Earth's solar cycle.

USING E-MAIL

CHAPTER OBJECTIVES:

Compose and send an e-mail message: Lesson 2.1

Specify special delivery options for an e-mail message: Lesson 2.2

Receive, sort, find, and delete messages: Lessons 2.3, 2.10, and 2.11

Reply to and forward an e-mail message: Lessons 2.4 and 2.5

Spellcheck an e-mail message before sending it: Lesson 2.6

Work with file attachments and hyperlinks: Lessons 2.7 through 2.9

Work with the Folder List: Lesson 2.12

Use Outlook Web Access: Lesson 2.13

CHAPTER TASK: CREATE AND RESPOND TO AN E-MAIL MESSAGE

Prerequisites

- Understand how to use menus, toolbars, dialog boxes, and shortcut keystrokes.
- Understand how to use the Navigation Pane and navigate within Outlook.

Unless you've been hiding out in a cave for the past 10 years, you already know that e-mail lets you send electronic messages to the staff at the office or to people all over the world. You probably also already know e-mail is fast (usually instantaneous) and economical (many e-mail accounts are completely free).

Sending and receiving e-mail messages is the biggest reason people use Outlook, so this is probably one of the most important chapters in the book. This chapter explains everything you need to know about e-mail: how to compose, send, and receive e-mail messages, how to reply to and forward e-mails, how to spellcheck an e-mail before sending it, and how to attach one or more files to an e-mail message. You will even learn how Outlook can help you find a misplaced e-mail message.

We have a lot of ground to cover in this chapter, so let's get started!

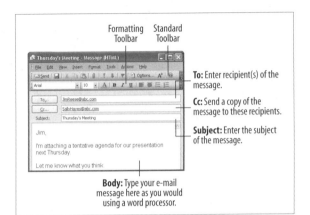

Figure 2-1. The New Message window.

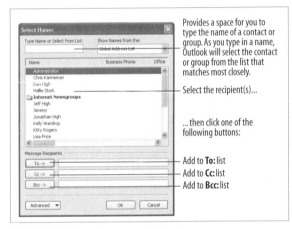

Figure 2-2. The Select Names dialog box.

We'll start this chapter off with a quick review of the most basic e-mail task of all: how to compose and send an e-mail message.

1 Make sure that you are in the Inbox folder—click the Mail button in the Navigation Pane if you're not.

The contents of the Inbox folder appear.

2 Click the ⌐New ▾ New Mail Message button on the toolbar.

 Other ways to compose a new message are to select File → New → Mail Message from the menu or to press Ctrl + Shift + M.

An Untitled – Message form appears, ready for you to compose a new message. First, you need to specify the recipient's e-mail address in the To field (see Figure 2-1). There are two ways to do this:

- If you know the e-mail address, type it into the To box.
- If you don't know the address, click the To button and select the address from your list of contacts.

In this exercise, we will use both methods to send the same message to two people. First let's enter an e-mail address directly into the To box...

3 Type your e-mail address into the To box.

If you need to send a message to more than one person, simply place a semicolon (;) between the recipients' e-mail addresses—for example: *JohnH@acme.com; BettyT@yahoo.com.*

Let's send this message to another person, this time using the address book to address the message.

4 Click the To button.

The Select Names dialog box appears, as shown in Figure 2-2.

5 Click the Show Names from the list arrow and select Contacts.

This will display the names and addresses in the Contacts folder.

6 Click the name of any recipient in the Name list and then click the To button.

If you need to send a message to more than one person, you can repeat this step to add the other recipients. When you're finished, move on to the next step.

7 Click OK.

The Select Recipients dialog box closes, and the recipient(s) appear in the To field.

8 (Optional) To send a *copy* of a message to someone, click in the Cc field and/or the Bcc field (instead of the To field) and repeat Steps 3–7 to enter their e-mail addresses.

Table 2-1 describes Carbon Copies (Cc) and Blind Carbon Copies (Bcc).

Next, you have to enter the subject of the message so your recipient(s) will know what your message is about. The subject will appear in the heading of the message in the recipient's inbox.

9 Click the Subject **field and type** Greetings from Timbuktu!

Now you can type the actual e-mail message.

10 Click the pointer in the body of the message and type:

Hi everyone – just wanted you all to know that my vacation in Timbuktu is going great so far!

Type the message as you would in a word processor. All the generic Windows commands such as cutting, copying, and pasting text are accessible in Outlook.

11 Click the ⊟Send Send button **on the toolbar when you're finished.**

The message is placed in the Outbox folder and will be sent the next time that you click the Send and Receive button.

> TIP *Another way to send an e-mail is to press* Alt + S.

12 Click the  Send/Receive button **on the toolbar.**

> TIP *Another way to send and receive e-mail is to press* Ctrl + M.

Outlook sends all the messages that are stored in the Outbox folder and retrieves any new e-mail messages that it finds on the e-mail server.

Table 2-1. Ways to address an e-mail message

Address	Description
To	Sends the message to the recipient you specify (required).
Carbon Copy (Cc)	Sends a copy of the message to a recipient who is not directly involved, but might be interested in the message.
Blind Carbon Copy (Bcc)	Sends a copy of the message to a recipient without anyone else knowing that she received the message. You need to select View → Bcc Field from the menu to use the Bcc Field.

QUICK REFERENCE

TO COMPOSE A MESSAGE:

1. CLICK THE INBOX FOLDER IN THE NAVIGATION PANE.

2. CLICK THE NEW MAIL MESSAGE BUTTON ON THE TOOLBAR.

3. TYPE THE RECIPIENT'S ADDRESS IN THE TO FIELD.

   OR...

   CLICK THE TO BUTTON TO THE LEFT OF THE TO BOX, CLICK THE NAME OF THE RECIPIENT IN THE NAME LIST, THEN CLICK THE TO BUTTON. CLICK OK WHEN YOU'RE FINISHED.

4. CLICK THE SUBJECT BOX AND ENTER THE MESSAGE'S SUBJECT.

5. CLICK THE POINTER IN THE LOWER PANE AND TYPE THE MESSAGE.

6. CLICK THE SEND BUTTON ON THE TOOLBAR TO SEND THE MESSAGE.

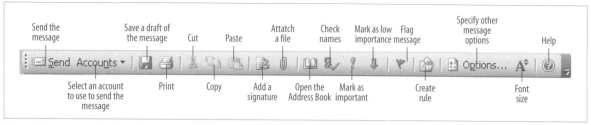

Figure 2-3. The Standard toolbar.

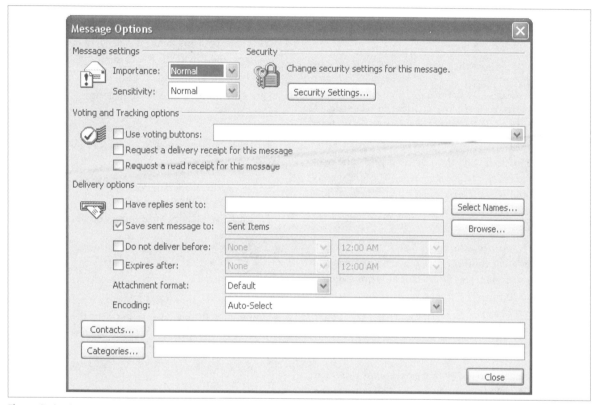

Figure 2-4. The Message Options dialog box lets you specify such options as the message's level of importance and sensitivity.

Most of the letters you mail are probably delivered by the postal service and require a first-class stamp. Sometimes you may need to mail a letter or package that requires special delivery options, such as parcel insurance, certification that the letter was received, or overnight delivery. Similarly, you can specify options for your e-mail messages. You can mark messages as urgent, specify a delivery receipt for e-mail messages, or request that messages be encoded so that they can be read by the intended recipient(s) only.

1 Click the  New Mail Message button on the toolbar.

> *TIP*
>
> *Other ways to compose a new message are to select File → New → Mail Message from the menu or to press Ctrl + Shift + M.*

First, we'll compose another e-mail message to ourselves.

2 Create the following e-mail message:

To: (Enter your own e-mail address here)
Subject: Help from Timbuktu!
Body: Please send money and start trying to get me another passport! I lost my wallet!

An e-mail message this important needs some special delivery options! To specify options for an e-mail message, click the Options button on the Standard toolbar (see Figure 2-3).

3 Click the Options button on the toolbar.

The Message Options dialog box appears, as shown in Figure 2-4.

> **TIP** *Another way to change a message's options is to select* View → Options *from the menu.*

You want to mark this message as urgent, and you want to receive notification of when the message is delivered and when the recipient opens the e-mail to read it. Let's start with marking the message as high importance.

> **NOTE** *If you are using Outlook in an Internet Only environment, some of the options will not appear in the Message Options dialog box.*

4 Click the ⌄ Importance drop-down arrow and select High.

> **TIP** *Another way to mark a message as urgent is to click the* Importance: High button *on the toolbar.*

Actually, you don't have to open the Message Options dialog box at all to mark a message as urgent. Simply click the 🔼 Importance: High button on the toolbar instead.

Next, you want to request both a delivery receipt and a read receipt for the message. Here's the difference between the two:

• **Delivery Receipt:** Outlook will send you notification when the message is successfully delivered to the recipient (which is usually almost instantaneous).

• **Read Receipt:** Outlook will send you notification when the recipient opens and (hopefully) reads the message.

5 Check both the Request a delivery receipt for this message and the Request a read receipt for this message boxes.

Those are all the options we need for this particular e-mail.

6 Click Close to close the Message Options dialog box.

Let's send our urgent message!

7 Click the Send button on the toolbar.

> **TIP** *Another way to send an e-mail is to press* Alt + S.

Depending on how Outlook is configured on your computer, you may have to perform the next step to send the e-mail message out immediately.

8 Click the 📧 Send/Receive ▾ Send/Receive button on the toolbar.

Outlook sends all the messages that are stored in the Outbox folder and retrieves any new e-mail messages it finds on the e-mail server.

Table 2-2 describes the different message options.

Table 2-2. Message options

Option	Description
Importance	Specifies whether the message is of high, normal, or low importance.
Sensitivity	Displays a tag indicating how the recipient should treat the message.
Security Settings	Encodes the message so it is not readable by anyone except the recipient(s).
Use voting buttons	Allows the recipient to quickly answer a sender's question by use of voting buttons. Outlook can then tabulate the results of the vote for the sender.

Table 2-2. Message options (Continued)

Option	Description
Request a delivery receipt for this message	Returns a message to you verifying the date and time the message arrived at the Inbox of the recipient.
Request a read receipt for this message	Returns a message to you verifying the date and time the message was opened by the recipient.
Have replies sent to	Sends replies to this message to someone else, such as an assistant.
Save sent message to	Saves a copy of the sent message in the specified folder.
Do not deliver before	Keeps the message in your Outbox folder until the date and time you specify.
Expires after	Makes the message unavailable after the specified date and time.

QUICK REFERENCE

TO SPECIFY MESSAGE OPTIONS:

1. CLICK THE NEW MAIL MESSAGE BUTTON ON THE TOOLBAR AND CREATE THE MESSAGE.

2. CLICK THE OPTIONS BUTTON.

3. SPECIFY THE MESSAGE OPTIONS AND CLICK OK.

TO MARK A MESSAGE AS URGENT:

• CLICK THE IMPORTANCE: HIGH BUTTON ON THE TOOLBAR.

Messages that have not been opened appear in **bold** and have a closed envelope icon ✉ next to them. A paper clip 📎 indicates an attached file.

This area displays the messages in the highlighted folder. Click or double-click the message you want to read.

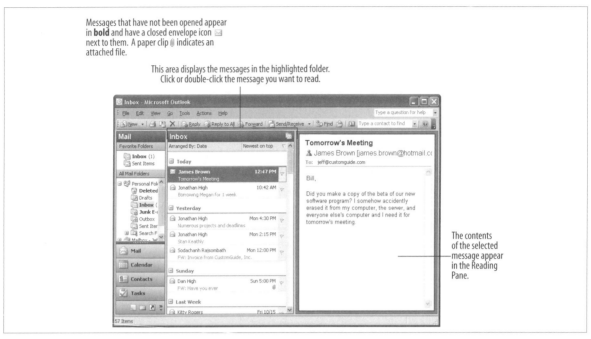

The contents of the selected message appear in the Reading Pane.

Figure 2-5. The Inbox window.

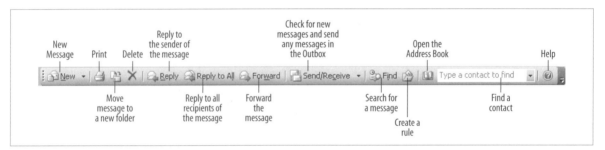

New Message | Print | Delete | Reply to the sender of the message | Check for new messages and send any messages in the Outbox | Open the Address Book | Help

Move message to a new folder | Reply to all recipients of the message | Forward the message | Search for a message | Find a contact | Create a rule

Figure 2-6. The Standard toolbar in Inbox View.

This lesson explains how to receive, read, and sort your e-mail messages in Outlook. When you receive e-mail messages, they appear in the Inbox. Normally, Outlook automatically checks your mail server for new messages every 10 minutes (although you can change this setting). If Outlook finds any new messages on your mail server, it downloads them and saves them to your Inbox. You can force Outlook to check for new messages by clicking the Send and Receive button on the toolbar. Let's check to see if you have any new e-mail.

1 Click the [Send/Receive] Send/Receive button on the toolbar.

Other ways to send an e-mail are to press *Ctrl* **+** *M* **or to select** *Tools → Send/Receive* **and then choose your account from the menu.**

You should receive at least one message (the message you sent to yourself in the previous lesson). Any new, unread messages appear in **bold** and have a closed envelope icon (✉) next to them. All messages have one or more icons to indicate their status, importance, and contents. Table 2-3 lists these icons and what they mean.

The next few steps explain how to open and read a message.

2 Click the message you want to read.

The contents of the message appear in the Reading Pane of the Inbox window, as shown in Figure 2-5. You can also open a message in its own window by double-clicking the message.

3 Double-click the Greetings from Timbuktu! message.

The message appears in its own window. You can close the message window when you're finished reading it by clicking the window's close button.

4 Close the Message window by clicking its Close button.

Once you have received a message, there are several things that you can do with the message: reply to it, forward it, view or download any attachments, print the message, or delete the message. (Figure 2-6 shows the Inbox View Standard toolbar, which offers short

cuts to take these actions.) We'll cover all of these topics later in the chapter.

When your Inbox is full of messages, it can be difficult to find what you're looking for. Try arranging the messages to sort the items to an easier view.

5 Click the Arranged By: column heading and select From.

 TIP *Another way to arrange messages is to select View → Arrange By and select an option from the menu.*

The messages are sorted by the sender.

6 Click the Arranged By: column heading and select Date.

This time the messages are sorted chronologically by when they were received.

See Table 2-4 to view other ways to arrange your messages.

Table 2-3. Message icons

Icon	Icon name	Description
✉	Unopened Message	This message has not yet been read or opened.
✉	Opened Message	This message has been read (or at least opened).
✉	Reply	You have replied to this e-mail message.
✉	Forward	You have forwarded this e-mail message.
◊	Attachment	This message has one or more files attached to it.
!	Urgent	This message is marked as urgent—better look at it fast!
⚑	Flagged	This message has been flagged to remind you about something.

Table 2-4. Arrange By options

Arrange By	Description
Date	Arranges messages by date, starting with today moving forward.
Conversation	Arranges messages by conversation topic.
From	Arranges messages by sender.
To	Arranges messages by recipient.
Folder	Arranges messages by the folders they are stored in.
Size	Arranges messages by size.
Subject	Arranges messages by topic.

Table 2-4. Arrange By options

Arrange By	Description
Type	Arranges messages by type.
Flag	Arranges messages by flag status.
Attachments	Arranges messages by whether or not they have an attachment.
E-mail Account	Arranges messages by e-mail account.
Importance	Arranges messages by importance.
Categories	Arranges messages by assigned categories.

QUICK REFERENCE

TO RECEIVE AND READ E-MAIL MESSAGES:

1. CLICK THE INBOX FOLDER IN THE NAVIGATION PANE.

2. CLICK THE SEND/RECEIVE BUTTON ON THE TOOLBAR.

3. CLICK OR DOUBLE-CLICK THE MESSAGE YOU WANT TO READ.

TO SORT MESSAGES:

• CLICK THE ARRANGED BY COLUMN HEADING AND SELECT THE OPTION YOU WANT TO USE TO SORT THE INBOX.

OR...

• SELECT VIEW → ARRANGE BY AND SELECT AN OPTION FROM THE MENU.

Replying to a Message

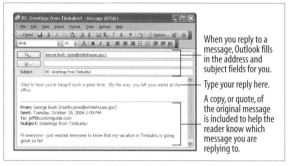

When you reply to a message, Outlook fills in the address and subject fields for you.

Type your reply here.

A copy, or quote, of the original message is included to help the reader know which message you are replying to.

Figure 2-7. It's easy to reply to a message.

You can reply to an e-mail message just like you would answer a letter. Replying to an e-mail message is incredibly easy—you don't even need to know the person's e-mail address. Just click the Reply button, write your response, and Outlook takes care of the rest.

This lesson explains how to reply to an e-mail.

1 Select the Greetings from Timbuktu! message that you sent to yourself earlier.

Next, you need to decide who you want to respond to. You have two choices:

*  **Reply:** Sends the reply only to the author of the message.

* **Reply to All:** Sends the reply to everyone who received the message.

2 Click the Reply button on the toolbar.

A new Message form appears where you can type your reply. Outlook automatically fills in the recipient's e-mail address, subject line, and body of the message in the new Message form—although you can change this information if you want.

Now all you have to do is enter a response to the message (see Figure 2-7).

3 Type Glad to hear you're having such a great time. By the way, you left your wallet here at the office.

We're ready to send the message.

4 Click the Send button on the toolbar.

The message is sent to the Outbox folder and will be sent the next time that you click the Send and Receive button.

Actually, some people think replying to an e-mail message is *too easy*. If you don't respond to your e-mail messages, no one is going to believe your "I received your message but I haven't had time to write back" and "I'm sorry, I somehow misplaced your address" excuses.

QUICK REFERENCE

TO REPLY TO A MESSAGE:

1. FIND AND OPEN THE MESSAGE TO WHICH YOU WANT TO REPLY.

2. CLICK THE REPLY OPTION YOU WANT TO USE:

   REPLY SENDS THE REPLY ONLY TO THE AUTHOR OF THE MESSAGE.

   REPLY TO ALL SENDS THE REPLY TO THE AUTHOR AND EVERYONE WHO RECEIVED THE MESSAGE.

3. TYPE YOUR REPLY AND CLICK THE SEND BUTTON ON THE TOOLBAR WHEN YOU'RE FINISHED.

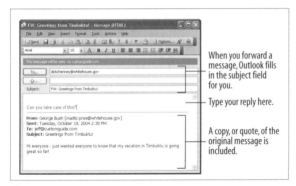

When you forward a message, Outlook fills in the subject field for you.

Type your reply here.

A copy, or quote, of the original message is included.

Figure 2-8. A message can be forwarded.

After you've read a message, you can add your own comments and forward it to someone else. Forwarding a message is very similar to replying to a message, except that you send the message on to someone else instead of back to the original sender. Besides the typical business correspondence, many people like to forward e-mails, called forwards, that contain jokes, inspirational (but almost always untrue) stories, and urban legends.

This lesson explains how to forward a message.

1 Select the Help from Timbuktu! **message that you created earlier.**

Here's how to forward the message to another recipient:

2 Click the 🖃 Forward Forward button **on the toolbar.**

A new Message form appears with the message you are forwarding. You need to specify the recipient to whom you want to send, or forward, the message.

3 Click the To button.

The Select Names dialog box appears.

4 Click the ☑ Show Names from the **down arrow and select** Contacts, **if necessary.**

This will display the names and addresses in the Contacts folder.

5 Click the name of any recipient in the Name list, click the To button, and then click OK.

The Select Recipients dialog box closes and the recipient(s) appear in the To field. You can also add your own comments about the message you are forwarding.

6 Click the message body area and type Can you take care of this?, **as shown in Figure 2-8.**

We don't really need to send this e-mail, so you can close it without saving any changes.

7 Close the message window and click No when asked if you want to save your changes.

QUICK REFERENCE

TO FORWARD A MESSAGE:

1. FIND AND SELECT THE MESSAGE YOU WANT TO FORWARD AND CLICK THE FORWARD BUTTON ON THE TOOLBAR.

2. ENTER THE RECIPIENT'S E-MAIL ADDRESS IN THE TO FIELD.

3. (OPTIONAL) ENTER YOUR OWN COMMENTS IN THE MESSAGE BODY AREA.

4. CLICK THE SEND BUTTON ON THE TOOLBAR.

Checking Your Spelling

Figure 2-9. The Spelling dialog box.

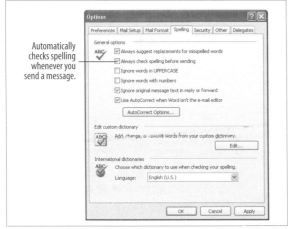

Automatically checks spelling whenever you send a message.

Figure 2-10. By selecting Tools → Options from the menu and clicking the Spelling tab, you can specify that Outlook automatically checks the spelling of your messages before sending them.

It's usually a good idea to spellcheck your messages before you send them. You can use Outlook's built-in spellchecker to find and correct any spelling errors that you might have made in your e-mails. E-mail messages often contain names and information the spellchecker may not recognize. When this happens, click either Ignore to ignore the word or Add to add the word to the custom spelling dictionary.

Outlook can also use Microsoft Word as its default e-mail editor. If this is the case, Word will underline suspected spelling errors in red. Simply right-click any incorrectly spelled words to make a correction, ignore the word, or add it to the dictionary.

1 Start the Notepad program by clicking the Windows Start button and selecting Programs → Accessories → Notepad from the menu.

The Notepad program appears. Notepad is a mini word processor that comes with Windows. Next, you need to open the document that contains the text you want to copy.

2 Select File → Open from the menu, navigate to your practice folder, then find and double-click the Lesson 2 file.

You want to copy the text in this letter and paste it into an e-mail message.

3 Press Ctrl + A to select all the text in the document.

Now you can copy the selected text to the Windows clipboard.

4 Press Ctrl + C to copy the document.

The selected text is copied from Notepad and placed on the Windows *Clipboard,* ready to be moved to a new location.

5 Close the Notepad program.

You should be back in Microsoft Outlook.

6 Click the New Mail Message button on the toolbar.

An Untitled – Message form appears, ready for you to enter a new message. You want to paste the text you copied from the Notepad program into the body of the new e-mail message.

7 Click the pointer in the body of the message and then click the Paste button on the toolbar.

Poof! The copied text appears at the insertion point. OK—time to check the spelling in this e-mail.

8 Select Tools → Spelling from the menu.

The Spelling dialog box appears, as shown in Figure 2-9. Because it can't find the word "auxilary" in its dictionary, the spellchecker flags it as a possible spelling error and lists a suggestion for the correct spelling of the word.

9 Click auxiliary in the Suggestions list and click Change.

Outlook makes the spelling correction for you. The next word Outlook flags, "Willes," isn't misspelled—the spellchecker just can't find it in its dictionary. There are two things you can do when the spellchecker doesn't recognize a correctly spelled word:

- **Ignore All:** Leaves the spelling as it is, and ignores that word throughout the rest of your presentation.
- **Add:** Adds the word to the spelling dictionary, so the spellchecker won't nag you about it during future spellchecks. Use this option for nonstandard words you use often.

Since "Willes" isn't a spelling error, you can tell the spellchecker to ignore it.

10 Click Ignore All to ignore all occurrences of "Willes" in the e-mail.

The spellchecker can't find any more incorrectly spelled words in the e-mail and displays the dialog box stating the spell check is complete.

11 Click OK.

Instead of having to select Tools → Spelling every time you want to run the spellchecker, you can tell Outlook to automatically check the spelling in your messages before you send them. If you're a terrible speller, as many of us are, the Automatic Spell Check feature is *highly recommended*.

12 Select Tools → Options from the main Outlook menu and click the Spelling tab.

The Options dialog box appears with the Spelling tab displayed, as shown in Figure 2-10.

13 Make sure the Always check spelling before sending checkbox is checked.

Now you can be sure that you won't forget to spellcheck a message before sending it!

14 Click Cancel to close the dialog box without saving any changes.

It's important to note that the spellchecker will not catch all of your spelling errors. For example, if you type the word "hat" when you mean to type "had," the spellchecker won't catch it because "hat" is a correctly spelled word.

QUICK REFERENCE

TO CHECK YOUR SPELLING:

- SELECT TOOLS → SPELLING FROM THE MENU.

OR...

- PRESS F7.

TO CORRECT SPELLING USING MICROSOFT WORD:

- RIGHT-CLICK THE SPELLING OR GRAMMAR ERROR AND SELECT THE CORRECTION FROM THE SHORTCUT MENU.

TO AUTOMATICALLY SPELL CHECK ALL NEW MESSAGES:

1. SELECT TOOLS → OPTIONS FROM THE MENU AND CLICK THE SPELLING TAB.

2. MAKE SURE THE ALWAYS CHECK SPELLING BEFORE SENDING CHECKBOX IS CHECKED.

3. CLICK OK.

Inserting a Hyperlink

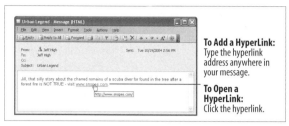

To Add a HyperLink:
Type the hyperlink address anywhere in your message.

To Open a HyperLink:
Click the hyperlink.

Figure 2-11. E-mails often contain hyperlinks, which point to web pages on the Internet.

Sometimes when you open an e-mail message, you may see one or more *hyperlinks*: blue, underlined text with the name of a web page, such as www.foxnews.com. If you want to look at that page, all you have to do is click the text and up pops your web browser with the web page you clicked. If you have ever been on the Internet, you've used hyperlinks to move between different web pages.

So how do you add a hyperlink to your own e-mail messages? Just type the hyperlink address anywhere in your message. Outlook is smart enough to recognize the address and formats it accordingly.

1 Click the New Mail Message button on the toolbar.

First, we'll compose an e-mail message to ourselves.

2 Create the following e-mail message:

To: (Enter your own e-mail address here)
Subject: Urban Legend
Body: Jill, That silly story about the charred remains of a scuba diver found in the tree after a forest fire is NOT TRUE – visit www.snopes.com.

As soon as Outlook sees the familiar "www," it formats "www.snopes.com "as a hyperlink.

3 Send the e-mail by clicking the Send button and then the Send/Receive button on the toolbar.

You should receive the message you just sent yourself.

4 Select the Urban Legend message.

If you want to see the page behind a hyperlink, simply click the hyperlink.

5 Click the www.snopes.com hyperlink, as shown in Figure 2-11.

If everything on your computer is set up correctly, your web browser should open the quite interesting Urban Legends Reference web page.

6 Close your web browser.

QUICK REFERENCE

TO OPEN A HYPERLINK:
* CLICK THE HYPERLINK.

TO INSERT A HYPERLINK IN AN E-MAIL MESSAGE:
* TYPE THE HYPERLINK ADDRESS ANYWHERE IN THE MESSAGE, USING THE CORRECT FORMAT (I.E., "WWW.MICROSOFT.COM").

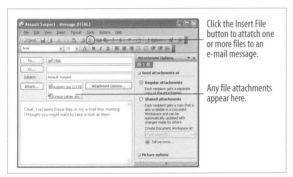

Click the Insert File button to attach one or more files to an e-mail message.

Any file attachments appear here.

Figure 2-12. You can attach one or more files, called attachments, to an e-mail message.

One of the most powerful and useful features of e-mail is the ability to attach one or more files to a message. Such files are called *attachments* and can be pictures, documents, and more. The recipient of an attachment opens the attached file in the program in which it was created. In this lesson, you will learn how to attach a file to an e-mail message.

1 Click the New Mail Message button on the toolbar.

First we'll compose another e-mail message to ourselves.

2 Create the following e-mail message:

To: (Enter your own e-mail address here.)
Subject: Assault suspect
Body: Chief, I received these files in my e-mail this morning. I thought you might want to take a look at them.

It's a good idea to leave some space between your message and any attachments.

3 Press Enter.

OK! You're ready to attach a file to this e-mail message. Here's how:

4 Click the 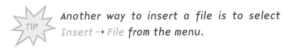 Insert File button on the toolbar.

> **TIP** Another way to insert a file is to select Insert → File from the menu.

The Insert File dialog box appears. Now you have to find the file you want to attach.

5 Navigate to the folder where your practice files are located.

Use the [Practice ▼] "Look in" list and Up One Level button 📁 to navigate to the various drives and folders on your computer.

6 Find and double-click the Lineup Letter file.

An icon representing the Lineup Letter appears at the top of the e-mail. You can attach more than one file to an e-mail—just repeat the procedures in Steps 4–6.

7 Repeat Steps 4–6 and attach the Suspect file.

8 Send the e-mail by clicking the Send button on the toolbar.

QUICK REFERENCE

TO ATTACH A FILE TO AN E-MAIL:

1. CLICK THE NEW MAIL MESSAGE BUTTON ON THE TOOLBAR AND CREATE THE MESSAGE.

2. CLICK THE INSERT FILE BUTTON ON THE TOOLBAR.

   OR...

   SELECT INSERT → FILE FROM THE MENU.

3. BROWSE TO, FIND, AND DOUBLE-CLICK THE FILE YOU WANT TO ATTACH.

4. TO ATTACH ADDITIONAL FILES, REPEAT STEPS 2 AND 3.

To view an attachment, select the file you want to open.

A paper clip 📎 indicates an attached file.

Figure 2-13. E-mail messages with a 📎 paper clip icon have attachments.

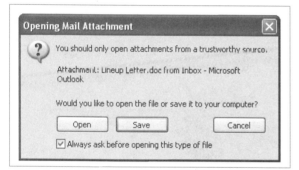

Figure 2-14. Outlook gives you the option of opening an attachment or saving it to a file on your hard disk.

In the previous lesson, you learned how to attach a file to an e-mail message. In this lesson, you will learn how to view an e-mail attachment and save it to your hard disk. Figure 2-13 shows an example of an e-mail with an attached file. Let's get started.

1 **Click the** Send/Receive button **on the toolbar.**

You should receive the message you sent to yourself in the previous lesson. Notice the message has a 📎 paper clip icon next it, indicating that the message contains an attachment.

2 **Select the** Assault Suspect **message in the Inbox pane.**

Several icons appear on the message header in the Reading Pane. To view the message's attachment(s), simply double-click the file you want to view.

3 **Double-click the** 📄 *Lineup Letter.doc* **file.**

The Opening Mail Attachment dialog box appears, as shown in Figure 2-14. Outlook displays the Opening Mail Attachment dialog box when it's not sure what to do with an attachment. You have two choices:

- **Open it:** Opens the file in the program that created it (if it's installed on your computer). Since some files can contain viruses, it is recommended that you use the Save option to save files to your hard disk and scan them using an anti-virus program before opening them.

- **Save it to your computer:** Saves the file to your hard disk. Make sure you keep track of where you save the file or you may not be able to find it later.

For this lesson, we'll open the *Lineup Letter.doc* file.

4 **Select the** Open **option.**

Outlook opens the Lineup Letter in Microsoft Word.

5 **Close Microsoft Word.**

Sometimes Outlook will ask you what you want to do with an attachment. Let's try opening the suspect file.

6 **Double-click the** *suspect.jpg* **file.**

Outlook opens the *suspect.jpg* file in a graphics program (provided you have one installed on your computer).

7 **Close the** *suspect.jpg* **window.**

You're back in Microsoft Outlook.

Attachments are sometimes easier to work with when the e-mail is opened in its own form.

8 **Double-click the** Assault Suspect **message in the Inbox pane.**

The Assault Suspect message opens in its own window. You can easily save any attachment to your hard disk.

9 **Right-click the** Suspect **attachment and select** Save As **from the shortcut menu.**

The Save Attachment dialog box appears. You don't need to save the Suspect attachment to the hard disk, so you can close the Save Attachment dialog box.

10 Click Cancel to close the Save Attachment dialog box and then close the Assault Suspect message window.

One final note on attachments: if you've been watching the news the past few years, you've undoubtedly heard about computer viruses and the havoc they can wreak. Many computer viruses are spread as e-mail attachments. For example, the dreaded "Melissa" and "I Love You" viruses that shut down thousands of computers a few years ago were both e-mail attachments. So how do you avoid such things? First, never open an attachment that looks suspicious or that is from someone you don't know. Second, make sure you have a good anti-virus program installed on your computer and that you save files to your hard disk before opening them.

QUICK REFERENCE

TO OPEN AN ATTACHMENT:

• OPEN THE E-MAIL BY CLICKING IT IN THE INBOX PANE, THEN DOUBLE-CLICK THE ATTACHMENT YOU WANT TO VIEW AND SELECT OPEN.

TO SAVE AN ATTACHMENT TO YOUR HARD DISK:

1. OPEN THE E-MAIL BY DOUBLE-CLICKING IT, THEN RIGHT-CLICK THE ATTACHMENT AND SELECT SAVE AS FROM THE SHORTCUT MENU.

2. SPECIFY A FILENAME AND LOCATION FOR THE ATTACHMENT AND CLICK OK.

Finding Messages

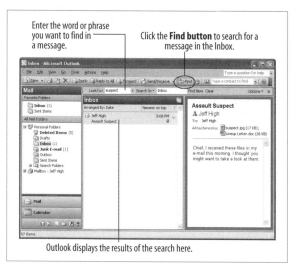

Enter the word or phrase you want to find in a message.

Click the **Find button** to search for a message in the Inbox.

Outlook displays the results of the search here.

Figure 2-15. Outlook's Find feature lets you find e-mail messages that contain a specified word or phrase.

The longer you use Outlook, the more cluttered your Inbox becomes, and the more difficult it is to find a specific e-mail message. Luckily, Outlook comes with a great Find feature, which can search for and track down your lost e-mails. Find searches the From field, Subject field, and message text of your e-mails for a specified word or phrase. Even if you can only remember a little bit about an e-mail message, Find can probably retrieve it.

In this lesson, you will learn how to use Outlook's Find feature to search for e-mail messages in your Inbox.

1 Click the 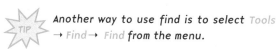 Find button on the toolbar.

> **TIP** *Another way to use find is to select* Tools → Find → Find *from the menu.*

The Find pane appears at the top of the message window. Normally, all you have to do is type the word or phrase you're looking for in the "Look for" box and click Find Now.

2 Type suspect in the Look for box and make sure the Search all text in each message box, located under Options, is checked.

The "Search all text in each message" box ensures that Outlook looks in the actual text of the messages for the specified word or phrase. Let's see how many e-mail messages contain the word "suspect."

3 Click the Find Now button.

Outlook searches the Inbox for messages that contain the word "suspect" and displays the results in the Inbox pane, as shown in Figure 2-15.

You can close the Find pane when you're finished using it.

4 Click the × Close button, located on the right side of the Find pane.

The Find pane closes and Outlook once again displays all the messages in your Inbox.

The Find feature is a lot more advanced than it looks. By clicking the Advanced Find button, you can search for messages specifically by date, subject, importance, and more.

QUICK REFERENCE

TO FIND A MESSAGE:

1. CLICK THE FIND BUTTON ON THE TOOLBAR.
   OR...
   SELECT TOOLS → FIND → FIND FROM THE MENU.

2. ENTER THE TEXT YOU WANT TO SEARCH FOR IN THE LOOK FOR BOX. ENSURE THAT THE SEARCH ALL TEXT IN EACH MESSAGE BOX IS CHECKED UNDER OPTIONS TO SEARCH THE ACTUAL TEXT IN YOUR E-MAIL MESSAGES.

3. CLICK FIND NOW.

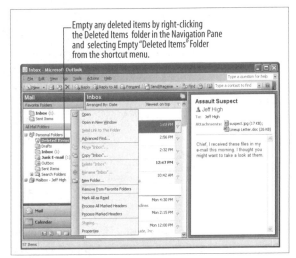

Empty any deleted items by right-clicking the Deleted Items folder in the Navigation Pane and selecting Empty "Deleted Items" Folder from the shortcut menu.

Figure 2-16. The Deleted Items folder stores all your deleted e-mail messages—as well as other deleted Outlook items.

If you are extremely organized and routinely clear the Inbox of old e-mail messages, finding messages shouldn't be a problem. When you delete an e-mail (or any Outlook item), Outlook places it in the Deleted Items folder. Just like the Windows Recycle Bin, the Deleted Items folder contains deleted Outlook items. If you change your mind and decide you need a deleted message, it's easy to find and retrieve it. This lesson will show you how to open the Deleted Items folder, restore a deleted message, and empty the Deleted Items folder.

1 Delete the Assault Suspect message by selecting it and pressing Delete.

Outlook removes the Assault Suspect message from the Inbox and places it in the Deleted Items folder.

2 Switch to the Deleted Items folder by clicking the Deleted Items folder in the Navigation Pane (see Figure 2-16).

The Deleted Items folder displays all the messages you have recently deleted. If you accidentally delete a message, you can easily retrieve it.

3 Select the Assault Suspect message, then click the Move to Folder button on the toolbar and select Inbox.

 Another way to move an item to a folder is to open the folder list and drag the item to the desired folder.

Outlook moves the Assault Suspect message back to the Inbox. Occasionally, you will want to empty the Deleted Items folder. Here's how:

4 Right-click the Deleted Items folder in the Navigation Pane, select Empty "Deleted Items" Folder from the shortcut menu, and click Yes to confirm the deletion.

Outlook permanently deletes the contents of the Deleted Items folder.

You can also have Outlook automatically empty the Deleted Items folder every time you quit Outlook. Simply select Tools → Options from the menu, click the Other tab, and check the "Empty the Deleted Items folder upon exiting" checkbox.

QUICK REFERENCE

TO DELETE A MESSAGE:

• SELECT THE MESSAGE AND CLICK THE DELETE BUTTON ON THE TOOLBAR.

OR...

• SELECT THE MESSAGE AND PRESS THE DELETE KEY.

TO VIEW DELETED ITEMS:

• CLICK THE DELETED ITEMS BUTTON IN THE NAVIGATION PANE.

TO EMPTY THE DELETED ITEMS FOLDER:

• RIGHT-CLICK THE DELETED ITEMS BUTTON IN THE NAVIGATION PANE, SELECT EMPTY "DELETED ITEMS" FOLDER FROM THE SHORTCUT MENU, AND CLICK YES TO CONFIRM THE DELETION.

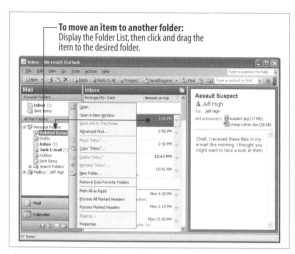

To move an item to another folder:
Display the Folder List, then click and drag the item to the desired folder.

Figure 2-17. The Folder List allows you to display and work with your Outlook folders.

This lesson introduces the Folder List, which you will use to display and work with your Outlook folders. The Folder List is especially important for several reasons when you're working with e-mail:

- **The Folder List contains folders that do not appear in the Navigation Pane.** The most important of these folders help you to manage your e-mail by storing sent messages and deleted messages. See Table 2-5 for a more detailed description of these special e-mail folders.

- **The Folder List helps you organize and manage your Outlook items.** In addition to the default folders, you can create your own folders to store items that are related in some way. For example, if you want to organize your correspondence on a particular fund-raising project, you could create a separate Fund-raiser folder in which to store the fund-raiser e-mail messages.

- **To view information in public folders on the network.** If you use Outlook in a workgroup environment, you can view information in shared and public folders, if the proper permissions have been delegated to you. This is useful for working and collaborating with other colleagues.

In this lesson you will learn how to open and view Outlook's Folder List.

1 Make sure that you are in the Inbox folder—click the Mail button in the Navigation Pane if you're not.

The Inbox, as you know by now, is where Outlook stores any messages you receive. There are several other e-mail related folders, as described in Table 2-5. To view these folders, you need to display the Folder List.

2 Click the Folder List button in the bottom of the Navigation Pane.

> **TIP**
> *Another way to display the folder list is to select Go → Folder List from the menu.*

The Folder List appears, as shown in Figure 2-17. Let's look at the contents of another folder.

3 Click the Sent Items folder in the Folder List.

The Sent Items folder stores copies of messages that you have sent in the past few weeks. You should be able to find the messages you sent in the previous lessons here.

You can move messages from one folder to another by dragging the message to the desired folder in the Folder List.

4 Click any message you created in the previous few lessons, and drag the message to the Deleted Items folder in the Folder List.

We're finished using the Folder List for now, so move on to the next step and close it.

5 Close the Folder List by clicking the Mail button in the Navigation Pane.

The Folder List closes.

You normally use the Folder List to view and manage your e-mail messages. For example, you might open the Folder List to view the contents of the Sent Items folders, which stores copies of all the e-mail messages you have sent.

Table 2-5. E-mail-related folders

Folder	Folder name	Description
	Inbox	Stores the messages you've received.
	Outbox	Temporarily stores any messages that you've composed that have not been sent.
	Sent Items	Stores copies of messages you have sent.
	Deleted Items	Stores messages that you've deleted.
	Drafts	Stores draft messages that you haven't completed yet.

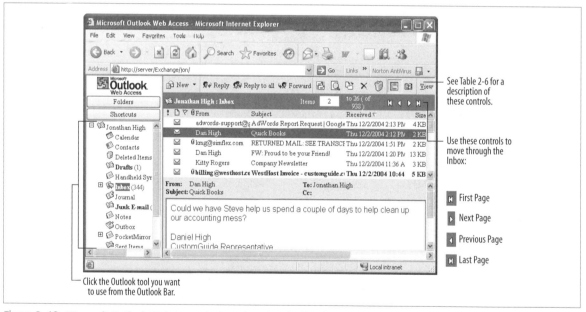

Figure 2-18. Outlook Web Access logon screen.

Figure 2-19. Microsoft Outlook Web Access looks and works a lot like the ordinary version of Outlook.

If your organization uses Microsoft Outlook, it probably also uses *Microsoft Exchange Server* to manage everyone's e-mail accounts. You don't have to know much about Microsoft Exchange (leave that headache to your network administrators!) other than the fact that it has one incredibly useful feature: Outlook Web Access.

Outlook Web Access lets you send and receive e-mail when you are away from the office by using a simple web browser. In other words, if you have access to the Internet, you can still send and receive e-mail messages using your Outlook account. If you've ever used Hotmail or any other free e-mail service, you probably already have a good idea of how Outlook Web Access works.

Once you're connected, Outlook Web Access acts like a stripped-down version of Microsoft Outlook. Here's how to use it:

1 Contact your IT department and see if your organization supports Outlook Web Access. If it does, ask them for the URL (web address) you need to access it and write it down.

These web addresses may be something simple, such as *mail.mycompany.com*, or incredibly confusing, such as *195.39.49.34/exchange*. Don't be surprised if your organization *doesn't* support Outlook Web Access, as it can raise many security issues.

2 Open any web browser and type the URL for your organization's Outlook Web Access.

If everything works the way it's supposed to, you should see the dialog box shown in Figure 2-18.

3 Enter your Username and Password and click OK.

The Outlook Web Access screen should appear, as shown in Figure 2-19. From here, Outlook Web Access looks and works like a basic version of Microsoft Outlook. Use the controls shown in Figure 2-19 and in Table 2-6 to send and receive e-mail messages and have access to your Contacts, Calendar, and Tasks List.

Table 2-6. The Microsoft Outlook Web Access toolbar

Button	Button name	Description
New	New	Create a new message, appointment, or task.
Reply	Reply	Reply to the sender of the selected message.
Reply to all	Reply to All	Reply to all recipients of the selected message.
Forward	Forward	Forward the selected message to another user.
	Send/Receive	Send your outgoing messages and check for new messages.
	Search	Search for an e-mail, appointment, or task.
	Move	Move the selected item to another folder.
	Delete	Delete the selected item.
	Empty Deleted Items	Empty the Deleted Items folder.
	Display Preview Pane	Displays the message Preview Pane.
	Address Book	Opens the Outlook Address book.
View Messages	View	Specify what is displayed in the Inbox.

QUICK REFERENCE

TO USE OUTLOOK WEB ACCESS:

1. FIND AND WRITE DOWN THE URL FOR YOUR ORGANIZATION'S OUTLOOK WEB ACCESS PAGE.

2. OPEN ANY WEB BROWSER AND TYPE THE URL (WEB ADDRESS) FOR YOUR ORGANIZATION'S OUTLOOK WEB ACCESS PAGE.

3. ENTER YOUR USERNAME AND PASSWORD AND CLICK OK.

Chapter Two Review

Lesson Summary

Composing and Sending E-mail

To Compose a Message: Click the Inbox folder in the Navigation Pane and click the New Mail Message button on the toolbar. Type the recipient's address in the To field or click the To button to the left of the To box, click the name of the recipient in the Name list, and then click the To button. Click the Subject box and enter the message's subject, click the pointer in the lower pane, and type the message. Click the Send button on the toolbar to send the message.

Specifying Message Options

To Specify Message Options: Click the New Mail Message button on the toolbar and create the message. Click the Options button, specify the message options, and click OK.

To Mark a Message as Urgent: Click the Importance: High button on the toolbar.

Receiving and Sorting Messages

To Receive and Read E-mail Messages: Click the Inbox folder in the Navigation Pane, click the Send/Receive button on the toolbar, and then click or double-click the message you want to read.

To Sort Messages: Click the Arranged By column heading and select the option you want to use to sort the Inbox. Or, select View → Arrange By and select an option from the menu.

Replying to a Message

To Reply to a Message: Find and open the message you want to reply to, and then click the reply option you want to use:

Reply sends the reply only to the author of the message.

Reply to All sends the reply to everyone who received the message.

Type your reply and click the Send button on the toolbar when you're finished.

Forwarding a Message

To Forward a Message: Find and select the message you want to forward and click the Forward Message button on the toolbar. Enter the recipient's e-mail address in the To field. (Optional) Enter your own comments in the message body area. Click the Send button on the toolbar.

Checking Your Spelling

To Check Your Spelling: Select Tools → Spelling from the menu, or press F7.

To Check Spelling using Microsoft Word: Right-click the spelling or grammar error and select the correction from the shortcut menu.

To Automatically Spell Check All New Messages: Select Tools → Options from the menu and click the Spelling tab, make sure the Always check spelling before sending checkbox is checked, and click OK.

Inserting a Hyperlink

To Open a Hyperlink: Click the hyperlink.

To Insert a Hyperlink in an E-mail Message: Type the hyperlink address anywhere in the message, using the correct format (i.e., www.microsoft.com).

Attaching a File to a Message

To Attach a File to an E-mail: Click the New Mail Message button on the toolbar and create the message. Click the Insert File button on the toolbar or select Insert → File from the menu. Browse to, find, and double-click the file you want to attach.

Opening an Attachment

To Open an Attachment: Open the e-mail by clicking it in the Inbox pane, then double-click the attachment you want to view and select Open.

To Save an Attachment to Your Hard Disk: Open the e-mail by double-clicking it, then right-click the attachment and select Save As from the shortcut menu. Specify a filename and location for the attachment and click OK.

Finding Messages

To Find a Message: Click the Find button on the toolbar or select Tools → Find → Find from the menu. Enter the text you want to search for in the Look for box. Check the Search all text in each message box under Options on the righthand side to search the actual text in your e-mail messages. Click Find Now.

Deleting Messages

To Delete a Message: Select the message and click the Delete button on the toolbar or press the Delete key.

To View Deleted Items: Click the Deleted Items folder in the Navigation Pane.

To Empty the Deleted Items Folder: Right-click the Deleted Items folder in the Navigation Pane, select Empty "Deleted Items" Folder from the shortcut menu, and click Yes to confirm the deletion.

Exploring the Folder List

To Display the Folder List: Click the Folder button in the Navigation Pane or select Go → Folder List from the menu.

To View Messages You've Sent: Open the Folder List and click the Sent Items folder.

To View Draft Messages: Open the Folder List and click the Drafts folder.

Using Outlook Web Access

To Use Outlook Web Access: Find and write down the URL for your organization's Outlook Web Access page. Open any web browser and type the URL (web address) for your organization's Outlook Web Access page. Enter your username and password and click OK.

Quiz

1. Which of the following is NOT a message option?
   A. Importance
   B. Sensitivity
   C. Language translation
   D. Tell me when this message has been read

2. All messages have one or more icons to indicate their status, importance, and contents. Which of the following statements is NOT true?
   A. A paper clip icon indicates the message has one or more files attached to it.
   B. A flag icon indicates the message is marked as urgent.
   C. A sealed envelope icon indicates the message has not yet been read or opened.
   D. An open envelope icon indicates the message has been read (or at least opened).

3. To reply to a message, click the Forward button on the toolbar (True or False?)

4. You've just received an e-mail titled "I Love You!" from someone you don't know. The message has an attachment. What do you do?
   A. Open the attachment immediately and see what it is!
   B. Forward the e-mail to your significant other to show them that at least other people appreciate you.
   C. The e-mail may likely contain a virus, so treat the e-mail and its attachment with extreme caution. Either delete it or save it to your hard disk but ONLY if you have an up-to-date anti-virus program installed.
   D. Pull the personal ad you posted last month from the Internet.

5. Outlook automatically highlights misspelled words with a wavy red underline. To correct a misspelling, simply right-click the incorrectly spelled word and select a correction from the shortcut menu. (True or False?)

6. You can have Outlook automatically check for spelling errors in all your new e-mails by selecting Tools → Options from the menu and clicking the Spelling tab. (True or False?)

7. To insert a hyperlink to a web page in an e-mail message, simply type an address using the correct format. (i.e., www.microsoft.com) (True or False?)

8. Which of the following statements are *not* true? (Select all that apply)

A. To see all of your folders in Outlook, click the Folder List button in the Navigation Pane.

B. Outlook's Find command searches only the From and Subject fields of your e-mail messages for the word or phrase you specify.

C. When you delete an item, Outlook places it in the Windows Recycle Bin, along with any other deleted files.

D. You can move items between folders by dragging and dropping.

Homework

1. Start the Notepad program (Click the Start button, select Programs → Accessories → Notepad).

2. Click the Open button on the Standard toolbar (or select File → Open from the menu). Browse to your practice folder and open the Homework 2 file.

3. Select all the text in the Homework 2 document and click the Copy button on the toolbar (or press Ctrl + C).

4. Close Notepad and start Microsoft Outlook.

5. Go to the Inbox and create a new e-mail message using the following information:

To: feedback@microsoft.com
Subject: Outlook Suggestions

6. Paste the text you copied in Step 3 in the e-mail message body.

7. Spellcheck the e-mail message and correct any spelling errors that you find.

8. Change the Importance Level of the e-mail message to Low.

9. Send the e-mail message to Microsoft.

Quiz Answers

1. C. Unfortunately, built-in language translation is not a message option.

2. B. A flag icon indicates a flagged message. An exclamation point icon indicates the message is marked as urgent.

3. False. You reply to a message by clicking the Reply button on the toolbar, of course.

4. C. While an e-mail titled "I Love You" with an attachment *could* come from a secret admirer, it's much more likely that it contains a virus. Either delete the message or save the file to your hard disk, but ONLY if you have an up-to-date anti-virus program installed.

5. False. Other Microsoft Office programs may highlight misspelled words with a red wavy underline, but in Outlook you have to spellcheck your e-mails by selecting Tools → Spelling from the menu or by pressing F7.

6. True. You can have Outlook automatically check for spelling errors in all your new e-mails by selecting Tools → Options from the menu and clicking the Spelling tab.

7. True. You can insert a hyperlink in an e-mail message simply by entering the hyperlink, using the current format—for example, www.microsoft.com.

8. B and C. B: By checking the "Search all text in each message" box in the Find panel, you can search the actual text in your e-mail messages. C: Outlook places deleted items in the Deleted Items folder—not in the Windows Recycle Bin.

CHAPTER 3

USING THE ADDRESS BOOK

CHAPTER OBJECTIVES:

Learn about the Address Book: Lesson 3.1

Add a new entry to the Address Book: Lesson 3.2

Search the Address Book and edit entries: Lesson 3.3

Create a distribution list: Lesson 3.4

Delete both a contact and a distribution list: Lesson 3.5

CHAPTER TASK: CREATE BOTH A CONTACT AND A DISTRIBUTION LIST

Prerequisites

- Understand how to use menus, toolbars, dialog boxes, and shortcut keystrokes.
- Understand how to use the Navigation Pane and navigate within Outlook.
- Understand how to compose and work with e-mail messages.

Outlook's Address Book is similar to a phone directory, except that instead of listing only names and phone numbers, the Address Book can store people's e-mail addresses, departments, addresses, and more. The Address Book is an important feature, because in addition to looking up people's addresses and phone numbers, you can use it to address e-mails as well.

Using the Address Book and Contacts List is easy. In this chapter, you will learn how to use the Address Book to look up an address, how to use a distribution list to send the same e-mail message to several people at once, and how to create and delete both Address Book entries and distribution lists. Let's get started!

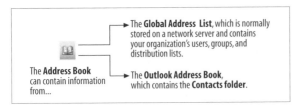

Figure 3-1. The Address Book can contain information from several types of sources.

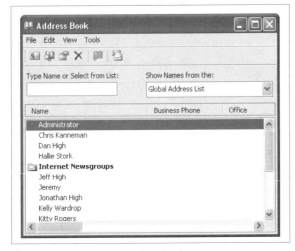

Figure 3-2. The Address Book dialog box.

Unless you correspond with just two or three different people, it's almost impossible to memorize all of the phone numbers, addresses, and e-mails of everyone that you know. Fortunately, if you use Outlook's Address Book, you don't have to.

The Address Book can get its information from one or more sources (see Figure 3-1), including Internet directory services and third-party address books. Here are the two most common sources that the Address Book uses:

- **The Global Address List:** If you use Outlook in a networked environment, the Global Address Book contains your organization's users, groups, and distribution lists. A network administrator usually manages the Global Address book, so you can't make any changes to it. The Global Address book is similar to a large telephone directory that is available for everyone to use.

- **The Outlook Address Book:** The Outlook Address Book is similar to a address book or "little black book" that is available for personal use only. There is a subcategory in the Outlook Address Book: the Contacts folder. Both personal contacts and distribution lists are stored in the Contacts folder. A distribution list is much like a party invitation list that was compiled using a much broader information source, such as your little black book or a phone book.

The Outlook Address Book is important to familiarize yourself with because you will come across a number of dialog boxes and toolbars that include the Address Book button.

Clicking the Address Book button gives you quick access to your Address Book so that you can use its information in the current view.

1 Click the 📖 Address Book button **on the toolbar.**

> **TIP** *Another way to open the Address Book is to press Ctrl + Shift + B.*

The Address Book dialog box appears, as shown in Figure 3-2.

We'll learn how to fully utilize the Address Book in the next couple of lessons, so go ahead and close it for the time being.

2 Click the Close button **on the Address Book dialog box.**

The Address Book dialog box closes and you return to the Microsoft Outlook program window.

QUICK REFERENCE

TO OPEN THE ADDRESS BOOK:

• CLICK THE ADDRESS BOOK BUTTON ON THE TOOLBAR.

OR...

• PRESS CTRL + SHIFT+ B.

TO CLOSE THE ADDRESS BOOK:

• CLICK THE CLOSE BUTTON.

Adding New Entries

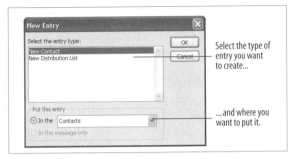

Figure 3-3. The New Entry dialog box.

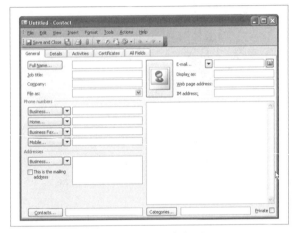

Figure 3-4. The Untitled – Contact dialog box.

Using the Outlook Address book saves you from having to memorize multiple sets of personal information. All you have to do is enter the names and e-mail addresses of the people to whom you send messages regularly, and you'll never have to remember another obscure e-mail address again.

This lesson will show you how to add an entry to the Outlook Address Book.

1 Click the 📖 Address Book button **on the toolbar.**

The Address Book window appears.

2 Click the 📇 New Entry button **on the toolbar.**

Another way to create a new contact is to press Ctrl + Shift + C.

The New Entry dialog box appears, as shown in Figure 3-3.

First, you need to specify where you want to save the new Address Book entry. Most of the time you will want to save entries in the Contacts folder.

3 Ensure that New Contact **is selected in the "Select the entry type" text box, click the** Put this entry **list arrow, select** Contacts **from the list, and click** OK**.**

The Untitled - Contact window appears, as shown in Figure 3-4.

4 Enter the contact information into the appropriate **categories.**

To add additional information about the recipient, such as their department, birthday, or manager's name, click the appropriate tabs and enter the information.

When you are finished, save the entry.

5 Click the Save and Close button **on the toolbar.**

You return to the Outlook Address Book window.

6 Click the Show Names from the: **list arrow and select** Contacts **from the list.**

The entry you just made appears in the window.

7 Click the Close button **on the Address Book window.**

You return to the Microsoft Outlook program window.

When you add entries to the Address Book, you can add as much or as little information as you want. For example, you might enter your Uncle Bob's address, phone number, and birthday, whereas the entry for your friend Susie contains just her e-mail address and name.

Most of the time, you will only want to add Contacts and Distribution lists to your Contacts folder. You can also add entries to your Personal Address Book—if it's installed on your system. Table 3-1 describes the most common Address Book entries.

Table 3-1. Types of Address Book entries

Entry	Description
Contacts	
Contact	Adds a contact to Outlook's Contacts folder.
Distribution List	Composed of several contacts so you can send an e-mail message to many people at once.
Personal Address Book	
cc: Mail Address	Sends e-mail messages to Outlook cc: mail users.
Fax Address	Sends faxes to the specified phone number.
Microsoft Mail Address	Sends e-mail messages to Microsoft Exchange users.
MacMail Address	Sends e-mail messages to MacMail users.
Internet Address	Sends e-mail messages to users on the Internet (using typical *name@domain.com* e-mail address).
X.400 Address	Sends e-mail messages to X.400 users.
Other Address	Use other address entries if you don't have a person's e-mail address, but still want to store their name, address, and phone number.
Personal Distribution List	Composed of several Address Book entries so you can send an e-mail message to several people at once.

QUICK REFERENCE

TO ADD AN ENTRY TO THE ADDRESS BOOK:

1. CLICK THE ADDRESS BOOK BUTTON ON THE TOOLBAR.

2. CLICK THE NEW BUTTON ON THE TOOLBAR.

   OR...

   PRESS CTRL + SHIFT + C.

3. SELECT THE TYPE OF CONTACT YOU WANT TO ENTER AND WHICH ADDRESS BOOK YOU WANT TO ENTER IT IN.

4. ENTER THE CONTACT INFORMATION.

5. CLICK THE SAVE AND CLOSE BUTTON.

   OR...

   PRESS ALT + S WHEN YOU'RE FINISHED.

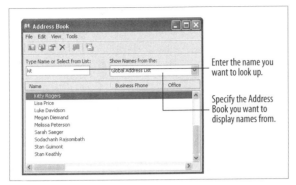

Figure 3-5. The Address Book dialog box.

Enter the name you want to look up.

Specify the Address Book you want to display names from.

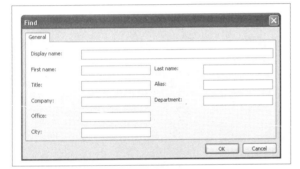

Figure 3-6. The Find dialog box.

Finding a name in the Address Book is a lot easier than looking one up in the phone book. All you have to do is type the name that you want to look up, and voila—there it is! You don't even have to enter the entire name. If you enter the first few letters, the Address Book will retrieve any similar names.

1 Click the 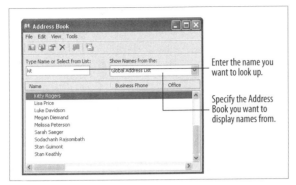 Address Book button **on the toolbar.**

The Address Book window appears, as shown in Figure 3-5.

You can usually find a name by typing it into the "Type Name or Select from List" box.

2 Click the Show Names from the: **list arrow and select** Contacts.

A list of your personal contacts appears on the screen.

3 Start typing your name in the Type Name or Select from List **box.**

When you enter a name in the "Type Name or Select from List" box, that name is automatically checked against the names in your Address Book, and matching entries are selected. When the Address Book has enough information, it should select your name. When this happens, move on to the next step.

4 Find your name in the list and double-click it.

The Contact window appears for your address entry. Information found in the Contact window is organized and grouped by different tabs.

5 Click the various tabs in the Contact window. Close the window when you're finished.

There is another way to find names in the Address Book: use the Find Items button. If you can't remember a contact's name, you can probably find it with this button. For instance, you may remember that a contact's name begins with "Gr," but you can't remember if it is "Grossman," "Grouch," or "Grinch." The Find Items button will help you out. Let's try it with your name.

6 Make sure Contacts **is selected from the drop-down list and click the** Find Items button **on the toolbar.**

The Find dialog box appears, as shown in Figure 3-6.

7 Enter any information you know about the contact, such as their first or last name, and click OK.

Your name should appear as a search result in the Address Book dialog box.

Now let's close the Address Book.

8 Click the Close button **to close the Address Book dialog box.**

QUICK REFERENCE

TO SEARCH THE ADDRESS BOOK:

1. CLICK THE ADDRESS BOOK BUTTON ON THE TOOLBAR.

2. START TYPING THE NAME IN THE TYPE NAME OR SELECT FROM LIST TEXT BOX.

   OR...

1. CLICK THE ADDRESS BOOK BUTTON ON THE TOOLBAR.

2. CLICK THE FIND ITEMS BUTTON.

3. ENTER ANY INFORMATION YOU KNOW ABOUT THE CONTACT, SUCH AS THEIR FIRST OR LAST NAME, AND CLICK OK.

TO EDIT AN ADDRESS BOOK ENTRY:

1. FIND AND DOUBLE-CLICK THE ENTRY.

2. MAKE THE NECESSARY CHANGES.

3. CLICK OK AND CLOSE THE ADDRESS BOOK DIALOG BOX.

Creating a Distribution List

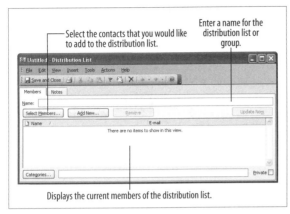

Select the contacts that you would like to add to the distribution list.

Enter a name for the distribution list or group.

Displays the current members of the distribution list.

Figure 3-7. The Distribution List dialog box.

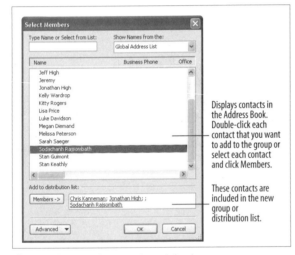

Displays contacts in the Address Book. Double-click each contact that you want to add to the group or select each contact and click Members.

These contacts are included in the new group or distribution list.

Figure 3-8. The Select Members dialog box.

A distribution list or group is an Address Book entry comprised of several names from the Address Book. Use distribution lists to send an e-mail message to each member of a group in a single mailing. You can use distribution lists to quickly send e-mails to:

• All employees in the same department or organization
• Members on the same project or committee
• A group of friends

Distribution lists show up as items in your Address Book and Contacts list the same way that a person's name does. To address an e-mail message using a distribution list, follow the same procedures that you would with any other contact.

In this lesson, you will learn how to create a distribution list that you can use to send e-mails to multiple recipients.

1 Click the New button **list arrow on the toolbar and select** Distribution List.

> TIP
> *Another way to create a distribution list is to select* File → New → Distribution List *from the menu.*

The Distribution List dialog box appears, as shown in Figure 3-7.

> ⁝ NOTE ⁝
> *Distribution lists and groups are the same things—so don't be confused when you see Outlook interchanging these terms.*

First, we need to give our new group, or distribution list, a name.

2 Type Luau Committee Members **in the** Name **box.**

Always try to give your group a meaningful name so that it makes sense to both you and to other Outlook users.

Let's add some members to this group.

3 Click Select Members.

The Select Members dialog box appears, as shown in Figure 3-8.

Now, all that you have to do is double-click the contact names that you want to add to your distribution list.

4 Find and double-click your name from the list.

Outlook adds your name to the Luau Committee Members distribution list.

5 Add two or three more contacts of your choice to the distribution list.

That's all there is to creating a distribution list!

6 Click OK to close the Select Members dialog box.

The Select Members dialog box closes, and you're once again looking at the Distribution List dialog box.

7 Click the Save and Close button on the toolbar to save your distribution list.

The Distribution List dialog box closes.

8 Click the Address Book button on the toolbar.

The Address Book dialog box appears.

9 Click the Show Names from the: list arrow and select Contacts.

This displays the contents of your Contacts Folder. Notice that your new distribution list appears among your contacts.

10 Close the Address Book dialog box.

Your group of personal contacts probably is constantly changing. Luckily, you can easily edit any distribution list. Let's move on to the next lesson to learn how.

QUICK REFERENCE

TO CREATE A DISTRIBUTION LIST:

1. CLICK THE NEW BUTTON LIST ARROW ON THE TOOLBAR AND SELECT DISTRIBUTION LIST.

2. ENTER A NAME FOR THE DISTRIBUTION LIST IN THE NAME BOX.

3. CLICK SELECT MEMBERS.

4. FIND AND DOUBLE-CLICK THE NAMES YOU WANT TO ADD TO THE DISTRIBUTION LIST. CLICK OK WHEN YOU'RE FINISHED.

5. CLICK THE SAVE AND CLOSE BUTTON ON THE TOOLBAR.

Deleting Contacts and Distribution Lists

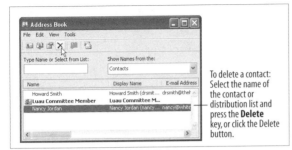

To delete a contact: Select the name of the contact or distribution list and press the **Delete** key, or click the Delete button.

Figure 3-9. You can easily delete contacts and distribution lists from the Address Book.

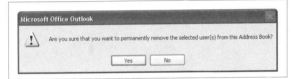

Figure 3-10. Outlook asks you to confirm any Address Book deletions.

You can delete any entry from your Contacts folder as well as distribution lists from your Personal Address Book. However, unless you're the corporate network administrator, you can't delete any Global Address List entries from the Address Book.

In this lesson, you will learn how to delete both a contact and a distribution list from your Contacts folder.

1 Click the Address Book button on the toolbar.

The Address Book dialog box appears.

2 Click the Show Names from the: list arrow and select Contacts.

The Address Book now displays only entries from your Contacts folder.

Deleting a contact couldn't be easier—here's what you have to do:

3 Find and select your name from the list, then click the Delete button on the toolbar.

Outlook asks you to confirm the deletion, as shown in Figure 3-10.

4 Click Yes to confirm the deletion.

Outlook deletes your contact entry from the Address Book and the Contacts list.

You can delete distribution lists from the Personal Address Book just as easily. Let's try it.

5 Find and select the Luau Committee Members distribution list from the Personal Address Book list, then click the Delete button on the toolbar.

Another way to delete a distribution list or contact is to select the contact or distribution list and press Delete.

Once again, you need to confirm the deletion.

6 Click Yes to confirm the deletion.

Outlook deletes the Luau Committee Members distribution list from the Contacts folder without touching any of its members.

7 Close the Address Book.

Congratulations! You've just finished another chapter and are one step closer to complete mastery of Microsoft Outlook!

QUICK REFERENCE

TO DELETE A CONTACT OR DISTRIBUTION LIST:

1. CLICK THE ADDRESS BOOK BUTTON ON THE TOOLBAR.

2. FIND AND SELECT THE CONTACT OR DISTRIBUTION LIST THAT YOU WANT TO DELETE.

3. CLICK THE DELETE BUTTON ON THE TOOLBAR.

   OR...

   PRESS DELETE.

   OR...

   RIGHT-CLICK THE CONTACT OR DISTRIBUTION LIST AND SELECT DELETE FROM THE SHORTCUT MENU.

4. CLICK YES TO CONFIRM THE DELETION.

Lesson Summary

Introduction to the Address Book

To Open the Address Book: Click the Address Book button on the toolbar or press Ctrl + Shift+ B.

Adding New Entries

To Add an Entry to the Address Book: Click the Address Book button on the toolbar, click the New button on the toolbar, and select the type of entry you want to add as well as the folder you want. Enter the information about the contact. Click OK and close the Address Book.

Searching the Address Book and Editing Entries

To Search the Address Book: Click the Address Book button on the toolbar, and enter the name you want to search for in the Type Name or Select from List box.

To Edit an Address Book Entry: Find and double-click the entry, make the necessary changes, click OK, and close the Address Book.

Creating a Distribution List

To Create a Distribution List: Click the New button list arrow on the toolbar, select Distribution List, and enter a name for the distribution list in the Name box. Click Select Members, find and double-click the names you want to add to the distribution list, and click OK when you're finished. Click the Save and Close button on the toolbar.

Deleting Contacts and Distribution Lists

To Delete a Contact or Distribution List: Click the Address Book button on the toolbar. Then, find and select the contact or distribution list you want to delete. Click the Delete button on the toolbar, or press the Delete key.

Quiz

1. Which of the following are NOT sources from which the Address Book gets its information? (Select all that apply)
   A. The Outlook Address Book (Outlook's Contacts List)
   B. The Global Address List
   C. The Yahoo! Global Address Book
   D. The national postal service's database

2. When you install Microsoft Outlook, Outlook automatically configures the Address Book for you. (True or False?)

3. In the Address Book, you can create… (Select all that apply)
   A. Contacts
   B. Task Requests
   C. Distribution Lists
   D. Mail merge templates

4. A distribution list is an Address Book entry comprised of several names from the Address Book. You use distribution lists to send an e-mail message to each member in the group in a single mailing. (True or False?)

5. You can open the Address Book by… (Select all that apply)
   A. Clicking the Address Book button on the toolbar.
   B. Clicking the Address Book button in the Navigation Pane.
   C. Pressing Ctrl + Shift + B.
   D. Clicking a To:, Cc:, or similar button that appears in an Outlook dialog box.

Homework

1. Start Microsoft Outlook.

2. Click the Inbox folder in the Navigation Pane and click the Address Book button on the toolbar.

3. Create a new contact entry in the Address Book using the following information:

   First: George
   Last: Bush
   E-mail: georgebush@whitehouse.gov

4. Create another contact entry in the Address Book using the following information:

   First: Dick
   Last: Cheney
   E-mail: dickcheney@whitehouse.gov

5. Create a distribution list named "White House" with both George Bush and Dick Cheney as members.

6. Delete the "White House" distribution list.

7. Use the Address Book's find feature to find any contacts whose last name is "Bush."

Quiz Answers

1. C and D. These are not sources for the Address Book.

2. False. If only this were true, as configuring the Address Book is one of the most difficult and technical tasks you will likely ever undertake.

3. A and C. You can create contacts and distribution lists in the Address Book.

4. True. A distribution list is an Address Book entry comprised of several names from the Address Book.

5. A, C, and D. Any of these will open the Address Book.

CHAPTER 4
USING THE CONTACTS LIST

CHAPTER OBJECTIVES:

Add a contact: Lesson 4.1

Edit and delete a contact: Lesson 4.2

Add an e-mail sender to the Contacts list: Lesson 4.3

Map a contact's address on the Internet: Lesson 4.4

Change views to display the Contacts list in different ways: Lesson 4.5

Use the Actions menu: Lesson 4.6

Print the Contacts list: Lesson 4.7

CHAPTER TASK: ADD, MODIFY, AND WORK WITH A CONTACT ENTRY

Prerequisites

• Understand how to use menus, toolbars, dialog boxes, and shortcut keystrokes.
• Understand how to use the Navigation Pane and navigate within Outlook.

In the old days, people kept track of their contacts in a device called a Rolodex. A Rolodex was a small box filled with note cards. Contact information was typed or scribbled on each card, and the cards were arranged alphabetically by the contact's name. You would then spin a knob on the side of the box to rotate the cards to find a person. The Rolodex seems like a primitive way to manage contact information, but this was the best way to do things until computers came along.

The Contacts list is a "technological Rolodex" database that keeps track of names, addresses, and phone numbers. Once you have entered a person's name into Outlook, the possibilities are endless. You can instantly find, e-mail or print contact information, or even create a map to a contact's business or home address.

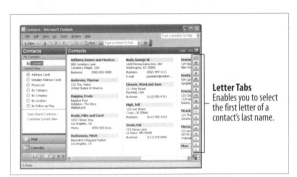

Figure 4-1. The Contacts list shows information about all of your existing contacts at once.

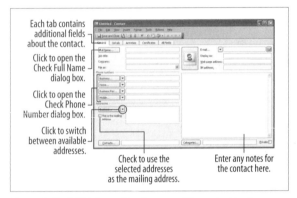

Each tab contains additional fields about the contact.

Click to open the Check Full Name dialog box.

Click to open the Check Phone Number dialog box.

Click to switch between available addresses.

Check to use the selected addresses as the mailing address.

Enter any notes for the contact here.

Figure 4-2. Add information for a specific contact in the Contact window.

Just like your little black book or a Rolodex, the Contacts list contains information about people and organizations with whom you interact. The Contacts list lets you enter as much or as little information about your contacts as you want, such as their name, phone numbers, addresses—even their web address or birthday! You can then use the information in the Contacts list with the other Outlook tools. For example, with a few clicks of the mouse, you can send an e-mail to a contact or schedule an appointment with her. You can even use the Contacts list with other programs. For instance, you could store all the information in your Contacts list on a Palm organizer.

This lesson is a quick review of the Contacts list. You'll learn how to find your way around the Contacts list and how to add a new contact. Ready? Let's get started…

1 Switch to the Contacts list by clicking the Contacts button in the Navigation Pane.

Outlook switches to Contacts view, as shown in Figure 4-1.

2 Click the New Contact button on the toolbar.

TIP *Another way to create a new contact is to press Ctrl + Shift + C.*

The Untitled - Contact window appears, as shown in Figure 4-2. It's up to you how much information you enter about a contact.

3 Click in the Full Name box and type Ms. Nancy Jordan.

Normally Outlook is pretty smart about determining a person's first name, last name, title, and so on. Occasionally, however, an unusual or improperly entered name will confuse Outlook, and the Check Full Name dialog box will appear, asking you to clarify which is the first name, last name, and title. You can summon the Check Full Name dialog box yourself by clicking the Full Name button—although you normally shouldn't need to do this.

4 Click the Full Name button.

The Full Name dialog box appears. Everything looks fine here.

5 Click OK to close the Full Name box.

Next, we need to enter the Company name.

6 Click in the Company box and type North Shore Travel.

Next, let's enter Ms. Jordan's business phone number and e-mail address.

7 Click in the Business box and type (202) 555-1414; click in the E-mail box and enter your e-mail address.

You can also use the Tab key to move between the fields in the contact window—press Tab to move to the next field and press Shift + Tab to move to the previous field.

Move on to the next step and enter the address for this contact.

8 Click in the Address box and enter the following address:

    1600 Pennsylvania Avenue NW
    Washington, DC 20500

You may have noticed that a lot of boxes in the Contacts window have list arrows next to them. These buttons are used if a contact has more than one phone number, e-mail account, or address. For example, clicking the list arrow next to the Address box would let you display a contact's home address.

9 Click the Address list arrow.

A list appears with the various addresses you can display. For this exercise, you just need to enter the business address.

10 Click anywhere outside the list to close it without selecting any options.

Just like the Full Name box, the Address box has a special Check Address dialog box you can use to help you enter foreign or confusing addresses—just click the Address button to use it.

We've finished entering all the information for this contact, so you can save your changes and close the New Contact window.

11 Click the Save and Close button on the toolbar.

The Contact window closes and the new Nancy Jordan contact appears in the Contacts list.

QUICK REFERENCE

TO VIEW THE CONTACTS LIST:

- CLICK THE CONTACTS BUTTON IN THE NAVIGATION PANE.

TO CREATE A NEW CONTACT:

1. CLICK THE NEW CONTACT BUTTON OR PRESS CTRL + SHIFT + C.

2. ENTER THE INFORMATION ABOUT THE CONTACT.

3. CLICK THE SAVE AND CLOSE BUTTON OR PRESS ALT + S WHEN YOU'RE FINISHED.

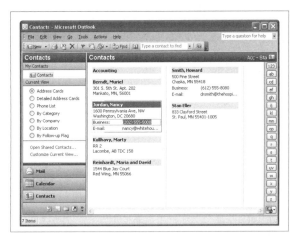

Figure 4-3. You can edit contact information directly in Contacts View…

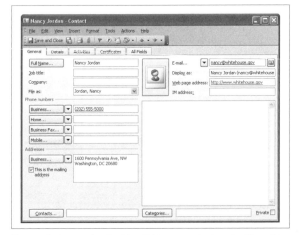

Figure 4-4. …or by double-clicking a contact and editing it in the Contact window.

It's easy to change information about your contacts. You can edit contact information by double-clicking a contact to open it in the Contacts window, or you can also edit information about a contact directly in Contacts View. The latter method is more time-efficient; simply select the entry you wish to edit and make your changes in place.

1 Click the Jordan, Nancy contact in the Contacts window.

Next, you need to select the text you want to change. For this lesson, we will change Nancy Jordan's business number.

2 Select the business number for the "Jordan, Nancy" contact and replace it with the number (202) 555-9000, as shown in Figure 4-3.

You can also edit a contact by displaying the Contact window. This may be necessary when the contact information that you want to edit isn't readily available in Contacts view.

You can assign up to three addresses for a contact by using a different label for each address.

To open a contact in the Contact window, simply double-click the contact.

3 Double-click the Jordan, Nancy contact.

The Jordan, Nancy contact appears in the Contact window, as shown in Figure 4-4. Let's add Nancy's home address to her contact information.

4 Click the Address list arrow and select Home.

Now you can enter Nancy's home address.

5 Click in the Address box and enter the following address:

```
1600 Pennsylvania Avenue NW
Washington, DC 20500
```

6 Click the Address list arrow and select Business.

Outlook displays the business address.

If a company has a web page, you can enter its URL in the web page address box.

7 Click in the web page address box and type www.whitehouse.gov.

⌇ NOTE ⌇   *Make sure you enter .gov at the end of this web address.*

To view the web page, simply open the contact and click the web address.

8 Click the www.whitehouse.gov web address.

Outlook launches your web browser and displays the web page.

9 Close your web browser program.

You should be back in Microsoft Outlook.

Notice that the Contact window is organized into several tabs: General, Details, Activities, Certificates, and All Fields. Ninety-five percent of the time, you will find all the fields you need on the General tab. But sometimes you may want to enter additional information about a contact, such as her birthday, which department she works in, or the name of her spouse.

When you want to enter more detailed information about a contact, click the Details tab.

10 Click each of the tabs listed in Table 4-1 and read their descriptions.

We're finished editing the Nancy Jordan contact.

11 Click the Save and Close button on the toolbar.

Table 4-1 describes the purpose of the tabs you'll find in the Contact window.

Table 4-1. The Contact window tabs

Contact tab	Description
General	Contains basic information such as the contact's name, phone numbers, address, and e-mail.
Details	Contains detailed information such as the contact's spouse, manager, birthday, etc.
Activities	Tracks your activities with the contact, such as calls and e-mails.
Certificates	Stores digital IDs for the contact so that you can send him or her encrypted e-mail.
All Fields	Allows you to create and use your own custom fields for the contact.

QUICK REFERENCE

TO EDIT A CONTACT:

- IF THE INFORMATION YOU WANT TO MODIFY APPEARS IN THE CONTACTS LIST, SELECT THE CONTACT AND MODIFY ITS INFORMATION IN PLACE.

OR...

1. DOUBLE-CLICK THE CONTACT YOU WANT TO EDIT.

2. MAKE THE NECESSARY CHANGES.

3. CLICK THE SAVE AND CLOSE BUTTON ON THE TOOLBAR OR PRESS ALT + S WHEN YOU'RE FINISHED.

TO DELETE A CONTACT:

- SELECT THE CONTACT AND CLICK THE DELETE BUTTON ON THE TOOLBAR.

OR...

- SELECT THE CONTACT AND PRESS THE DELETE KEY.

Adding an E-mail Sender to the Contacts List

Figure 4-5. Adding a contact by clicking and dragging.

To add an e-mail sender's name and e-mail address to the Contacts list, click and drag the e-mail item to the Contacts button in the Navigation Pane.

You may receive an e-mail message from someone you want to add to your Contacts list. To add an e-mail sender's name and e-mail address to your Contacts list, simply drag the e-mail to the Contacts button in the Navigation Pane (see Figure 4-5). Outlook will add the sender's name and e-mail address to the Contacts list—and you can add any additional information yourself.

1 Click the Mail button in the Navigation Pane.

The Inbox appears.

2 Create the following e-mail message:

To: (Enter your own e-mail address here)
Subject: Message to myself

You're ready to send the message.

3 Click the Send button on the toolbar.

The message window closes and Outlook sends the e-mail to the Outbox.

4 Click the Send/Receive button on the toolbar.

You should receive the message you sent to yourself. You can quickly add the name and e-mail address of any e-mail sender by dragging an e-mail message from them to the Contacts button in the Navigation Pane.

5 Click and drag the Message to myself e-mail to the Contacts button in the Navigation Pane.

The new Contact window appears with the name and e-mail address of the sender of the selected e-mail message. You can also add additional information about the contact, such as a phone number.

Normally, you would click the Save and Close button on the toolbar, but here we will delete the contact because we don't need it.

6 Close the Contact box without saving the changes.

QUICK REFERENCE

TO ADD AN E-MAIL SENDER TO THE CONTACTS LIST:

1. CLICK THE MAIL BUTTON IN THE NAVIGATION PANE.

2. CLICK AND DRAG AN E-MAIL FROM THE PERSON YOU WANT TO ADD TO THE CONTACTS LIST TO THE CONTACTS BUTTON IN THE NAVIGATION PANE.

3. ENTER ANY ADDITIONAL INFORMATION TO THE CONTACT.

4. CLICK THE SAVE AND CLOSE BUTTON ON THE TOOLBAR OR PRESS ALT + S WHEN YOU'RE FINISHED.

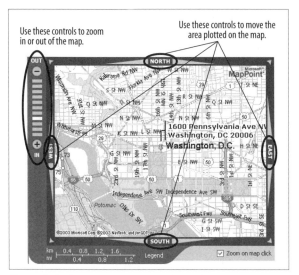

Use these controls to zoom in or out of the map.

Use these controls to move the area plotted on the map.

Figure 4-6. If you're connected to the Internet, Outlook can plot any address in the Contacts list on a detailed map.

Are you good at finding addresses that you have never visited before? No? Don't worry—if you're connected to the Internet, Outlook can pinpoint any U.S. or Canadian address on a detailed map stored in the Contacts list.

In this lesson, you will learn how to plot the address of a contact on an Internet-based map.

1 Click the Contacts button in the Navigation Pane.

The Contacts list appears.

First, you need to open the contact whose address you want to map on the Internet.

2 Find and double-click the Jordan, Nancy contact.

The Nancy Jordan contact appears in its own window. Since you have no idea where 1600 Pennsylvania Avenue is, you decide to map it out on the Internet.

3 Click the Display Map of Address button on the toolbar.

TIP *Another way to plot an address is to select* Actions → Display Map of Address *from the menu.*

Outlook opens your web browser, and if you're connected to the Internet, displays a map (as shown in Figure 4-6). You can use the controls to zoom in or out of the map or to move to the plotted area.

NOTE *Outlook can plot the address only if you have entered it correctly and completely. For example, Outlook will not be able to plot a location that doesn't include a street address. As of this writing, Outlook can only plot U.S. and Canadian addresses. So if you need directions to a contact in Liberia, you're out of luck!*

4 Close your web browser.

You're back in Microsoft Outlook.

5 Close the Contact window.

QUICK REFERENCE

TO MAP A CONTACT'S ADDRESS ON THE INTERNET:

1. FIND AND DOUBLE-CLICK THE CONTACT.

2. CLICK THE DISPLAY MAP OF ADDRESS BUTTON ON THE TOOLBAR.

OR...

SELECT ACTIONS → DISPLAY MAP OF ADDRESS FROM THE MENU.

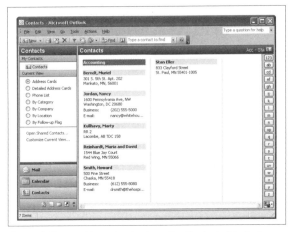

Figure 4-7. In Address Cards view, the Contacts list displays contacts on individual cards.

Figure 4-8. In Phone List view, the Contacts list displays more contacts on the screen at once.

Outlook is flexible enough to keep all of your contacts in the same place but sort and display them differently, depending on the kind of work you're doing. Like other folders in Outlook, the Contacts list has several different ways, called *views*, to look at the same information. Outlook's views are very useful when it comes to organizing the Contacts list. You can use these views to:

- Display more detailed information about each contact with fewer contacts on the screen at once (Address Cards).

- Display more contacts on the screen at once with less detailed information about each contact (Phone List).

- Organize and sort your contacts by their category, company, location, or follow-up flag (By Category, By Company, By Location, or By Follow Up Flag).

In this lesson, you will learn how to utilize Outlook's views to help you sort and organize the Contacts list.

1 Click the Contacts button in the Navigation Pane.

The Contacts list appears.

2 Click the Phone List option under the Current View menu in the Navigation Pane.

Other ways to change views are to select View → Arrange By → Current View *from the menu and select the desired view, or to select* Tools → Organize *from the menu, select* Using Views, *and then select the desired view.*

Phone List view displays contacts in a list with their company name as well as their business, business fax, home, and mobile phone numbers. Phone List view also displays more contacts on the screen at a time, as shown in Figure 4-8.

3 Switch between each of the Contact views and refer to Table 4-2 to read about their descriptions.

You can also change views by selecting View → Arrange By → Current View and then choosing the desired view from the menu. When you've finished, move on to the next step.

4 Click the Address Cards option in the Current View list in the Navigation Pane.

Your Contacts list is once again displayed in the no-nonsense Address Cards view, as shown in Figure 4-7.

Here are the preset Contacts list views that are available. Most people seem to use the Address Cards view (the default view for the Contacts list) or Phone List view to display the Contacts list.

Table 4-2. Available Contact views

View	Displays
Address Cards	Displays contacts on individual cards with one mailing address as well as business and home phone numbers. This is the default view for the Contacts list.
Detailed Address Cards	This is the most detailed view of the Contacts list. Displays everything on individual cards: business and home addresses, phone numbers, and any other information.
Phone List	Displays contacts in a list with company name, business phone number, business fax number, and home phone number. Phone List View displays more contacts on the screen at a time but has less detailed information.
By Category	Displays your contacts in a table and organizes and sorts contacts by category.
By Company	Displays your contacts in a table and organizes and sorts contacts by company.
By Location	Displays your contacts in a table and organizes and sorts contacts by country.
By Follow Up Flag	You remind yourself about getting back to important contacts by flagging them. Flagged View organizes contacts according to which kinds of flags are set. We'll discuss how to flag items in Outlook later on.

QUICK REFERENCE

TO CHANGE VIEWS:

1. CLICK THE CONTACTS BUTTON IN THE NAVIGATION PANE.

2. SELECT THE VIEW YOU WANT FROM THE CURRENT VIEW MENU OR SELECT VIEW → ARRANGE BY → CURRENT VIEW FROM THE MENU AND THEN SELECT ONE OF THE VIEWS DESCRIBED IN TABLE 4-2.

Using the Actions Menu

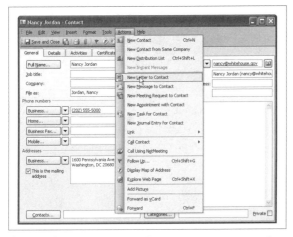

Figure 4-9. The Actions menu lets you create a new e-mail or letter addressed to the selected contact.

The Actions menu is particularly powerful when you're using the Contacts list. With just a few clicks of the mouse, you can create an e-mail or letter addressed to a selected contact. You can also use the Actions menu to schedule a meeting with a contact, assign a task to a contact, or even dial a contact's phone number! To use the Actions menu, you simply need to select or open a contact, select Actions from the menu, and then select one of the commands listed in Table 4-3.

In this lesson, you will learn about how to use the Actions menu while in the Contacts list.

1 Find and double-click any contact from the Contacts list.

The contact opens in its own window. Let's take a closer look at the Actions menu.

2 Select Actions from the menu bar.

The Actions menu appears, as shown in Figure 4-9. As you can see, there are a lot of useful commands here.

3 Select New Letter to Contact from the menu.

Poof! Up pops Microsoft Word with the Letter Wizard, ready to help you write a letter to the selected contact. The Letter Wizard is supposed to make it easier to write a letter, but to be perfectly honest, most people find the Letter Wizard more annoying than helpful.

4 Click Finish to close the Letter Wizard.

The Letter Wizard dialog box closes.

What do you know…there's a letter addressed to your contact.

5 Close Microsoft Word without saving the new document.

You should be back in Microsoft Outlook.

The New Letter to Contact option is only one of the many useful commands you can find in the Actions menu. Table 4-3 lists all the commands located in the Actions menu.

Table 4-3. The Actions menu

Menu	Description
New Contact	Creates a new contact.
New Contact from Same Company	Creates a new contact with the same company as the selected contact.
New Distribution List	Creates a new distribution list for e-mailing purposes.
New Instant Message	Sends an instant message to the contact (if your network and computer are configured with these options).
New Letter to Contact	Creates a letter in Microsoft Word addressed to the contact.
New Message to Contact	Creates an e-mail message addressed to the contact.
New Meeting Request with Contact	Creates a meeting request addressed to the selected contact.

Table 4-3. The Actions menu (Continued)

Menu	Description
New Appointment with Contact	Creates a new appointment with the contact.
New Task for Contact	Creates a task request addressed to the contact.
New Journal Entry for Contact	Creates a journal entry related to the contact.
Link	Links or attaches files or other Outlook items to the contact.
Call Contact	Opens the automatic phone dialer to dial the contact's number.
Call Using NetMeeting	Opens NetMeeting and starts a new call.
Follow Up	Flags the contact to indicate that a follow-up action is required.
Display Map of Address	Plots the contact's address on an Internet-based map.
Explore Web Page	Displays the contact's web page (if any) in your web browser.
Add Picture	Adds a picture to the contact.
Forward as vCard	E-mails the selected contact as an electronic business card.
Forward	E-mails the contact information to another Outlook user.

QUICK REFERENCE

TO USE THE ACTIONS MENU WITH A CONTACT:

1. SELECT OR DOUBLE-CLICK THE CONTACT TO OPEN IT.

2. SELECT ACTIONS FROM THE MENU BAR AND THEN SELECT THE DESIRED ACTION FROM THE MENU.

Printing the Contacts List

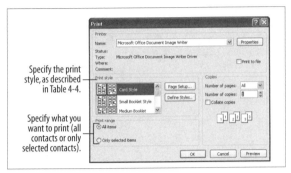

Specify the print style, as described in Table 4-4.

Specify what you want to print (all contacts or only selected contacts).

Figure 4-10. The Print dialog box lets you specify a print style and number of copies.

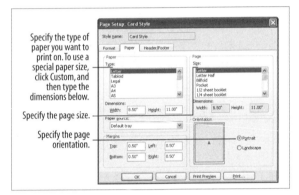

Specify the type of paper you want to print on. To use a special paper size, click Custom, and then type the dimensions below.

Specify the page size.

Specify the page orientation.

Figure 4-11. The Page Setup dialog box lets you change the paper size, orientation, and header and/or footer.

Even in an increasingly digital world, some people still like to have a printed hard copy of their Contacts list. So much for the paperless office! Printing your Contacts list is no different from printing anything else in Outlook, except for a few unique options of which you need to be aware. You can customize the Contacts list print settings so that your printed list looks exactly how you want it to. For example, you can select a print style from card, booklet, memo, or phone directory formats, as well as select which contacts you want to print.

In this lesson, you will learn how to print a hard copy of Outlook's Contacts list.

1 Make sure you are still in the Contacts list and click the Print button on the toolbar.

> *Other ways to print are to press Ctrl + P or to select File → Print from the menu.*

The Print dialog box appears, as shown in Figure 4-10. The Print dialog box is similar to other print dialog boxes except for a few Contacts list–related features. By default, Outlook will print all the contacts in the Contacts list.

You can print only selected contacts by holding down the Ctrl key as you click each contact that you want to print. When you've finished selecting the contacts you want to print, open the Print dialog box by clicking the Print button on the toolbar and selecting the "Only selected items" option.

Notice the "Print style" section. Here you can specify the format of your printout using the styles described in Table 4-4. If none of the styles meet your needs, you can create your own.

2 Select Phone Directory Style from the "Print style" list and click Page Setup.

The Page Setup dialog box appears. Here you can change the print layout, paper size, and orientation, and even add a header and/or footer to your printout.

3 Click the Paper tab.

The Paper tab appears, as shown in Figure 4-11. If you use a Franklin® planner, you can specify the type of paper on which you want to print. You can also select the paper's orientation: Landscape or Portrait.

4 Click the Print Preview button.

This is what your Contacts list will look like when printed. You don't need to print your Contacts list at this time, so you can close any open dialog boxes.

5 Click the Close button for both the Page Setup and Print dialog boxes.

We breezed through the Page Setup dialog box in this lesson, but you may want to look at Table 4-4 to become better acquainted with the Page Setup dialog box and its many useful and powerful options.

Table 4-4. Contact print styles

Print style	Style name	Description
	Card	This prints all cards one at a time from top to bottom on the page, two columns wide, with six blank cards printed at the end, and with letter tabs and headings on a standard 8.5 × 11-inch piece of paper.
	Small Booklet	This is a printout arranged in a way that can be cut and stapled to form a small-sized paper booklet. When you print a booklet, the page layout and page numbering are arranged automatically. Contains contact name, phone number, and address information.
	Medium Booklet	This is a printout arranged in a way that can be cut and stapled to form a medium-sized paper booklet. Contains contact name, phone number, and address information.
	Memo	This is a printout with detailed information about the contact.
	Phone Directory	This is a nicely condensed directory that shows only the contacts' names and phone numbers.

QUICK REFERENCE

TO PRINT THE CONTACTS LIST:

1. CLICK THE PRINT BUTTON ON THE TOOLBAR.

   OR...

   SELECT FILE → PRINT FROM THE MENU.

   OR...

   PRESS CTRL + P.

2. SPECIFY THE DESIRED PRINT OPTIONS AND CLICK OK.

TO CHANGE THE PAPER SIZE/TYPE:

1. OPEN THE PRINT DIALOG BOX.

2. CLICK THE PAGE SETUP BUTTON.

3. CLICK THE PAPER TAB AND MAKE THE NECESSARY CHANGES.

TO ADD A HEADER AND/OR FOOTER:

1. OPEN THE PRINT DIALOG BOX.

2. CLICK THE PAGE SETUP BUTTON.

3. CLICK THE HEADER/FOOTER TAB AND MAKE THE NECESSARY CHANGES.

Chapter Four Review

Lesson Summary

Adding a Contact

To View the Contacts List: Click the Contacts button in the Navigation Pane.

To Create a New Contact: Click the New Contact button or press Ctrl + Shift + C. Enter the information about the contact and click the Save and Close button or press Alt + S when you're finished.

Editing and Deleting Contacts

To Edit a Contact (In Place): If the information you want to modify appears in the Contacts list, select the contact, and modify its information in place.

To Edit a Contact (Within a Window): Double-click the contact you want to edit and make the necessary changes. Click the Save and Close button on the toolbar or press Alt + S when you're finished.

To Delete a Contact: Select the contact and click the Delete button on the toolbar, or press the Delete key.

Adding an E-mail Sender to the Contacts List

To Add an E-mail Sender to the Contacts List: Click the Mail button in the Navigation Pane and then click and drag an e-mail from the person you want to add to the Contacts list to the Contacts button in the Navigation Pane. Enter any additional information to the contact and then click the Save and Close button on the toolbar or press Alt + S when you're finished.

Mapping a Contact's Address on the Internet

To Map a Contact's Address on the Internet: Find and double-click the contact, click the Display Map of Address button on the toolbar, or select Actions → Display Map of Address from the menu.

Changing Views

Click the Contacts button in the Navigation Pane. Select the view you want from the Current View menu or select View → Arrange By → Current View from the menu and select the desired view.

Using the Actions Menu

To Use the Actions Menu with a Contact: Double-click the contact to open it, and then select Actions from the menu bar and select the desired action from the menu.

Printing the Contacts List

To Print the Contacts list: Click the Print button on the toolbar; or select File → Print from the menu; or press Ctrl + P. Specify the desired print options and click OK.

To Change the Paper Size/Type: Open the Print dialog box, click the Page Setup button, and click the Paper tab.

To Add a Header and/or Footer: Open the Print dialog box, click the Page Setup button, click the Header/Footer tab, and make the necessary changes.

Quiz

1. When you add an entry to the Contacts list, you must include the following: First Name, Last Name, Address, City, State, and Postal Code. (True or False?)

2. Which of the following statements is NOT true?

    A. If you're connected to the Internet, you can plot a contact's address on a map.

    B. The Actions menu lets you quickly send e-mails, letters, meeting requests, and tasks to a selected contact.

    C. You can quickly add an e-mail sender to the Contacts list by dragging an e-mail from them to the Contacts button.

    D. Outlook can print the Contacts list on 8.5 × 11-inch paper only—which makes it unsuitable for use in Franklin® Day planners.

3. Which of the following is NOT a Contact View?

    A. Detailed Address Cards

    B. By State

    C. By Company

    D. Phone List

Homework

1. Start Microsoft Outlook.

2. Click the Contacts button in the Navigation Pane.

3. Create a new contact using the following information:

   First: Mickey
   Last: Mouse
   Address: 220 Celebration Place
   Kissimmee, Florida 34747

4. If your computer is connected to the Internet, plot Mickey's address on a map.

5. Practice switching between the various Contact Views located under the Views → Current View menu. Switch back to Address Cards View when you're finished.

6. Delete the Mickey Mouse contact and exit Microsoft Outlook.

Quiz Answers

1. False. You can include as much or as little information as you want about a contact.

2. D. Outlook can print your Contacts list on just about any paper size and style.

3. B. There isn't a preset By State Contact View.

CHAPTER 5
USING THE CALENDAR

CHAPTER OBJECTIVES:

Schedule and reschedule an appointment: Lessons 5.1 and 5.3

Schedule an all-day event: Lesson 5.4

Set an appointment reminder: Lesson 5.5

Copy an appointment: Lesson 5.6

Configure Calendar options: Lesson 5.7

Create a recurring appointment: Lesson 5.8

Print the Calendar: Lesson 5.9

Arrange and color-code appointments and events: Lessons 5.10 and 5.12

View the TaskPad: Lesson 5.13

Change views to display the Calendar in different ways: Lessons 5.2, 5.11, and 5.14

CHAPTER TASK: CREATE, MODIFY, AND RESCHEDULE AN APPOINTMENT

Prerequisites

- Understand how to use menus, toolbars, dialog boxes, and shortcut keystrokes.
- Understand how to use the Navigation Pane and navigate within Outlook.

From the ancient Chinese to the Aztecs to the Romans, a time-keeping mechanism like a calendar has always been an essential part of life. Now, in the 21st century, with our soccer practices, masseuse appointments, and empowerment seminars, a trusty calendar is more important than ever. Outlook's powerful, yet user-friendly, Calendar is the answer to the typical 21st-century schedule.

Coming in at a close second to e-mail, the Calendar is one of the most used tools in Microsoft Outlook. The Calendar lets you keep track of appointments (like a visit to the dentist), and events (like a vacation). It's amazingly simple to add or reschedule an appointment or event in the Calendar. Once you've entered your schedule into the Calendar, you can display it in Daily, Weekly, or Monthly view.

In this chapter, you'll learn how to create and reschedule appointments and events, how to add a reminder to your appointments so that you don't forget about them, and how to view your schedule using the various Calendar views. You will also learn how to create a recurring appointment, such as a weekly staff meeting. Outlook's Calendar is one of those tools that, once you start using it, you'll wonder how you ever got along without. Let's not waste any more time discussing the Calendar—turn the page and let's start using it!

Scheduling an Appointment

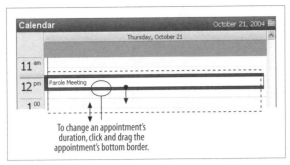

Figure 5-1. You can add and edit an appointment directly in Day and Week views.

Figure 5-2. The drop-down calendar lets you select a date for your appointment.

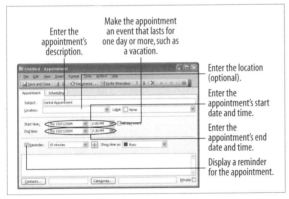

Figure 5-3. The New Appointment form.

The day's already over?! All of that precious time—where did it all go? The current version of Outlook's Calendar can't give you any extra time, but it can help you manage the time you have so that you can (hopefully) spend your day more productively. Outlook's Calendar is great for keeping track of your appointments and events:

- An **appointment** is any scheduled activity that happens within a one-day time period. When you schedule an appointment, the Calendar blocks off the

specified time span—for example, from 10:00 AM to 11:30 AM.

- An **event** is any appointment that lasts one or more 24-hour days, such as a conference or vacation. Events are not displayed as blocked-out time periods.

There are two ways to enter an appointment:

- **The quick way** to enter an appointment is to view the Calendar in a format that shows the hours of the day in a column. To enter your appointment, just click the start time, type a description, and specify the duration—as shown in Figure 5-1.

- **The complete way** to enter an appointment is by clicking the New Appointment button on the toolbar, entering the information about the appointment, and then clicking the Save and Close button when you're finished. This method lets you add details about the meeting's location, notes about the agenda, and a reminder about the appointment, as shown in Figure 5-3.

In this lesson, you'll learn how to schedule appointments using both methods.

1 Switch to the Calendar folder by clicking the Calendar button in the Navigation Pane.

First, we'll schedule an appointment using the quick and easy method—something you need to be in either the Day or Week view to do.

2 Click the Day View button on the toolbar.

The Calendar displays one day at a time, with the hours in a column.

3 Click to the right of the 9:00 AM and type Parole Meeting.

By default, new appointments last 30 minutes. If your appointment is shorter or longer, you must change the end time. You can do this by selecting the appointment and then clicking and dragging its bottom border.

4 With the Parole Meeting still selected, click and drag the appointment's bottom border to 10:30 AM.

Let's move on to the complete way to create appointments.

5 Click the New ▾ New Appointment button **on the toolbar.**

> TIP *Another way to create a new appointment is to press* Ctrl + Shift + A.

The Appointment window appears, as shown in Figure 5-3. This where you add the what, where, and when information about your appointment.

6 **Click in the** Subject **box and type** Dental Appointment.

That's the "what" part of the appointment. Now for the "where."

7 **Click the** Location **box and type** Dr. Poe's Office, 50th St.

Actually, entering the location of your appointment is completely optional. If you know your appointment's location, you can just leave the Location box blank.

8 **Click the first** Start time arrow **(the date arrow).**

A tiny drop-down calendar appears, as shown in Figure 5-2. You can use this calendar to select a date by clicking the date that you want. You can select different months by clicking the calendar's advance and previous arrows.

9 **Click the calendar's** ▸ advance arrow.

The calendar advances one month. Now let's select a date.

10 **Select the first Friday of the month.**

The drop-down calendar disappears and the selected date appears in the date field. The end time has also changed to the selected date.

11 **Click the second** ⊽ Start time arrow **(the time arrow) and select** 10:00 AM.

The start time is now set at 10:00 AM, and the end time automatically adjusts to 10:30 AM. This appointment lasts two hours, so we need to change the end time.

12 **Click the second** ⊽ End time arrow **(the time arrow) and select** 12:00 PM.

That's all the information we need for this particular appointment. Let's save it.

13 **Click the** Save and Close button **on the toolbar.**

> TIP *Another way to save and close is to press* Alt + S.

Outlook saves the new appointment—but where is it? That's the topic of the next lesson!

QUICK REFERENCE

TO SWITCH TO THE CALENDAR:

- CLICK THE CALENDAR BUTTON IN THE NAVIGATION PANE.

TO SCHEDULE AN APPOINTMENT:

- IN DAY OR WEEK VIEW, SELECT THE APPOINTMENT'S DATE AND TIME AND ENTER THE APPOINTMENT'S DESCRIPTION.

OR...

1. CLICK THE NEW APPOINTMENT BUTTON OR PRESS CTRL + N.

2. ENTER THE APPOINTMENT AND ITS DATE AND TIME.

3. CLICK THE SAVE AND CLOSE BUTTON OR PRESS ALT + S WHEN YOU'RE FINISHED.

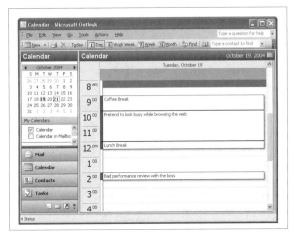

Figure 5-4. The Calendar in Day view.

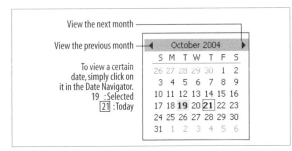

Figure 5-5. The Date Navigator is a small calendar that appears in all Calendar views and lets you select the day, week, or month that you want to display.

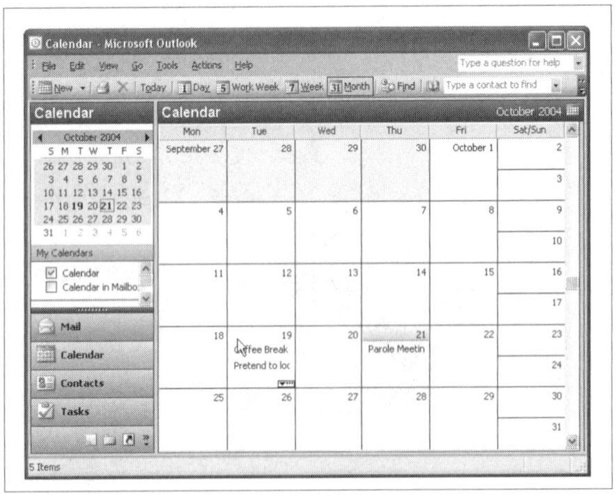

Figure 5-6. The Calendar in Month view.

A monthly calendar is useful for seeing the days of your appointments, but not very helpful when you want to see the details of your daily schedule. On the other hand, a daily planner is useful for scheduling the details of your

busy day, but not for the big picture of your upcoming appointments. Outlook's calendar gives you the best of both worlds. Simply click one of the view buttons on the toolbar to display the following views:

- **Day View:** Displays one day at a time. You can easily see when your appointments start and end and when you have free time. You can only see appointments for the selected day.

- **Work Week View:** Displays a weekly calendar, without weekends. You can see when your appointments start and end, and when you have free time. You can only see appointments for the selected five business days.

- **Week View:** Displays a weekly calendar, including weekends. You can only see appointments for the selected week. It's not easy to see your busy and free times.

- **Month View:** Displays a monthly calendar. Month view does not display much information about your appointments, such as how long they are and what time they are over. In Month view, you use the scroll bar to move from month to month.

In this lesson, you will learn to use each of these views. In addition, you'll learn how to change the date! Let's get started.

1 Make sure you are in Calendar view and click the Day View button on the toolbar.

Day view is great for when you want to look over your daily appointments. Outlook displays when your appointments' start and end times are and when you have free time.

The Date Navigator is displayed to the left of the Appointment area, as shown Figure 5-4. The Date Navigator shows the current month, today's date, and the selected date. You can use the Date Navigator to move to different dates, enabling you to view or add appointments on other days. Dates displayed in bold have at least one appointment, the date with the red border around it is the current date, and the date highlighted in yellow is the date that is currently selected.

2 Click the Date Navigator's ▸ advance arrow.

The Date Navigator scrolls to the next month.

3 Click any date in the Date Navigator.

The Appointment area displays any appointments for the selected day. Let's try switching to Work Week view.

4 Click the Work Week View button on the toolbar.

Work Week view is similar to Day view, except instead of displaying a single day, Work Week view displays the five business days in the selected week.

5 Click the Week View button on the toolbar.

Week view displays a seven-day weekly calendar. Week view displays the start times and the durations of the appointments in the selected week.

6 Click the Month View button on the toolbar.

Month view is laid out just like the calendar that you might have hanging on your wall at home. This view lets you look at the "big picture." Month view doesn't have a lot of room to work with, so it displays appointments in a truncated format and does not display their start times or durations.

Let's try deleting the dental appointment that we added in the previous lesson.

7 Use the Date Navigator, as shown in Figure 5-5, to select the date of the dental appointment that you added in the previous lesson.

Find the appointment? Great—here's how to delete it:

8 Click the dental appointment and delete it by clicking the Delete button on the toolbar.

> Another way to delete an appointment is to select the appointment and press the Delete key.

Poof! The appointment vanishes from the calendar.

You can keep yourself more organized than ever before by using different Calendar views.

QUICK REFERENCE

TO SWITCH BETWEEN CALENDAR VIEWS:

CLICK ONE OF THE FOLLOWING BUTTONS ON THE TOOLBAR:

- DAY VIEW DISPLAYS ONE DAY AT A TIME.

- WORK WEEK VIEW DISPLAYS A WEEKLY CALENDAR WITHOUT WEEKENDS.

- WEEK VIEW DISPLAYS A WEEKLY CALENDAR INCLUDING WEEKENDS.

- MONTH VIEW DISPLAYS A MONTHLY CALENDAR.

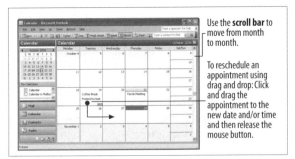

Use the **scroll bar** to move from month to month.

To reschedule an appointment using drag and drop: Click and drag the appointment to the new date and/or time and then release the mouse button.

Figure 5-7. Dragging and dropping is probably the fastest and most straightforward way to reschedule an appointment.

Unfortunately, things don't always work out the way we want them to—especially when it comes to appointments. Coworkers cancel appointments at the last minute, traffic slows down even the shortest of commutes, and doctor appointments almost always run late. Fortunately for us, rescheduling an appointment in Outlook is a very simple task that will not add any stress to your already hectic workday.

There are two ways to reschedule an appointment in Outlook:

- **Dragging and Dropping the Appointment:** This is probably the most common and easiest way to reschedule an appointment. You're probably already familiar with dragging and dropping if you have ever dragged a file to the Windows Recycle Bin or to another folder. To reschedule an appointment by dragging and dropping:

  1. If necessary, switch Calendar views.

  2. Select the appointment.

  3. Click and drag the appointment to the new date and time.

- **Opening and Editing the Appointment:** You can double-click any appointment to display its appointment form. From there, you can change the date and/ or time of the appointment. To save the changes you make, click the Save and Close button on the toolbar.

In this lesson, you will learn how to reschedule an appointment using both of these methods.

1 Make sure that you are in Calendar view. If you're not, click the Calendar button in the Navigation Pane.

First, we need to add a new appointment.

2 Click the New Appointment button on the toolbar.

The Appointment window appears. You should already know the basic procedure for adding a new appointment.

3 Schedule an appointment using the following information:

Subject: Physical Exam
Start Time: 7:30 AM, April 1, 2004
End Time: 8:30 AM, April 1, 2004

Make sure that you click the Save and Close button when you're finished!

April 1, 2004 arrives. You're just about to drag yourself out of bed when you hear the weather report on TV. To your surprise, five feet of snow fell last night and everybody's snowed in! Obviously you won't be going anywhere today, so you'll need to reschedule your physical exam for next week.

We'll reschedule this appointment using the drag-and-drop technique (see Figure 5-7). First, you need to be able to see the original appointment and the destination date and/or time for when you want to reschedule it. You need to be in Month view to reschedule this particular appointment, using drag and drop.

4 Click the Month View button on the toolbar and use the Vertical scroll bar to move to April 2004.

You should be able to see the appointment you added in Step 3.

Now, let's reschedule the appointment.

5 Click the Physical Exam appointment in the April 1 box, drag it to the April 8 box, and release the mouse button.

The appointment has been rescheduled for 7:30 AM on April 8, 2004. Had you wanted to change the time as well, you would have needed to be in Day or Week view, or you would have had to use the open and edit method to reschedule the appointment.

Whoops! April Fool! Evidently the weather crew at your local news station thought it would be funny to play a joke on those who hadn't had a chance to look out the window. It's 65 degrees and sunny—there's no snow anywhere. Time to reschedule that physical exam again.

This time, we will use the open and edit method to reschedule the appointment.

6 Double-click the Physical Exam appointment.

The appointment appears in its own form. Rescheduling an appointment is not much different than creating a new one—all you have to do is select the new start and end times and dates.

7 Click the first ☑ Start time arrow and select April 1, 2004 from the calendar.

Now, all you have to do is save the rescheduled appointment. We don't need to save this appointment, so it's time to finish up.

8 Click the Delete button on the toolbar and click Yes in the dialog box.

That's it! You've just learned the basics about adding, viewing, and rescheduling appointments.

QUICK REFERENCE

TO RESCHEDULE AN APPOINTMENT:

1. SWITCH TO MONTH VIEW.

2. CLICK AND DRAG THE APPOINTMENT TO THE NEW DATE.

OR...

1. DOUBLE-CLICK THE APPOINTMENT TO OPEN IT.

2. MODIFY THE APPOINTMENT'S START TIME, END TIME, AND DATE.

3. CLICK THE SAVE AND CLOSE BUTTON OR PRESS ALT + S WHEN YOU'RE FINISHED.

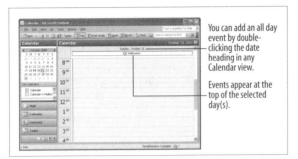

You can add an all day event by double-clicking the date heading in any Calendar view.

Events appear at the top of the selected day(s).

Figure 5-8. An event is any appointment that lasts one or more full days.

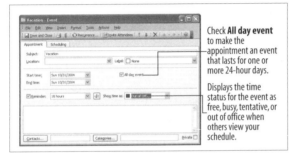

Check **All day event** to make the appointment an event that lasts for one or more 24-hour days.

Displays the time status for the event as free, busy, tentative, or out of office when others view your schedule.

Figure 5-9. To create an event, simply create an appointment and check the "All day event" box.

Events are important dates that last one or more days. Some examples are conferences, holidays, and vacations. Because they don't have start and stop times, events appear as banners in your Calendar, as shown in Figure 5-8. Events do not occupy blocks of time in the Calendar, unless you specify that you will be out of the office during the event.

1 Make sure you're in Calendar view and click the New Appointment button **on the toolbar.**

The procedure for scheduling an event is the same as scheduling an appointment.

2 In the Subject **box, type** Vacation.

Next, you have to specify when the event starts and ends.

3 Type 1/1 **in the** Start time **box and** 1/5 **in the** End time **box.**

Finally, you need to tell Outlook that this is an all-day event and not an appointment.

4 Check the All day event **box, as shown in Figure 5-9.**

Events don't occupy blocks of time in the Calendar, unless you specify that you will be out of the office during the event.

5 Click the Show time as **list arrow and select** Out of Office.

Now, the event will be blocked off when other people view your schedule.

6 Click the Save and Close button **on the toolbar.**

QUICK REFERENCE

TO SCHEDULE AN EVENT:

1. CLICK THE NEW APPOINTMENT BUTTON.

   OR...

   PRESS CTRL + N.

2. ENTER THE APPOINTMENT AND ITS DATE.

3. CHECK THE ALL DAY EVENT BOX.

4. CLICK THE SAVE AND CLOSE BUTTON OR PRESS ALT + S WHEN YOU'RE FINISHED.

OR...

• DOUBLE-CLICK THE DATE HEADING IN ANY CALENDAR VIEW AND ENTER THE EVENT.

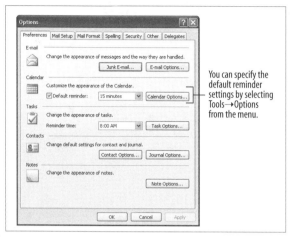

You can specify the default reminder settings by selecting Tools→Options from the menu.

Figure 5-10. You can specify if you want to be reminded of all appointments in the Options dialog box.

Figure 5-11. Check the Reminder box to be reminded of an appointment.

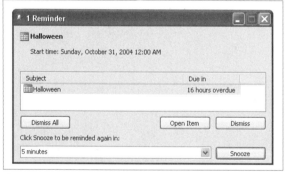

Figure 5-12. The Reminder dialog box appears to alert you of impending appointments.

Are you very forgetful? If so, you may want Outlook to remind you of your appointments. A reminder sounds an alarm and displays a dialog box prior to an appointment. You can specify how many minutes before an appointment you want a reminder to appear and the sound that plays for a reminder. Appointments with reminders have a ⚘ icon in them.

1 Click the New Appointment button on the toolbar and schedule an appointment using the following information:

Subject: Wake Up
Start Time: 10 minutes from whatever time it is now

Next, you need to turn on the reminder (if it isn't already selected).

2 Click the Reminder checkbox, click the list arrow, and select 5 minutes from the list.

By default, you will be reminded 15 minutes before that pending appointment. You can change the amount of time prior to the appointment that the reminder appears by selecting a new time from the list located to the right of the Reminder checkbox (see Figure 5-11).

3 Click the Save and Close button on the toolbar.

In several minutes, you should hear a chime and see the Reminder dialog box, as shown in Figure 5-12. When the Reminder dialog box appears, you have several choices:

- **Dismiss:** Closes the Reminder and will not display further reminders.
- **Snooze:** Displays the reminder again after the amount of time you select has passed.
- **Open Item:** Opens the appointment the reminder is regarding.

4 Click Dismiss.

Outlook closes the Reminder dialog box.

Depending on your setup, Outlook may automatically add a reminder to all of your new appointments. You can change this default setting by selecting Tools → Options from the menu, clicking the Preferences tab, and changing the Default Reminder settings in the Calendar section, as shown in Figure 5-10.

QUICK REFERENCE

TO SET A REMINDER:

1. CLICK THE NEW APPOINTMENT BUTTON, OR PRESS CTRL + N.

2. ENTER THE APPOINTMENT AND ITS DATE AND TIME.

3. CLICK THE REMINDER CHECKBOX. YOU CAN CHANGE THE AMOUNT OF TIME PRIOR TO THE APPOINTMENT BY SELECTING A NEW TIME FROM THE LIST LOCATED TO THE RIGHT OF THE REMINDER CHECKBOX.

4. CLICK THE SAVE AND CLOSE BUTTON, OR PRESS ALT + S WHEN YOU'RE FINISHED.

TO CHANGE THE DEFAULT REMINDER SETTINGS:

- SELECT TOOLS → OPTIONS FROM THE MENU AND CHANGE THE DEFAULT REMINDER SETTINGS IN THE CALENDAR SECTION.

Copying Appointments

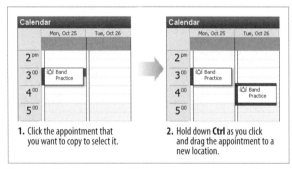

1. Click the appointment that you want to copy to select it.

2. Hold down **Ctrl** as you click and drag the appointment to a new location.

Figure 5-13. You can quickly create several instances of the same appointment by copying the appointment.

Sometimes, you may have several appointments at the same place—but on different days and at different times. For example, perhaps your son has a football game at 5:00 PM on Tuesday and 4:30 PM on Friday. Instead of manually creating two or more individual appointments, you can save yourself some time by creating one appointment and then copying it to the remaining day(s) and/or time(s).

You can copy any appointment by first selecting the appointment you want to copy and then holding down Ctrl as you click and drag the appointment to the desired location.

In this lesson, you will learn how to copy an appointment.

1 **Click the** Work Week View button **on the toolbar.**

The Calendar displays your current work week.

2 **Click to the right of** 3:00 PM **on** Monday **and type** Band Practice.

Since band practice currently lasts a grueling 60 minutes, you must change its end time.

3 **With the Band Practice appointment still selected, click and drag its bottom border to** 4:00 PM.

Instead of manually entering several more Band Practice appointments, you can copy the existing appointment to the desired date(s) and time(s). To copy an appointment, hold down Ctrl as you click and drag the appointment to a new location. Let's try it!

4 **With the Band Practice appointment still selected, press** Ctrl **as you click and drag the appointment to** 4:00 PM Tuesday**, as shown in Figure 5-13.**

The Band Practice appointment is copied to the new time slot.

If an appointment repeats at regular intervals, such as a meeting that is held on the first Tuesday of every month, you should create a single *recurring* appointment instead of copying and creating several individual appointments. We'll cover that topic in another lesson.

QUICK REFERENCE

TO COPY AN APPOINTMENT:

1. SWITCH TO A CALENDAR VIEW THAT DISPLAYS BOTH THE ORIGINAL DATE AND TIME AND THE NEW DATE AND TIME.

2. CLICK THE APPOINTMENT TO SELECT IT.

3. HOLD DOWN THE CTRL KEY AS YOU CLICK AND DRAG THE APPOINTMENT TO THE DESIRED DATE AND TIME.

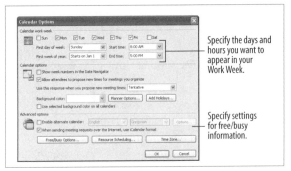

Specify the days and hours you want to appear in your Work Week.

Specify settings for free/busy information.

Figure 5-14. The Calendar Options dialog box lets you customize your work week options, calendar display options, and more.

Do you work for a business whose business hours are 5:00 AM to 4:00 PM Monday through Saturday? Poor you. At least you can configure Outlook's Calendar to better display your company's horrible...er, unique, schedule. The Calendar Option dialog box lets you specify the days and hours in your work week, how the calendar displays busy and free time, and more.

In this lesson, you will learn how to configure the Calendar to suit your own unique schedule and needs.

1 Select Tools → Options from the menu.

The Options dialog box appears.

2 Click the Preferences tab, if necessary, and click the Calendar Options button.

The Calendar Options dialog box appears, as shown in Figure 5-14. Most of the options listed here are self-explanatory.

For this lesson, we will change the Calendar's Start Time to 5:00 AM.

3 Click the Start time list arrow and select 5:00 AM.

You can close any open dialog boxes.

4 Click OK, OK to close both the Calendar Options and Options dialog boxes.

You may need to switch to Day view to see the changes.

5 Click the Day button on the toolbar, if necessary.

The Calendar's start time is now 5:00 AM—hope you're a morning person! Let's change the start time back to 8:00 AM.

6 Repeat Steps 1–4 and change the Start time back to 8:00 AM.

In addition to the start and end times, you can use the Calendar Options dialog box to specify holidays that you want to add to your Calendar, configure meeting request options, and more.

QUICK REFERENCE

TO CONFIGURE THE CALENDAR'S OPTIONS:

1. SELECT TOOLS → OPTIONS FROM THE MENU.

2. CLICK THE PREFERENCES TAB, IF NECESSARY, AND CLICK THE CALENDAR OPTIONS BUTTON.

3. MAKE THE NECESSARY CHANGES IN THE CALENDAR OPTIONS DIALOG BOX.

4. CLICK OK, OK WHEN YOU'RE FINISHED.

Working with Recurring Appointments

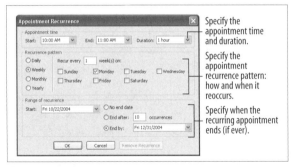

Figure 5-15. The Appointment Recurrence dialog box.

Specify the appointment time and duration.

Specify the appointment recurrence pattern: how and when it reoccurs.

Specify when the recurring appointment ends (if ever).

Figure 5-16. When you delete a recurring appointment, Outlook asks if you want to delete all occurrences of the appointment, or just the selected appointment.

With Microsoft Outlook, you can easily enter a *recurring* appointment that appears at regular intervals: same time, same place. For example, if you have a staff meeting that occurs at 10:00 AM the first Monday of every month, you need only to create one recurring appointment instead of creating dozens of separate appointments. Recurring appointments are identified with an ↻ icon.

The process of creating a recurring appointment is straightforward and easy. Rescheduling or deleting a recurring appointment is a little more tricky. When you reschedule a recurring appointment, you must specify if you want to reschedule just one instance of the appointment, such as a meeting that has been rescheduled for the week, or all instances of the appointment, such as a meeting that is permanently moved from Thursdays to Fridays.

1 Click the New Appointment button on the toolbar.

The Appointment form appears. You already know the procedure for adding a new appointment.

2 Schedule an appointment using the following information:

Subject: Staff Meeting
Start Time: 10:00 AM on Friday of the current week
End Time: 11:00 AM on Friday of the current week

This staff meeting is held at 10:00 AM every Friday, so it makes sense to make it a recurring appointment. Here's how:

3 Double-click the Staff Meeting appointment and click the Recurrence... Recurrence button on the toolbar.

Other ways to create a recurring appointment are to select Actions → Recurrence from the menu or to press Ctrl + G.

The Appointment Recurrence dialog box appears, as shown in Figure 5-15. The Appointment Recurrence dialog box is where you tell Outlook when and how often the appointment should recur. You have several choices here:

- **Daily:** Appointments that recur every day or work day.

- **Weekly:** Appointments that recur on the same day(s) of the week, such as a staff meeting that occurs every Friday or a payday which occurs every other Thursday.

- **Monthly:** Appointments that recur on a monthly basis, such as a departmental meeting that occurs on the first Friday of every month or an inventory audit that occurs on the 5th of every month.

- **Yearly:** Appointments that recur on an annual basis, such as a holiday or birthday.

Since this appointment recurs every Friday, you want to select the Weekly option.

4 In the Recurrence pattern section, select the Weekly and Friday options.

The "Recur every ___ weeks" box lets you specify the time period you want to pass before repeating the appointment. Because there is a 1 in this box, the appointment will repeat every week.

The bottom of the Appointment Recurrence dialog box lets you specify when the recurring appointment will stop recurring (if ever). We don't need to specify an end date for our recurring appointment, so we can leave the No End date option selected.

One way of modifying a rescheduled appointment without changing previous appointments is to change the recurring appointment's end date to the current date, and then create a new recurring appointment with the new date, time, and recurrence pattern.

5 Click OK.

The Appointment Recurrence dialog box closes.

6 Click the Save and Close button on the toolbar.

Outlook saves the recurring appointment.

7 Click the Month View button on the toolbar.

Notice the recurring appointment appears at 10:00 AM on every Friday.

As you've seen, creating recurring appointments is quite easy, but modifying and deleting them is a little trickier. Here's why:

8 Select any Staff Meeting appointment and press Delete.

As soon as you try to delete the Staff Meeting appointment, a dialog box like the one shown in Figure 5-16 appears. When you reschedule or delete a recurring appointment, you have to tell Outlook if you want to reschedule or delete just one instance or all instances of the appointment.

9 Select the Delete the series option and click OK.

⸗ NOTE ⸗ *Be extremely careful when you delete or modify all occurrences of a recurring appointment. All occurrences means all occurrences—even if they have already occurred! If you use the Calendar to keep track of your past appointments, modifying or deleting a recurring appointment will delete and modify occurrences in the past and you will lose your record of the appointment. This is one of Outlook's all-time worst features. Hopefully, it will be remedied in the next version of the program.*

Recurring appointments become more useful the more you employ them. Many people find it useful to enter all their regular appointments, such as classes or regular recreational events, as recurring appointments to prevent them from scheduling conflicting appointments.

QUICK REFERENCE

TO CREATE A RECURRING APPOINTMENT:

1. CLICK THE NEW APPOINTMENT BUTTON.

   OR...

   PRESS CTRL + N.

2. ENTER THE APPOINTMENT AND ITS DATE AND TIME.

3. CLICK THE RECURRENCE BUTTON ON THE TOOLBAR.

4. SPECIFY THE RECURRENCE PATTERN AND DURATION. CLICK OK WHEN YOU'RE FINISHED.

5. CLICK THE SAVE AND CLOSE BUTTON ON THE TOOLBAR OR PRESS ALT + S TO SAVE THE APPOINTMENT.

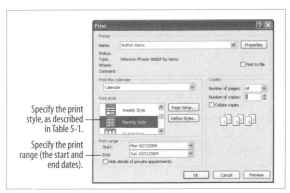

Specify the print style, as described in Table 5-1.

Specify the print range (the start and end dates).

Figure 5-17. The Print dialog box lets you specify a print style and date range.

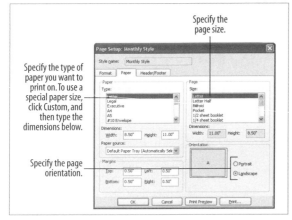

Specify the page size.

Specify the type of paper you want to print on. To use a special paper size, click Custom, and then type the dimensions below.

Specify the page orientation.

Figure 5-18. The Page Setup dialog box lets you change the paper size, orientation, and header and/or footer.

Printing the Calendar is no different than printing anything else in Outlook, except for a few unique Calendar-related options of which you need to be aware. You can customize the Calendar print settings so your printed calendar looks the way you want. For example, you can specify Daily, Weekly, or Monthly formats and the range of dates you want to print.

In this lesson, you will learn how to print a hard copy of Outlook's Calendar.

1 Make sure you are still in Calendar view and click the Print button on the toolbar.

> *Other ways to print are to select File →
> Print from the menu or to press Ctrl + P.*

The Print dialog box appears, as shown in Figure 5-17. The Outlook Print dialog box is similar to other print dialog boxes except for a few Calendar-related features. By default, Outlook will print the current month. You can change the Print range by specifying a start and end date.

2 Click the Start list arrow and select January 1, 2004 from the calendar.

Now let's specify the end date.

3 Click the End list arrow and select January 31, 2004 from the calendar.

The calendar disappears and the date appears in the End text box.

Notice the "Print style" section. Here, you can specify the format of your printout using the styles described in Table 5-1. If none of these styles suit your needs, you can always create your own.

4 Select Monthly Style from the "Print style" list and click Page Setup.

The Page Setup dialog box appears. This is where you can change the print layout, paper size, and orientation, and even add a header and/or footer to your printout.

5 Click the Paper tab.

The Paper tab appears, as shown in Figure 5-18. If you use a Franklin® planner, you can specify paper specially designed for your planner. You can also select the paper's orientation: Portrait or Landscape.

6 Click Print Preview.

This is how your calendar will look when printed. You don't need to print the calendar at this time, so you can close any open dialog boxes.

7 Click the Close button on the toolbar at the top of the screen.

You return to the Outlook Calendar.

We breezed through the Page Setup dialog box in this lesson, so you may want to take some time to better acquaint yourself with its many useful options. For example, you can use the Page Setup dialog box to include your Task Pad on your printed calendar.

Table 5-1. Calendar print styles

Print style	Style name	Description
	Daily	Prints one day per page, from 7:00 AM to 7:00 PM, with tasks and notes areas. This is the most detailed calendar style.
	Weekly	Prints one week per page without tasks and notes areas.
	Monthly	Prints a calendar similar to the type you hang on your wall: one month per page without tasks and notes areas.
	Tri-Fold	This is a printout broken into three parts: one displays the hours and appointments in the selected day; one displays the task list; and one displays the appointments in a selected week.
	Calendar Details	This is a printout of all calendar items that are currently displayed, arranged in a list format.

QUICK REFERENCE

TO PRINT THE CALENDAR:

1. CLICK THE PRINT BUTTON ON THE TOOLBAR.

   OR...

   SELECT FILE → PRINT FROM THE MENU.

   OR...

   PRESS CTRL + P.

2. SPECIFY THE DESIRED PRINT OPTIONS AND CLICK OK.

TO CHANGE THE PAPER SIZE/TYPE:

1. OPEN THE PRINT DIALOG BOX.

2. CLICK THE PAGE SETUP BUTTON.

3. CLICK THE PAPER TAB AND MAKE THE NECESSARY CHANGES.

TO ADD A HEADER AND/OR FOOTER:

1. OPEN THE PRINT DIALOG BOX.

2. CLICK THE PAGE SETUP BUTTON.

3. CLICK THE HEADER/FOOTER TAB AND MAKE THE NECESSARY CHANGES.

Color-Coding Appointments

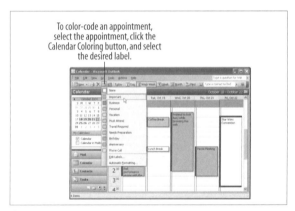

To color-code an appointment,
select the appointment, click the
Calendar Coloring button, and select
the desired label.

Figure 5-19. If you have a busy schedule, you can color-code your appointments to make Outlook's Calendar easier to read.

You can also color-code an
appointment by selecting it
from the Label list in
the Appointment window

Figure 5-20. Color-coding appointments in the Appointment window.

Figure 5-21. The Edit Calendar Labels dialog box.

Outlook's Calendar can sometimes get confusing and cluttered if you're a busy person who has lots of scheduled appointments and meetings. Because every appointment looks the same, it can be difficult to distinguish which appointments are important (such as watching Monday night football) and which ones aren't.

Fortunately, Microsoft Outlook has the perfect solution: color-coding your appointments. Outlook 2003 comes with 10 preset color-coded labels that you can use to categorize your appointments.

This lesson explains how to color-code your appointments.

1 Make sure you are still in Calendar view and select the appointment you want to color-code.

Here's how to color-code an appointment:

2 Click the [icon] Calendar Coloring button on the toolbar and select the desired color, as shown in Figure 5-19. (You can also color-code your appointments via the Label list in the Appointment window, as shown in Figure 5-20.)

Outlook applies the selected color to the appointment.

The preset color-code labels are quite generic and you will almost certainly want to modify several of them. Here's how:

3 Select Edit → Label → Edit Labels from the menu.

The Edit Calendar Labels dialog box appears, as shown in Figure 5-21. Now you can easily edit any of the 10 preset labels.

4 Edit the labels as desired. Click OK when you're finished.

That's all there is to applying color-coded labels to your appointments!

QUICK REFERENCE

TO APPLY COLOR-CODING TO AN APPOINTMENT:

1. SELECT THE APPOINTMENT THAT YOU WANT TO COLOR-CODE.

2. CLICK THE CALENDAR COLORING BUTTON ON THE TOOLBAR AND SELECT THE DESIRED COLOR.

TO EDIT THE PRESET LABELS:

1. SELECT EDIT → LABEL → EDIT LABELS FROM THE MENU.

2. EDIT THE LABELS AS DESIRED.

3. CLICK OK WHEN YOU'RE FINISHED.

The available Calendar views displayed in the Navigation Pane.

Figure 5-22. The Calendar in Day/Week/Month view with the available Calendar views displayed in the Navigation Pane.

Figure 5-23. Active Appointments view displays a list of all appointments and meetings beginning with the current date.

Besides Day, Work Week, Week, and Month views, the Calendar has several more ways of displaying your appointments. These additional views are quite useful in getting a bird's eye view of all your appointments. You can use additional views to:

• Display a list of all appointments and meetings and their details beginning today and going into the future.

• Display only events or recurring appointments in a list.

• Display all appointments by category in a list.

In this lesson, you will learn how to utilize the Calendar's additional views.

1 Make sure you are in Calendar view and select View → Arrange By → Current View → Active Appointments from the menu.

Active Appointments view displays a list of all appointments and meetings beginning today and going into the future, as shown in Figure 5-23. This

view is useful for when you want to see all of your upcoming appointments—in an easy-to-read list.

2 Switch between each of the Calendar views and refer to Table 5-2 to read their descriptions.

Remember: you open the Current view menu by selecting View → Current View from the menu. When you've finished, move on to the next step.

3 Select View → Arrange By → Current View → Day/Week/Month from the menu.

TIP *Another way to change views is to select Tools → Organize from the menu, click Using Views, and select a view from the list.*

The Calendar is once again displayed in the traditional view you've become familiar with.

If you think that this sounds like a tedious process, and would like a more convenient way of accessing these Calendar views, you're in luck! You can display them in the Navigation Pane.

4 Select View → Arrange By → Show Views In Navigation Pane from the menu.

All of the available Calendar views are now shown in the Navigation Pane, to the left of your Calendar, as shown in Figure 5-22. Now, all you have to do to change the current view is scroll down in the Navigation Pane to the view that you would like to activate, and select it.

You might not want the Calendar views displayed in your Navigation Pane all of the time, so let's hide them again.

5 Select View → Arrange By → Show Views In Navigation Pane from the menu.

The available Calendar views are removed from the Navigation Pane.

Table 5-2 describes each of the Calendar views.

Table 5-2. Available Calendar views

View	Displays
Day/Week/Month	Displays appointments, events, and meetings for days, weeks, or a month. Also includes a list of tasks. This view looks like a paper calendar or planner and is the Calendar's default view.
Day/Week/Month-With AutoPreview	The same as the Day/Week/Month view, except the first lines of text appear in the items.
Active Appointments	Displays a list of all appointments and meetings and their details beginning today and going into the future.
Events	Displays a list of all events and their details.
Annual Events	Displays a list of events that happen once a year and their details.
Recurring Appointments	Displays a list of recurring appointments and their details.
By Category	Displays a list of all Calendar items grouped by category, with details about them.

QUICK REFERENCE

TO CHANGE CALENDAR VIEWS:

- SELECT VIEW → ARRANGE BY → CURRENT VIEW FROM THE MENU AND SELECT ONE OF THE VIEWS DESCRIBED IN TABLE 5-2.

OR...

- SELECT TOOLS → ORGANIZE FROM THE MENU, CLICK USING VIEWS, AND SELECT A VIEW FROM THE LIST.

TO SHOW OR HIDE AVAILABLE CALENDAR VIEWS IN THE NAVIGATION PANE:

- SELECT VIEW → ARRANGE BY → SHOW VIEWS IN NAVIGATION PANE FROM THE MENU.

Arranging Appointments and Events

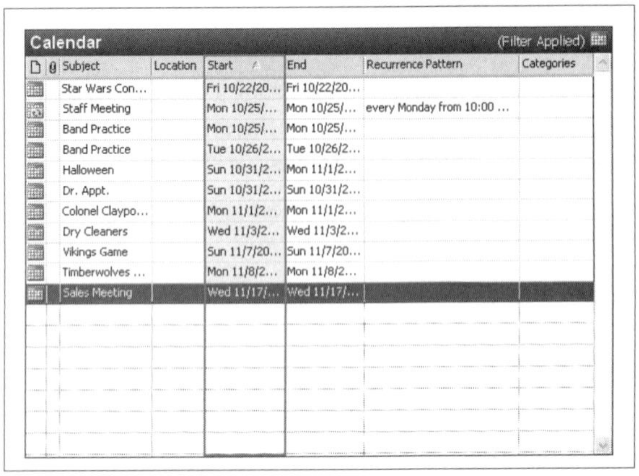

Figure 5-24. The Calendar in Active Appointments view and arranged by Date.

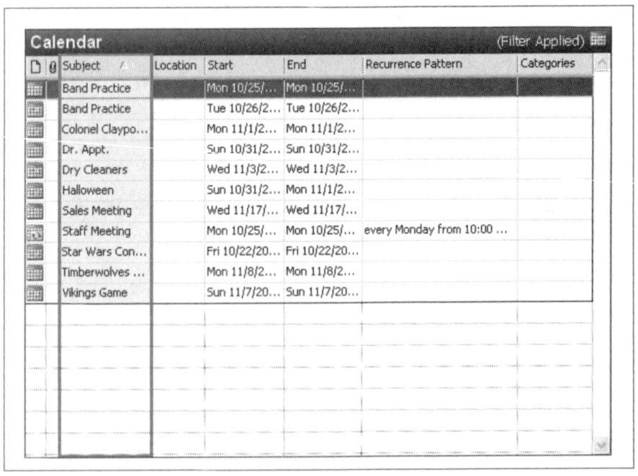

Figure 5-25. The Calendar in Active Appointments view and arranged by subject.

In the last lesson, we learned different ways of viewing our calendars. The Current view options are very helpful, but also very generalized. If you have a lot of active appointments in your calendar and you choose the Active Appointments view from the Current view submenu, you are going to have a lot to look at and sort through.

Luckily, Outlook 2003 offers many more ways to view your appointments and events. These options are found by selecting View → Arrange By from the menu. For example, you can arrange your appointments by date, subject, or importance.

Let's try some of these available Arrange By options! First, make sure the calendar is not in the Day/Week/Month or Day/Week/Month with AutoPreview view.

1 Select View → Arrange By → Current View → Active Appointments **from the menu.**

A list of all your active appointments/events appears. They are arranged by the date that the appointment/event occurs, because date is the default setting. If you have a lot of active appointments in your calendar, you now have a screen full of very loosely organized information, as shown in Figure 5-24.

Let's arrange them differently.

2 Select View → Arrange By → Subject **from the menu.**

Your appointments and events are now organized alphabetically by subject, as shown in Figure 5-25. This is handy for finding an appointment that you know the name of, but you can't quite remember the date. All you have to do is scroll down the list to find your appointment.

Some Arrange By options are much more useful than others. For example, it may be very useful for you to arrange your appointments and events by predetermined categories, but you do not have any appointments with attachments, so you would not want to choose this option.

Take a look at Table 5-3 and check out some of the other options in the Arrange By submenu. When you are finished, we are going to return the calendar to its default view.

3 Select View → Arrange By → Current View → Day/Week/Month **from the menu.**

The Calendar is once again displayed in the default view.

Table 5-3 describes each of the options available in the Arrange By submenu.

Table 5-3. Arrange By submenu options

Arrange By	Description
Date	Arranges appointments and events by date, starting with today moving forward.
Conversation	Arranges appointments and events by similarities.
From	Arranges appointments and events according to recipient.
To	Arranges appointments and events according to recipient.
Folder	Arranges appointments and events by the folders in which they are stored.
Size	Arranges appointments and events by size.
Subject	Arranges appointments and events by topic.
Type	Arranges appointments and events by type.
Flag	Arranges appointments and events by flag status.
Attachments	Arranges appointments and events by whether or not they have an attachment.
E-mail Account	Arranges appointments and events by e-mail account.
Importance	Arranges appointments and events by importance.
Categories	Arranges appointments and events by categories that you determine.

QUICK REFERENCE

TO CHANGE CALENDAR VIEWS:

• SELECT VIEW → ARRANGE BY FROM THE MENU AND
  SELECT ONE OF THE OPTIONS DESCRIBED IN
  TABLE 5-3.

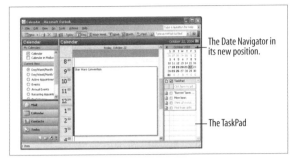

Figure 5-26. Microsoft Outlook in Calendar view with the TaskPad shown.

Figure 5-27. The TaskPad with a completed task.

Every day there are certain tasks that you need or want to accomplish. Sometimes it can be confusing just trying to remember what things you need to do, not to mention actually doing them. Outlook offers a solution to this problem: the Tasks list, which we'll learn more about in Chapter 6. In this lesson, however, we will focus on a more condensed version of the Tasks list, called the Task-Pad, that you can use alongside your Calendars.

The TaskPad is an abbreviated version of the Tasks list. When used in conjunction with the Calendar, you can view the items on your Tasks list while also viewing your scheduled appointments and events.

In this lesson, you will learn how to show the TaskPad, add new tasks, check off completed tasks, and change the view settings of the TaskPad.

⸬ NOTE ⸬   *In order to show the TaskPad, the Calendar must be in either Day/Week/Month view or Day/Week/Month With AutoPreview view.*

1   **Make sure that you are in Calendar view and select** View → Arrange By → Current View → Day/Week/ Month **from the menu.**

The Calendar is now shown in the default view.

2   **Select** View → TaskPad **from the menu.**

The TaskPad appears in the bottom righthand corner of the program window, as shown in Figure 5-26.

Now you can see all of the tasks that you need to accomplish, while still being able to take inventory of your current appointments and events. Also, notice that the Date Navigator has moved so that it is situated right above the TaskPad.

So you can see the TaskPad in the Calendar view, but can you actually use it? Of course you can! It's easy to add a new task or to check off a task that you have completed. First, let's add a new task.

3   **In the TaskPad pane, click the** Click here to add a new task **text box, type** Buy Susan a birthday gift, **and press** Enter.

The new task appears on the TaskPad, but wait! You stopped to buy the gift on the way into work. The task has been completed, so let's check it off.

4   **Check the** Buy Susan a birthday gift **checkbox.**

The task moves to the bottom of the list, fades, and is crossed-off, similar to the one shown in Figure 5-27. It sure feels good to accomplish something!

If you really have a lot of tasks to accomplish, you might consider organizing, or viewing, them differently.

5   **Select** View → TaskPad View → All Tasks **from the menu.**

This shows all of the tasks that you have in your calendar. This can be pretty overwhelming, but don't worry; there are lots of other ways to view the Task-Pad.

Refer to Table 5-4 to familiarize yourself with each of the available TaskPad views.

6   **Select** View → TaskPad View → Today's Tasks **from the menu.**

Today's Tasks is the default view for the TaskPad. When you select this view, only those tasks that are to be completed today are shown in TaskPad pane.

You hide the TaskPad the same way that you opened it.

7 Select View → TaskPad from the menu.

The TaskPad is removed from the Outlook program window and the Date Navigator moves back to the lefthand side of the window.

Table 5-4. Available TaskPad views

View	Description
All Tasks	Displays all tasks in the Calendar.
Today's Tasks	Displays only those tasks that must be accomplished today.
Active Tasks for Selected Days	When you select a certain day or days and then select this view, only the tasks to be completed on the selected days are shown.
Tasks for Next Seven Days	Displays all tasks that are to be completed within the next seven days.
Overdue Tasks	Displays only those tasks that are past their due dates.
Tasks Completed on Selected Days	When you select a certain day or days and then select this view, only the tasks that have already been completed on the selected days are shown.
Include Tasks with No Due Date	When this option is checked, only those tasks that have no set due date are shown—no matter which view you choose.
	When this option is unchecked, only those tasks that have set due dates are shown—no matter which view you choose.

QUICK REFERENCE

TO SHOW OR HIDE THE TASKPAD:

• SELECT VIEW → TASKPAD FROM THE MENU.

TO ADD A NEW TASK:

1. CLICK THE CLICK HERE TO ADD A NEW TASK TEXT BOX AND ENTER THE TASK.

2. PRESS ENTER.

TO CHECK OFF A COMPLETED TASK:

• CLICK THE CHECKBOX THAT IS LOCATED TO THE LEFT OF THE TASK THAT HAS BEEN COMPLETED.

TO CHANGE THE TASKPAD VIEW:

• SELECT VIEW → TASKPAD VIEW AND THEN SELECT THE DESIRED VIEW.

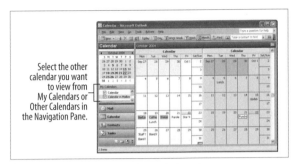

Select the other
calendar you want
to view from
My Calendars or
Other Calendars in
the Navigation Pane.

Figure 5-28. Viewing calendars side by side.

If you're trying to fit appointments into a tight schedule, it can be annoying and confusing having to switch back and forth between calendars while trying to find a time that's available. With Microsoft Outlook, now you can view two calendars at the same time, side by side, so they can be easily and effectively compared.

1 If necessary, click the Calendar button in the Navigation Pane.

The Calendar opens.

It's easiest to view all the appointments on a calendar in Month view.

2 Click the Month button on the toolbar.

Now select the other calendar you want to view at the same time.

3 In the Navigation Pane, click the checkbox of the calendar you want to view with the current calendar.

The calendars appear on your screen in different colors so they are easy to compare, as shown in Figure 5-28. The calendars have synchronized scrolling, so it's easy to navigate through both calendars at the same time.

When you're finished, go back to viewing one calendar.

4 In the Navigation Pane, click the checkbox of the calendar you want to hide.

The calendar closes and just one calendar fills the Outlook window.

You can do this with any two calendars in Outlook, even shared calendars (something you'll learn about later in Chapter 10).

QUICK REFERENCE

TO VIEW CALENDARS SIDE BY SIDE:

• IN THE NAVIGATION PANE, CLICK THE CHECKBOX OF THE CALENDAR YOU WANT TO VIEW WITH THE CURRENT CALENDAR.

Chapter 5 Review

Lesson Summary

Scheduling an Appointment

To View the Calendar: Click the Calendar button in the Navigation Pane.

To Schedule an Appointment Directly on the Calendar: From Day or Week view, select the appointment's date and time and enter the appointment's description.

To Schedule an Appointment in a Form: Click the New Appointment button or press Ctrl + N. Enter the appointment and its date and time and click the Save and Close button, or press Alt + S when you're finished.

Viewing the Calendar

To Switch Between Calendar Views: Click one of the following buttons on the toolbar: Day View displays one day at a time; Work Week View displays a weekly calendar without weekends; Week View displays a weekly calendar including weekends; and Month View displays a monthly calendar.

Editing and Rescheduling Appointments

To Reschedule an Appointment (Using Drag and Drop): Switch to a Calendar view that displays both the original date and time and the new date and time. Click the appointment to select it, and then click and drag the appointment to the new date and time.

To Reschedule an Appointment (Using the Appointment Form): Double-click the appointment to open it. Modify the appointment's start and end time, and then click the Save and Close button or press Alt + S when you're finished.

Scheduling an Event

To Schedule an Event: Click the New Appointment button or press Ctrl + N, enter the appointment and its date, select the All day event box, and click the Save and Close button or press Alt + S when you're finished. Alternatively, double-click the date heading in any Calendar view and enter the event.

Setting Reminders

To Set a Reminder: Open an existing appointment or create a new appointment by clicking the New Appointment button, or press Ctrl + N. Click the Reminder checkbox. You can change the amount of time prior to the appointment that the reminder appears by selecting a new time from the list arrow to the right of the Reminder checkbox. Click the Save and Close button or press Alt + S when you're finished.

To Change the Default Reminder Settings: Select Tools → Options from the menu and change the Default Reminder settings in the Calendar section.

Copying Appointments

Switch to a Calendar view that displays both the original date and time and the new date and time. Click the appointment to select it, then hold down the Ctrl key as you click and drag the appointment to the desired date and time.

Configuring Calendar Options

Select Tools → Options from the menu, click the Preferencmues tab if necessary, and click the Calendar Options button. Make the necessary changes in the Calendar Options dialog box, then click OK, OK when you're finished.

Working with Recurring Appointments

Open an existing appointment or create a new appointment by clicking the New Appointment button or press Ctrl + N. Click the Recurrence button on the toolbar and specify the recurrence pattern and duration. Click OK when you're finished. Click the Save and Close button on the toolbar or press Alt + S to save the appointment.

Printing the Calendar

To Print the Calendar: Click the Print button on the toolbar or select File → Print from the menu. Specify the desired print options and click OK.

To Change the Paper Size/Type: Open the Print dialog box, click the Page Setup button, and click the Paper tab.

To Add a Header and/or Footer: Open the Print dialog box, click the Page Setup button, click the Header/Footer tab, and make the necessary changes.

Color-Coding Appointments

To Apply Color-Coding to an Appointment: Select the appointment, click the Calendar Coloring button on the toolbar and select the desired color.

To Edit the Preset Color-Coded Labels: Select Edit → Label → Edit Labels from the menu. Edit the labels as desired. Click OK when you're finished.

Changing Calendar Views

To Change Views: Select View → Arrange By → Current View from the menu and select the desired view. Or, select Tools → Organize from the menu, click Using Views, and select a view from the list.

To Show or Hide Available Calendar Views in the Navigation Pane: Select View → Arrange By → Show Views In Navigation Pane from the menu.

Arranging Appointments and Events

Select View → Arrange By from the menu and select one of the options in the menu.

To use the Arrange By settings, your calendar must be in any view other than Day/Week/Month or Day/Week/Month with AutoPreview.

Viewing the TaskPad

To Show or Hide the TaskPad: Select View → TaskPad from the menu.

To Add a New Task: Click the Click here to add a new task text box and enter the task. Press Enter.

To Check Off a Completed Task: Check the checkbox that is located to the left of the task that has been completed.

To Change the TaskPad View: Select View → TaskPad View and then select the desired view.

Viewing Calendars Side by Side

In the Navigation Pane, check the checkbox of the calendar you want to view side by side with the current calendar.

Quiz

1. Which of the following is NOT a Calendar view?

   A. Day view

   B. Three-Day view

   C. Work Week view

   D. Week view

2. An event is a special type of appointment that cannot be rescheduled. (True or False?)

3. Which of the following statements are NOT true? (Select all that apply.)

   A. You can change the default reminder setting by selecting Tools → Options from the menu and changing the Default Reminder settings in the Calendar section of the Preferences tab.

   B. You can change the amount of time prior to the appointment that the reminder appears by selecting a new time from the ⌄ arrow to the right of the Reminder checkbox.

   C. When a reminder appears, the only option you have available is to click OK to close the Reminder dialog box.

   D. You can reschedule appointments by either clicking and dragging them to the desired time and/or date or opening them and then changing the time and/or date.

4. By opening the Options dialog box (select Tools → Options from the menu), you can change the days that appear in the Work Week view. (True or False?)

5. Which of the following appointments could you NOT schedule using Outlook's recurring appointment feature?

   A. An appointment held on the first Monday of every month.

   B. A birthday that falls on July 9th of every year.

   C. A mystical ceremony that occurs during each full moon.

   D. A status meeting held every other Thursday.

6. When you reschedule a recurring appointment, Outlook asks if you want to reschedule only future appointments or all appointments. (True or False?)

Homework

1. Start Microsoft Outlook and click the Calendar button in the Navigation Pane.

2. Practice switching between Day, Work Week, Week, and Month views.

3. Create an appointment using the following information:

   Subject: Halloween Party
   Start Time: 7:00 PM, October 31 of the current year
   End Time: 9:00 PM, October 31 of the current year

4. Save and Close the appointment.

5. Reschedule the Halloween Party appointment to 6:00 PM.

6. Make the Halloween Party into a recurring appointment that happens at the same time every October 31st.

7. Delete the Halloween Party appointment.

Quiz Answers

1. B. Day view, Work Week view, Week view, and Month view are the available Calendar views. There isn't a Three-Day view.

2. False. An event is any appointment that lasts one or more 24-hour days, such as a conference or vacation. It can be rescheduled.

3. C. When a reminder appears, you can click dismiss to close the reminder, click Snooze to display the reminder again after a specified amount of time has passed, or click Open Item to open the appointment.

4. True. You can change the days that appear in Outlook's Work Week view by selecting Tools → Options from the menu.

5. C. The current version of Outlook doesn't support recurring appointment based on lunar cycles.

6. False. This one should be true, but unfortunately it's not.

USING THE TASKS LIST

CHAPTER OBJECTIVES:

Create a new task: Lesson 6.1

Work with recurring and regenerating tasks: Lesson 6.2

Change views to display the Tasks list in different ways: Lesson 6.3

Change the way tasks are displayed: Lesson 6.4

CHAPTER TASK: CREATE, MODIFY, AND COMPLETE A TASK

Prerequisites

- Understand how to use menus, toolbars, dialog boxes, and shortcut keystrokes.
- Understand how to use the Navigation Pane and navigate within Outlook.

Even if you're not an organized person, you've probably scrawled a to-do list on a piece of paper to help you remember everything that you have to do. The problem with paper to-do lists is that they're easy to misplace and are often not right in front of you when you need them to tell you what needs to be done.

Now you can throw away your paper to-do lists, because Outlook's Tasks list is difficult to misplace (when was last time you couldn't find your computer?) and is always right in front of you.

Creating tasks in the Tasks list really isn't much more difficult than writing down a to-do list—hence the brevity of this chapter. Here, you will learn how to create a task, how to mark a task as complete once it's finished, and how to delete a task. You will also learn how to create a recurring task that appears at a specified interval, such as a reminder to get a weekly report in to your boss.

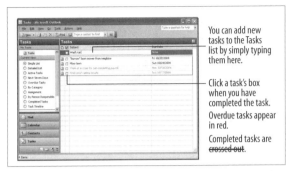

You can add new tasks to the Tasks list by simply typing them here.

Click a task's box when you have completed the task.

Overdue tasks appear in red.

Completed tasks are ~~crossed out~~.

Figure 6-1. The Tasks list helps you organize your daily tasks.

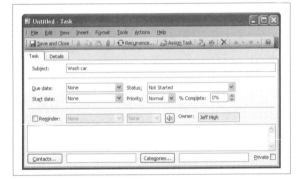

Figure 6-2. The Task dialog box lets you enter more detailed information about a task.

Writing down your tasks in a to-do list or task list makes them easier to remember and manage. To help you organize your tasks, Outlook comes with the Tasks list, as shown in Figure 6-1. As with most other Outlook items, you can make your tasks as simple or as detailed as needed. Here are a few notes about Outlook's Tasks list:

• You can assign priorities to your tasks. For example, you could give a "Pay rent" task a higher priority than a "Go shopping" task.

• You can assign start dates to your tasks for when they should appear as reminders in the Tasks list, and due dates for when the task must be completed. For example, a "Send out holiday cards" task might have a start date of December 10, 2004 and a due date of December 17, 2004.

• Tasks can be recurring. For example, you could create a "Do yoga stretches" task that appears in the Tasks list every Tuesday.

• Perhaps the most satisfying of all, tasks in the Tasks list can be crossed off when you've finished them.

In this lesson, you will learn how to use Outlook's Tasks list to manage your to-do's.

1 Switch to the Tasks list by clicking the Tasks button in the Navigation Pane.

Outlook displays the Tasks list. Although you can create a new task by clicking the New Task button on the toolbar, it's usually easier to create a new task by entering it directly in the Task view.

2 Click in the Click here to add a new Task box and type Wash car.

You can also specify a due date for the task.

3 Click in the Due date box to the right of the new task, click the Due date list arrow and select a future date from the calendar. Press Enter.

You can edit a task directly in the Task view, or by double-clicking the task and editing it in the Task dialog box.

4 Double-click the Wash car task.

The Wash car task appears in the Task dialog box, as shown in Figure 6-2. The Task dialog box lets you specify additional information about the task, such as the task's priority or the percentage of the task that is finished.

5 Click the Priority list arrow and select Low.

That's enough changes for now.

6 Click the Save and Close button on the toolbar.

Outlook saves the task and closes the Task dialog box.

As you complete tasks, you will want to mark them as complete without deleting them from the Tasks folder to keep a record of what you've accomplished. Here's how to mark a task as complete:

7 Check the empty checkbox to the left of the Wash car task.

A check mark appears in the checkbox and a line appears through the task to indicate that it is complete.

Eventually, you will want to delete some of your completed tasks. The procedure for deleting a task is no different from deleting any other Outlook item.

8 Click the Wash car **task then press** Delete.

Outlook deletes the task from the Tasks list and puts it in the Deleted Items folder.

Table 6-1 describes the fields you'll see in the Task dialog box.

Table 6-1. Fields in the Task dialog box

Field	Description
Due Date	Specifies the due date for when the task must be completed.
Start Date	Specifies the date when the task will appear in the Tasks list as a reminder.
Status	Specifies the status of the task: Not Started, In Progress, Completed, Waiting on Someone Else, or Deferred.
Priority	Specifies the importance level of the task: High, Normal, or Low.
% Complete	Specifies the percentage of the task that is finished.
Reminder	Displays a reminder for the item.
Owner	Specifies the name of the person who created the task. If the task is sent to another person, that person becomes the owner of the task.

QUICK REFERENCE

TO VIEW THE TASKS LIST:

• CLICK THE TASKS LIST BUTTON IN THE NAVIGATION PANE.

TO CREATE A NEW TASK:

• CLICK THE CLICK HERE TO ADD A NEW TASK BOX AND ENTER THE TASK AND ITS DUE DATE.

OR...

1. CLICK THE NEW TASK BUTTON OR PRESS CTRL + N.

2. ENTER INFORMATION ABOUT THE TASK.

3. CLICK THE SAVE AND CLOSE BUTTON OR PRESS ALT + S WHEN YOU'RE FINISHED.

TO MARK A TASK AS COMPLETE:

• CHECK THE BOX BY THE TASK.

TO DELETE A TASK:

• SELECT THE TASK AND CLICK THE DELETE BUTTON ON THE TOOLBAR.

OR...

• SELECT THE TASK AND PRESS THE DELETE KEY.

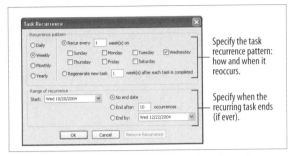

Figure 6-3. You can create a recurring task in the Task Recurrence dialog box.

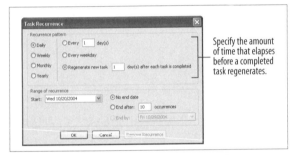

Figure 6-4. Choose how often you want the task to regenerate.

Do you have a task that occurs on a regular basis that you need to remind yourself about? Maybe you have to submit a progress report on the first Tuesday of each month or pay your electric bill on the 12th of every month. With Outlook, you can easily create a recurring task that appears at regular intervals, such as the first Thursday of every month.

You can also create a regenerating task, which reappears at regular intervals once you have completed it. For example, to keep yourself motivated, you might create a "Work Out" task that regenerates every day. Recurring and regenerating tasks are easy to identify because of their 🔁 icons.

This lesson will show you how to create a recurring task and a regenerating task.

1 Click the 📄 New ▾ New Task button on the toolbar.

> TIP *Other ways to add a new task are to select File → New → Task from the menu or to press Ctrl + Shift + K.*

The Untitled - Task window appears.

2 Click in the Subject box and type Deliver status report to boss.

Here's how to make this task recurring:

3 Click the Recurrence... Recurrence button on the toolbar.

> TIP *Other ways to create a recurring task are to select Actions → Recurrence from the menu or to press Ctrl + G.*

The Task Recurrence dialog box appears, as shown in Figure 6-3. This is where you tell Outlook when and how often the task recurs. You have several choices here:

- **Daily:** Tasks that recur every day or every work day.
- **Weekly:** Tasks that recur on the same day(s) of the week, such as a report due every Friday or a payroll due every other Thursday.
- **Monthly:** Tasks that recur on a monthly basis, such as an inventory audit that occurs on the 5th of every month.
- **Yearly:** Tasks that recur on an annual basis, such as tax-filing days.

Since this task recurs every Tuesday, you want to select the Weekly option.

4 In the Recurrence pattern section, select the Weekly and Friday options.

Make sure that Friday is the only day checked. The "Recur every ___ weeks" box lets you specify the time period you want to pass before the task repeats. Because there is a 1 in the "Recur every ___ weeks" box, the task will repeat every week.

The bottom of the Task Recurrence dialog box lets you specify when the recurring task will stop repeating (if ever). We don't need to specify an end date for this particular recurring task, so we can leave the "No end date" option selected.

5 Click OK.

The Task Recurrence dialog box closes.

6 Click the Save and Close button on the toolbar.

Regenerating tasks are similar to recurring tasks, except that regenerating tasks recur only once they have been marked as complete. Here's how to create a regenerating task:

7 Click the New Task button on the toolbar.

The Task window appears.

8 Click in the Subject box and type Work Out.

Here's how to make this into a regenerating task:

9 Click the Recurrence button on the toolbar.

The Task Recurrence dialog box reappears.

10 In the Recurrence pattern section, select the Daily and Regenerate new task options, as shown in Figure 6-4.

Congratulations! You've just created a regenerating task!

11 Click OK and then click the Save and Close button on the toolbar.

You've just created a recurring task and a regenerating task. Outlook will create a regenerating daily reminder to work out and a recurring weekly reminder to get that status report to your boss each Friday.

Table 6-2 describes different types of tasks.

Table 6-2. Task types

Type of task	Description	Example
Normal task	Occurs just once	Returning a phone call
Recurring task	Repeats at regular intervals, whether it has been marked as complete or not	Paying rent, submitting a weekly status report
Regenerating task	Repeats at regular intervals once it has been marked as complete	Mowing the lawn, changing oil in your car, working out

QUICK REFERENCE

TO CREATE A RECURRING TASK:

1. CREATE A NEW TASK OR DOUBLE-CLICK AN EXISTING TASK.

2. CLICK THE RECURRENCE BUTTON ON THE TOOLBAR.

3. SPECIFY THE RECURRENCE PATTERN AND DURATION. CLICK OK WHEN YOU'RE FINISHED.

4. CLICK THE SAVE AND CLOSE BUTTON ON THE TOOLBAR OR PRESS ALT + S TO SAVE THE TASK.

TO CREATE A REGENERATING TASK:

1. CREATE A NEW TASK OR DOUBLE-CLICK AN EXISTING TASK.

2. CLICK THE RECURRENCE BUTTON ON THE TOOLBAR.

3. SELECT THE REGENERATE OPTION AND SPECIFY WHEN THE TASK SHOULD REGENERATE. CLICK OK WHEN YOU'RE FINISHED.

4. CLICK THE SAVE AND CLOSE BUTTON ON THE TOOLBAR OR PRESS ALT + S TO SAVE THE TASK.

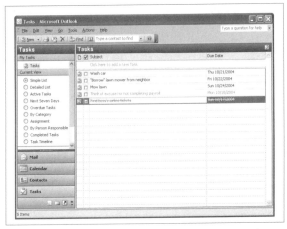

Figure 6-5. In Simple List view, the Tasks list displays only a few details so you can see your tasks at a quick glance.

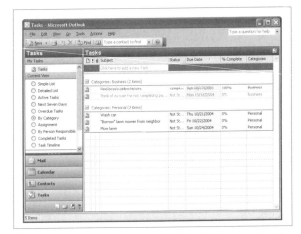

Figure 6-6. In Categories view, the Tasks list is grouped and organized by categories.

Like most other Outlook tools, there are several ways to view your Tasks list. For example, you can view your Tasks list by:

• Tasks that are due in the current week

• Tasks that are overdue

• Tasks by category—for example, to separate your business and personal to-do's

So which Tasks view is the best? That depends on the situation and on your own personal preference. Maybe you want to view all your completed tasks, or maybe only those tasks that are overdue. Outlook gives you 10 different preset ways to look at the items stored in your Tasks list. Let's take a look at some of them now.

1 Make sure you are in Task view.

2 Click the Detailed List option in the Current View menu in the Navigation Pane.

Now, we can see the tasks' due dates, percent complete, and category. This view is great when you are working on several projects and want to see how far away they are from being completed.

3 Switch between each of the views and refer to Table 6-3 to read about their descriptions.

Remember: open the Current View menu by selecting View → Arrange By → Current View from the menu. When you've finished move on to the next step.

4 Select View → Arrange By → Current View → Simple List from the menu.

> **TIP** Other ways to change views are to select View → Arrange By → Current View from the menu and select the desired view; or select Tools → Organize from the menu, select Using Views, and select the desired view.

You're back at the most common way of looking at the Tasks list.

Table 6-3 describes the views that are available for the Tasks list.

Table 6-3. Available Tasks list views

View	Displays
Simple List	Displays tasks in a list with only a few details so you can see your tasks at a quick glance.
Detailed List	Displays tasks in a list that shows many details about each task, including priority and percentage complete.
Active Tasks	Displays tasks that are incomplete (including ones that are overdue), in a list.
Next Seven Days	Displays tasks that are due in the next seven days, in a list.

Table 6-3. Available Tasks list views (Continued)

View	Displays
Overdue Tasks	Displays tasks that are overdue, in a list.
By Category	Displays tasks in a list, grouped by category and sorted by due date within each category.
Assignment	Displays tasks in a list that shows only the tasks that have been assigned to others, sorted by the task owner's name and due date.
By Person Responsible	Displays tasks in a list, grouped by the task owner's name and sorted by due date for each task owner.
Completed Tasks	Displays in a list all tasks that have been marked complete.
Task Timeline	Displays tasks, represented by icons, in chronological order by start date on a timeline. Tasks without start dates are arranged by due date.

QUICK REFERENCE

TO CHANGE VIEWS:

1. CLICK THE TASKS BUTTON IN THE NAVIGATION PANE.

2. SELECT THE VIEW YOU WANT FROM THE CURRENT VIEW MENU OR SELECT VIEW → ARRANGE BY → CURRENT VIEW FROM THE MENU AND SELECT ONE THE VIEWS DESCRIBED IN TABLE 6-3.

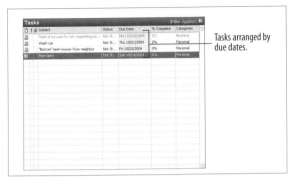

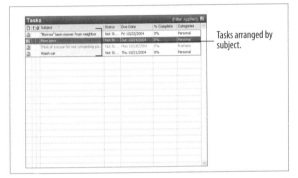

Outlook 2003 offers many ways to view your tasks. These options are found by selecting View → Arrange By from the menu. For example, you can arrange your tasks by date, subject, or importance.

⊰ NOTE ⊰ *The options listed in Figure 6-7 are not available in Task Timeline view. This is due to the fact that a timeline already has specific boundaries in terms of organization. It would be redundant to add another arrangement criteria.*

Let's try out some of the available Arrange By options! First, we need to make sure that the Task Pane is not in the Task Timeline view.

1 Select View → Arrange By → Current View → Active Tasks **from the menu.**

A list of all your active tasks appears. They are currently arranged by the due dates, because date is the default setting. If you have a lot of active tasks, you now have a screen full of very loosely organized information.

Let's arrange them differently.

2 Select View → Arrange By → Subject **from the menu.**

Your tasks are now organized alphabetically by subject, as shown in Figure 6-8. This is handy for finding a task that you know the name of, but you can't quite remember the due date. All you have to do is scroll down the list to find your task.

Some Arrange By options are much more useful than others. For example, it may be very useful for you to arrange your tasks by predetermined categories, but you do not have any tasks with attachments, so you would not want to choose this option.

Let's return the calendar to its default view.

3 Select View → Arrange By → Current View → Simple List **from the menu.**

The Tasks Pane is once again displayed in the default view.

Table 6-4 describes each of the options available in the Arrange By submenu.

Table 6-4. Arrange By submenu options

Arrange By	Description
Date	Arranges tasks by date, starting with today and moving forward.
Conversation	Arranges tasks by similarities.
From	Arranges tasks according to who created them.
To	Arranges tasks by recipient.
Folder	Arranges tasks by the folders in which they are stored.
Size	Arranges tasks by size.

Table 6-4. Arrange By submenu options (Continued)

Arrange By	Description
Subject	Arranges tasks by topic.
Type	Arranges tasks by type.
Flag	Arranges tasks by flag status.
Attachments	Arranges tasks by whether or not they have an attachment.
E-mail Account	Arranges tasks by e-mail account.
Importance	Arranges tasks by importance.
Categories	Arranges tasks by categories that you determine.

QUICK REFERENCE

TO CHANGE HOW TASKS ARE ARRANGED IN THE TASK PANE:

1. MAKE SURE THAT YOUR TASK PANE IS NOT IN TASK TIMELINE VIEW.

2. SELECT VIEW → CURRENT VIEW → ARRANGE BY FROM THE MENU AND MAKE A SELECTION.

Chapter Six Review

Lesson Summary

Using the Tasks List

To View the Tasks List: Click the Tasks button in the Navigation Pane.

To Create a New Task (Directly in the Tasks list): Click the Click here to add a new Task box and enter the task and its due date.

To Create a New Task (Using the Task Window): Click the New Task button or press Ctrl + N, enter the information about task, and click the Save and Close button or press Alt + S when you're finished.

To Mark a Task as Complete: Check the box by the task or open the task window and select the task.

To Delete a Task: Select the task and click the Delete button on the toolbar or select the task and press the Delete key.

Creating Recurring and Regenerating Tasks

To Create a Recurring Task: Create a new task or double-click an existing task. Click the Recurrence button on the toolbar, specify the recurrence pattern and duration, and click OK when you're finished. Click the Save and Close button on the toolbar or press Alt + S to save the task.

To Create a Regenerating Task: Create a new task or double-click an existing task. Click the Recurrence button on the toolbar, select the Regenerate option, specify when the task should regenerate, and click OK when you're finished. Click the Save and Close button on the toolbar or press Alt + S to save the task.

Changing Views

To Change Views: Click the Tasks button in the Navigation Pane. Select the view you want from the Current View menu or select View → Arrange By → Current View from the menu and select the desired view.

Arranging Tasks

To Change How Tasks are Arranged in the Task Pane: Make sure that the Task Pane is not in Task Timeline view, then select View → Current View → Arrange By from the menu and make a selection.

Quiz

1. Which of the following statements are NOT true? (Select all that apply.)

   A. One way to mark a task as complete is to check the box by the task

   B. Another way to mark a task as complete is to click the Mark Complete button on the toolbar when the task window is open

   C. Overdue tasks normally appear in bold

   D. Completed tasks are automatically sent to the Deleted Items folder

2. A _____ task repeats at regular intervals, whether it has been completed or not.

   A. Normal

   B. Repeating

   C. Recurring

   D. Regenerating

3. A _____ task repeats at regular intervals once it has been marked as complete.

   A. Normal

   B. Repeating

   C. Recurring

   D. Regenerating

Homework

1. Start Microsoft Outlook and click the Tasks button in the Navigation Pane.

2. Create a new task using the following information:

   Subject: Brush your teeth!
   Due Date: Tomorrow

3. Make the Brush your teeth! task into a recurring task that happens every day.

4. Double-click the Brush your teeth! task to open it.

5. Change the Brush your teeth! task's priority to High then close the Task form.

6. Delete the Brush your teeth! task.

Quiz Answers

1. C and D. C: Overdue tasks normally appear in red. D: Completed tasks are simply marked as complete—not deleted.

2. C. A recurring task repeats at regular intervals, whether it has been completed or not.

3. D. A regenerating task repeats at regular intervals once it has been marked as complete.

CHAPTER 7
USING THE JOURNAL

CHAPTER OBJECTIVES:

Automatically record items in the Journal: Lesson 7.1

Manually create a journal entry: Lesson 7.3

Open, modify, and delete a journal entry: Lesson 7.4

Create journal entries that relate to a contact: Lesson 7.5

Change views to display the Journal in different ways: Lessons 7.2 and 7.6

CHAPTER TASK: CREATE, MODIFY, AND WORK WITH A JOURNAL ENTRY

Prerequisites

- Understand how to use menus, toolbars, dialog boxes, and shortcut keystrokes.
- Understand how to use the Navigation Pane and navigate within Outlook.

Christopher Columbus kept a journal of his voyages to the New World, and Thomas Edison kept one about his various experiments and inventions. Now it's your turn! You can use Outlook's Journal to keep a log of your important daily activities. Then, when you're famous, future historians and students will look back and read about your exciting daily activities at the office!

In a nutshell, the Journal keeps track of three different types of activities:

- **Manually Created Activities:** You can manually create a journal entry, just like you would create an e-mail or task. Manually created journal entries can be about any type of activity you can think of: phone calls, meetings, important conversations, faxes, etc.
- **Contact-Related Activities:** Outlook can automatically record certain activities that are related to a particular contact. For example, you could configure the Journal to automatically track any e-mails sent to or received from Bob Smith.
- **Microsoft Office Documents:** The Journal can also automatically record any documents that you create or modify in any Microsoft Office program, such as Microsoft Excel, PowerPoint, or Word.

You will learn how to create and work with journal entries using all three methods in this chapter. You will also learn how to attach a file to a journal entry, how to use the Journal with the Contacts list to perform basic contact management, and how to display the Journal using the available preset views.

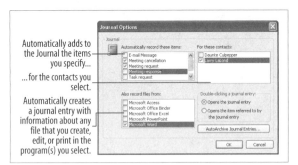

Automatically adds to the Journal the items you specify...

...for the contacts you select.

Automatically creates a journal entry with information about any file that you create, edit, or print in the program(s) you select.

Figure 7-1. The Journal Options dialog box.

The fastest and easiest way to create a journal entry is to do nothing. What?!? That's right—Outlook's Journal can automatically record information about any document you create, edit, or print from any Microsoft Office application. The Journal can also automatically track e-mail messages, meeting requests and responses, and task requests and responses to the contacts you specify. Before you can use Outlook's automatic Journal recording features, you have to turn them on. This lesson will show you how to do just that.

1 Select Tools → Options from the menu and click the Preferences tab if necessary.

The Options dialog box appears.

2 Click the Journal Options button located in the Contacts category.

The Journal Options dialog box appears, as shown in Figure 7-1. In the top half of the dialog box, you can specify the types of activities you want to automatically record and the names of the people in your Contacts list for which they are recorded. For example, you might want to record e-mail messages from your boss but not your mother, so you would only check your boss's name.

The bottom half of the dialog box lets you automatically record journal entries about files you create, open, close, and save from any Microsoft Office program, such as a Microsoft Word document or Microsoft Excel spreadsheet.

We're not going to make any changes to the journal in this lesson.

3 Click OK to close the Journal Options dialog box, and then click OK to close the Options dialog box.

So if Outlook's Journal can automatically record everything you do on your computer, why do most people decide NOT to use the automatic recording features? One word: *privacy*. Many people find the idea of Outlook keeping track of every Microsoft Office document they work on—including personal letters—a little disturbing. If other people occasionally use your computer, you may want to think twice before enabling all of the Journal's automatic recording features.

QUICK REFERENCE

TO AUTOMATICALLY RECORD JOURNAL ENTRIES:

1. SELECT TOOLS → OPTIONS FROM THE MENU, AND CLICK THE PREFERENCES TAB IF NECESSARY.

2. CLICK THE JOURNAL OPTIONS BUTTON.

3. SPECIFY THE ITEMS YOU WANT TO AUTOMATICALLY RECORD IN THE JOURNAL.

4. WHEN YOU'RE FINISHED, CLICK OK, OK.

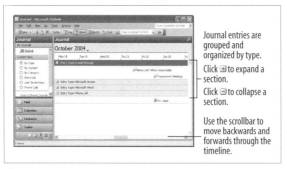

Journal entries are grouped and organized by type.

Click ⊞ to expand a section.

Click ⊟ to collapse a section.

Use the scrollbar to move backwards and forwards through the timeline.

Figure 7-2. The Journal normally organizes information into related groups.

The Journal displays its information on a timeline. A timeline makes it easy to view the chronological order of your activities. For example, perhaps you can't find an Excel spreadsheet that you worked on last week. You could use Outlook's Journal to view everything you've worked on in Microsoft Excel during the past week to find the spreadsheet.

The Journal has usually been one of Outlook's least used and least understood features—as a result, Microsoft has all but hidden it in Outlook 2003. Before we get started, here's how to add the Journal to the Navigation Pane.

1 Click the ⊟ Configure buttons button in the Navigation Pane.

A menu appears with options for configuring which and how many buttons appear in the Navigation Pane.

2 Select Add or Remove buttons → Journal from the menu.

The Journal button appears at the bottom of the Navigation Pane.

You can change the time scale used in the Journal by clicking any of the following buttons:

- 1 Day **Day:** View one day at time.
- 7 Week **Week:** View one week at a time.
- 31 Month **Month:** View one month a time.

Move on to the next step to learn more about how to view information in the Journal.

3 Click the Journal button in the Navigation Pane.

> TIP
>
> *Another way to open the journal is to click the Folder List button in the Navigation Pane to display the Folder List, and then click the Journal folder.*

The contents of the Journal appear, as shown in Figure 7-2 (your Journal will contain different information than the figure). The Journal normally displays its information in a *grouped view*, meaning items are organized into sections that you can expand or collapse to display or hide the items then contain. A plus symbol (+) or a minus symbol (-) beside a section means that it contains several journal entries. You can display a section's journal entries by clicking its plus sign.

> NOTE
>
> *Groups appear only if there are one or more entries included, so if you haven't used the Journal to log any Excel spreadsheets, a Microsoft Excel section won't appear in your timeline.*

4 Practice scrolling through the Journal timeline and expanding and collapsing any sections you find by clicking their + and - buttons.

QUICK REFERENCE

TO ADD A JOURNAL BUTTON TO THE NAVIGATION PANE:

1. CLICK THE CONFIGURE BUTTONS BUTTON IN THE NAVIGATION PANE.

2. SELECT ADD OR REMOVE BUTTONS → JOURNAL FROM THE MENU.

TO SWITCH TO THE JOURNAL:

• CLICK THE JOURNAL BUTTON IN THE NAVIGATION PANE, OR CLICK THE FOLDER LIST BUTTON IN THE NAVIGATION PANE TO DISPLAY THE FOLDER LIST AND THEN CLICK THE JOURNAL FOLDER.

TO SWITCH BETWEEN JOURNAL TIMELINE VIEWS:

CLICK ONE OF THE FOLLOWING BUTTONS ON THE TOOLBAR:

• DAY DISPLAYS ONE DAY AT A TIME.

• WEEK DISPLAYS ONE WEEK AT A TIME.

• MONTH DISPLAYS ONE MONTH AT A TIME.

TO EXPAND/COLLAPSE A JOURNAL SECTION:

• CLICK THE SECTION'S + OR - BUTTON.

Manually Creating a Journal Entry

Specify the type that best describes the journal entry so that you can find it later. To display the entry quickly, type its first letter.

Specify the start date, time, and duration of the activity. You can use the **Start Timer** to track the duration of the journal entry.

Enter the name of any contacts associated with the entry. Click **Contacts** to select names from a list.

Figure 7-3. The New Journal Entry form.

You can manually create Journal entries to record your phone calls, meetings, and documents on which you've worked. You'll learn how in this lesson.

1 While in Journal View, click the  New Journal Entry button on the toolbar.

> **TIP**
> *Another way to create a journal entry is to press Ctrl + Shift + J.*

The New Journal Entry form appears, as shown in Figure 7-3.

2 Click in the Subject box and type Company picnic.

Next, you need to specify what type of journal entry you're making.

3 Click the Entry type list arrow.

Up pops a list of the various types of activities that can be used to best describe the journal entry.

4 Select Phone call from the list.

Many activities are associated with a contact, such as letters, e-mail messages, or meetings. You can enter the names of one or more contacts associated with an item by entering their name(s) in the Contact box or by selecting them from the Address Book.

5 Click the Contacts button.

The Address Book appears. All you have to do here is find and double-click the name(s) you want to add to the entry. We don't need to select any names for now.

6 Click Cancel to close the Address Book.

If you want, you can record the duration of the activity. For example, how long a phone call lasts. You can do this by selecting an amount of time from the Duration list or by clicking the Start Timer button to track the duration of the journal entry.

7 Click the Duration list arrow and select 15 minutes.

Finally, you will usually want to write a brief note about the journal entry.

8 In the Notes box, type Need catering for company picnic.

9 Click the Save and Close button on the toolbar.

Outlook saves the journal entry and closes the Journal Entry form.

QUICK REFERENCE

TO MANUALLY CREATE A JOURNAL ENTRY:

1. CLICK THE NEW JOURNAL ENTRY BUTTON ON THE TOOLBAR.

2. ENTER THE SUBJECT IN THE SUBJECT BOX.

3. SELECT THE TYPE OF ENTRY FROM THE ENTRY TYPE LIST.

4. (OPTIONAL) ENTER THE NAMES OF ANY CONTACTS ASSOCIATED WITH THE JOURNAL ENTRY.

5. (OPTIONAL) ENTER THE ACTIVITY'S DURATION.

6. CLICK THE SAVE AND CLOSE BUTTON ON THE TOOLBAR OR PRESS ALT + S WHEN YOU'RE FINISHED.

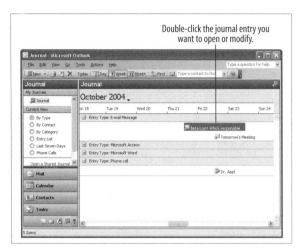

Figure 7-4. Like any other Microsoft Outlook item, you open journal entries by double-clicking them.

Journal entries are easy to move, open, and modify. When you modify a journal entry in Outlook, its associated item or document is not affected. Likewise, when you modify an item or document, any related journal entries are unaffected. For example, if you delete a journal entry regarding a Word document, the actual Word document is unaffected.

In this lesson, you will learn how to open, modify, and delete a journal entry. You will also learn how to go to an exact date in the Journal—particularly useful if you have hundreds of items in your Journal.

1 Select Go → Go to Date from the menu.

The Go to Date dialog box appears. There is only one thing you can do in the Go to Date dialog box: enter the date you want to go to.

2 Click the Date list arrow and select the current date from the calendar, then click OK.

The Journal moves to the specified date. Here's how to open a journal entry:

3 Find and double-click the Company picnic journal entry, located in the Phone call section [you may have to expand the phone call section by clicking its plus symbol (+)].

The journal entry opens in its own form.

4 Click the Start time list arrow and select tomorrow's date, then click the Save and Close button on the toolbar.

Outlook saves the modified journal entry. Notice that the "Company picnic" journal entry has moved on the timeline to reflect the date change.

If you no longer need a journal entry, you can select the entry and press the Delete key or click the Delete button on the toolbar to delete it.

5 Select the Company picnic journal entry and press Delete.

The Company picnic entry is deleted from the Journal.

QUICK REFERENCE

TO GO TO A SPECIFIC DATE:
* SELECT GO → GO TO DATE FROM THE MENU.

TO EDIT A JOURNAL ENTRY:
* DOUBLE-CLICK THE JOURNAL ENTRY.

TO DELETE A JOURNAL ENTRY:
* SELECT THE JOURNAL ENTRY AND CLICK THE DELETE BUTTON ON THE TOOLBAR.

OR...

* SELECT THE JOURNAL ENTRY AND PRESS THE DELETE KEY.

Figure 7-5. Most Outlook 2003 forms have a Contacts field where you can specify the name of one or more contacts associated with the item.

Figure 7-6. A contact's Activities tab contains any journal entries that relate to that contact.

Many people use the Journal together with their Contacts list to keep track of their activities with their contacts. For example, you could have the Journal keep track of all your phone calls to a particular client. Outlook's contact management features aren't quite as sophisticated as a full-featured contact management program, such as Symantic's Act, but they're often suitable for keeping track of your appointments, calls, and correspondence with a contact.

Microsoft has somewhat improved the contact management features in Outlook 2003—every appointment, journal entry, and task form now has a Contact field where you can easily specify the name(s) of the contact(s) associated with the Outlook item. You can also click the Contacts button, found near the bottom of these forms, to select one or more names from the Contacts list.

1 Click the Contacts button in the Navigation Pane.

Outlook switches to the Contacts list.

2 Click the New Contact button on the toolbar.

The Untitled - Contact window appears.

3 Create a new contact using the following information:

Full Name: Press, James
Company: McDonald's
Address: 229 North 2nd Street
         Minneapolis, MN 55417

4 Click the Save and Close button on the toolbar.

Outlook saves the new contact and closes the contact form.

5 Click the Journal button in the Navigation Pane.

You're back to the Journal. Let's create a new journal entry.

6 Click the New Journal Entry button on the toolbar.

The New Journal Entry form appears, as shown in Figure 7-5.

7 Click in the Subject box and type Call to Jim.

Next, you need to specify what type of journal entry you're making.

8 Click the Entry type list arrow.

Up pops a list of the various types of activities that best describe the journal entry.

9 Select Phone call from the list.

Many activities are associated with someone, such as letters, e-mail messages, or meetings. You can enter the names of one or more contacts associated with an item by entering their name(s) in the Contact box, or by selecting them from the Address Book.

10 Click the Contacts button.

The Select Contacts dialog box appears. Simply select the contact(s) that are related to the journal entry.

11 Find and double-click the Press, James contact.

The James Press contact appears in the Contacts field. Notice the James Press text is underlined. Double-clicking the name James Press opens the James Press contact in its own form.

We've finished creating the journal entry.

12 Click the Save and Close button on the toolbar.

Let's go back to the Contacts list.

13 Click the Contacts button in the Navigation Pane.

Next, we need to open the James Press contact.

14 Find and double-click the Press, James contact.

The James Press contact appears in its own form. You can view any journal entries for the contact by clicking the Activities tab.

15 Click the Activities tab.

The contents of the Activities tab appear, as shown in Figure 7-6. To open any contact-related item in its own form, just double-click it.

16 Close the contact form.

In all honesty, the integration between the Contacts list and the Journal could be much better. For example, the Journal records only certain types of activities for just the contacts that you select. Hopefully, Outlook's limited contact management features will get better in the next version of Outlook.

QUICK REFERENCE

TO CREATE A JOURNAL ENTRY RELATED TO A CONTACT:

1. CREATE THE JOURNAL ENTRY IN ITS OWN FORM BY CLICKING THE NEW JOURNAL ENTRY BUTTON ON THE TOOLBAR.

2. ENTER THE CONTACT(S) THAT ARE RELATED TO THE JOURNAL ENTRY IN THE CONTACTS FIELD. CLICK THE CONTACTS BUTTON TO SELECT THE CONTACT(S) FROM A LIST.

TO VIEW JOURNAL ENTRIES RELATED TO A CONTACT:

• FIND AND DOUBLE-CLICK THE CONTACT AND CLICK THE ACTIVITIES TAB.

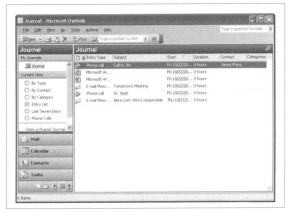

Figure 7-7. In Entry List view, the Journal displays its entries in a table format.

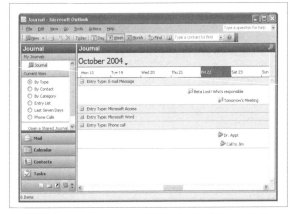

Figure 7-8. The Journal normally displays its information in a timeline, so you can see when each entry was created.

Like many other Outlook tools, there are several ways to view your Journal. For example, you can look at it through one of the following views:

• **Last Seven Days:** To view all journal entries that have occurred within the past seven days.

• **Contact:** To see all the e-mail messages you've sent to Bob Jones.

• **Category:** To separate your business and personal activities.

So which view is the best? That depends on the situation and your own personal preference. Maybe you want to view only those activities that have occurred during the past week, or maybe you want your journal entries grouped by contacts. Outlook gives you six different pre-set ways to look at the items stored in your Journal. Let's take a look at some of them now.

1 Make sure you're in Journal view.

2 In the Navigation Pane, click the Entry List option located in the Current View menu.

Other ways to change views are to select View → Arrange By → Current View from the menu and select the desired view; or to select Tools → Organize from the menu, select Using Views, and then select the desired view.

Entry List view displays all your Journal entries in a list, regardless of who, what, or when. This view is great for when you want to see *everything* in your Journal, as shown in Figure 7-7.

You can click any column heading to sort the information in the column in ascending or descending order.

3 Refer to Table 7-1 to familiarize yourself with these views by reading their descriptions.

Remember: open the Current View menu by selecting View → Arrange By → Current View from the menu. When you've finished, move on to the next step.

4 In the Navigation Pane, click the By Type option located in the Current View menu.

You're back to the most common way of looking at the Journal.

Table 7-1 offers a summary of the available Journal views.

Table 7-1. Available Journal views

View	Displays
By Type	Displays journal entries in a timeline, grouped according to their type.
By Contact	Displays journal entries in a timeline, grouped by the name of the person associated with the item.
By Category	Displays journal entries in a timeline, grouped according to their category.
Entry List	Displays all your journal entries in a list, regardless of who, what, or when.
Last Seven Days	Displays your most recent journal entries in a list.
Phone Calls	Displays your phone call journal entries in a list.

QUICK REFERENCE

TO CHANGE VIEWS:

1. MAKE SURE YOU ARE IN JOURNAL VIEW.

2. SELECT THE VIEW YOU WANT FROM THE CURRENT VIEW MENU OR SELECT VIEW → ARRANGE BY → CURRENT VIEW FROM THE MENU AND SELECT ONE OF THE VIEWS DESCRIBED IN TABLE 7-1.

Lesson Summary

Recording Items in the Journal Automatically

To Automatically Record Journal Entries: Select Tools → Options from the menu and click the Preferences tab, if necessary. Click the Journal Options button. Specify the items you want to automatically record in the journal. When you're finished, click OK, OK.

Viewing the Journal

To Switch to the Journal: Click the Journal button in the Navigation Pane or click the Folder List button in the Navigation Pane to display the Folder List. Then click the Journal folder.

To Switch between Journal Timeline Views: Click one of the following buttons on the toolbar: Day displays one day at a time; Week displays one week at a time; and Month displays one month at a time.

To Expand a Journal Section: Click the section's ⊞ button.

To Collapse a Journal Section: Click the section's ⊟ button.

Manually Creating a Journal Entry

To Manually Create a Journal Entry: Click the New Journal Entry button on the toolbar. Enter the subject in the Subject box and select the type of entry from the Entry type list. (Optional) Enter the names of any contacts associated with the journal entry and/or enter the duration of the activity. Click the Save and Close button on the toolbar or press Alt + S when you're finished.

Opening, Modifying, and Deleting a Journal Entry

To Go to a Specific Date: Select Go → Go to Date from the menu.

To Edit a Journal Entry: Double-click the journal entry.

To Delete a Journal Entry: Select the journal entry and click the Delete button on the toolbar or select the journal entry and press the Delete key.

Creating Journal Entries Related to a Contact

To Create a Journal Entry Related to a Contact: Create a new journal entry, click the Contacts button, and select a contact.

To View Journal Entries Related to a Contact: Find and double-click the contact and click the Activities tab.

Changing Journal Views

To Change Views: Select the view you want from the Current View menu or select View → Arrange By → Current View from the menu and select the desired view.

Quiz

1. Outlook can automatically record… (Select all that apply.)
   A. Documents created in or worked on in Microsoft Word.
   B. Worksheets created in or worked on in Microsoft Excel.
   C. E-mail messages sent to a specified contact.
   D. All e-mail messages, regardless of recipient.

2. The Journal automatically records when you create and send an e-mail message to someone in your Contacts list. (True or False?)

3. By default, the Journal displays its entries in which type of format?
   A. A table
   B. A weekly calendar
   C. A monthly calendar
   D. A timeline

4. Journal entries are modified by:

   A. Double-clicking the journal entry

   B. Journal entries cannot be modified

   C. Selecting Journal → Modify from the menu

   D. Saying the word "Modify" into your computer mouse

5. Each contact in the Contacts list has an Activities tab, which lets you add and/or view journal entries related to the contact. (True or False?)

Homework

1. Start Microsoft Outlook.

2. See what items the Journal automatically records. Select Tools → Options from the menu, click the Preferences tab, and then click the Journal Options button.

3. Click OK to close the Journal Options dialog box, then click OK to close the Options dialog box.

4. Click the Journal button in the Navigation Pane.

5. Create a journal entry using the following information:

   Subject: Call to mom
   Entry Type: Phone call

6. Delete the "Call to mom" journal entry.

Quiz Answers

1. A, B, and C. The Journal can record any files you create or modify in Microsoft Office. The Journal can also record e-mail messages sent to the contacts you specify—but to specified contacts only.

2. False. The Journal can automatically record e-mail messages sent to a contact, but *only* if you tell it to.

3. D. The Journal normally displays its entries in a timeline, so that it's easy to see when the entries were created.

4. A. Double-clicking opens a journal entry and allows you to modify it.

5. True. The Activities tab lets you add and/or view journal entries related to the contact.

CHAPTER 8
ADVANCED E-MAIL FEATURES

CHAPTER OBJECTIVES:

Save an unfinished message to the Drafts folder: Lesson 8.1

Recall a message: Lesson 8.2

Use the Out of Office Assistant: Lesson 8.3

Create and use stationery: Lesson 8.4

Create and insert a signature: Lessons 8.5 and 8.6

Deal with junk e-mail: Lesson 8.7

Add names to the Blocked and Safe Senders lists: Lesson 8.8

Format a message: Lessons 8.9 and 8.10

Change views to display the Inbox in different ways: Lessons 8.11 and 8.12

Change the e-mail format and default options: Lesson 8.13

Change the security settings: Lesson 8.14

CHAPTER TASK: WORK WITH MORE ADVANCED E-MAIL OPTIONS

Prerequisites

- Understand how to use menus, toolbars, dialog boxes, and shortcut keystrokes.
- Understand how to use the Navigation Pane and navigate within Outlook.
- Understand how to compose, send, and receive e-mail.

If you've gotten this far, you undoubtedly know how to send and receive e-mails, reply to and forward e-mails, and probably even how to attach one or more files to an e-mail. So, what else is there? This chapter is all about Outlook's more advanced e-mail features.

In this chapter, you will learn how to save an unfinished e-mail message to the Drafts folder so that you can come back and finish it later. You'll also learn how to use the Out of Office Assistant to notify people that you will be away from your computer for several days and cannot respond to their e-mails immediately. Finally, you'll learn all about how to format your messages by using different message formats, signatures, and stationery.

Are you ready to become a certified e-mail whiz? Turn the page, and let's get started!

Figure 8-1. You can save unfinished messages in the Drafts folder so that you can return to them later.

If you get interrupted while composing an e-mail message, all is not lost. You can save the unfinished e-mail message and return to it later. Unfinished messages are saved in the Drafts folder and are not sent. In this lesson, you will learn how to save an unfinished message and then go back to it at another time.

1 Click the Mail button in the Navigation Pane, then click the New Mail Message button on the toolbar.

First, we'll compose an e-mail message to ourselves.

2 Create the following e-mail message:

To: (Enter your own e-mail address here.)
Subject: Reactor Emergency Shutdown Code
Body: Barb, I just received your somewhat hysterical voicemail about some kind of nuclear meltdown. Anyway, the emergency shutdown code for the reactor is

Hey, what do you know? It's time for lunch! You had better save this e-mail message so that you can finish it later.

3 Click the Save button on the toolbar and close the Message window.

Other ways to save a draft are to close the Untitled Message window and click Yes to save your changes, or to press Ctrl + S.

Outlook saves the unfinished message in the Drafts folder. Let's see what's for lunch…

…wow, what a meal! You're stuffed! Let's get back to that unfinished message.

4 Click the Drafts folder in the All Mail Folders area of the Navigation Pane.

Outlook displays the contents of the Drafts folder, as shown in Figure 8-1.

5 Double-click the Reactor Emergency Shutdown Code message.

The message appears in its own window.

6 Click after the word "is" and type 3.

Now, you can send the message.

7 Send the e-mail by clicking the Send button and then the Send/Receive button on the toolbar.

QUICK REFERENCE

TO SAVE A DRAFT:
• CLICK THE SAVE BUTTON ON THE TOOLBAR.

OR…

• PRESS CTRL + S.

OR…

• CLOSE THE MESSAGE WINDOW AND CLICK YES WHEN PROMPTED TO SAVE YOUR CHANGES.

TO VIEW THE DRAFTS FOLDER:
• CLICK THE DRAFTS FOLDER IN THE ALL MAIL FOLDERS AREA OF THE NAVIGATION PANE.

Figure 8-2. The Recall This Message dialog box.

You're in trouble. The boss actually came through and gave you that raise you've been grumbling about for the past few months. What are you going do about the nasty resignation message that you just sent him? Don't start cleaning out your desk just yet. If you're in a workgroup environment, you can recall a sent message, as long as the recipient has not yet opened the message. You can choose to delete the unread message from the recipient's Inbox or replace the original message with a different one. The downside is that either way, Outlook will notify the recipient that you recalled the original message. You didn't think you could get off that easily, did you?

1 Click the Mail button in the Navigation Pane and click the Sent Items folder in the All Mail Folders area.

Outlook displays the messages you have sent.

2 Double-click the Reactor Emergency Shutdown Code message.

The message opens in its own window. Nobody is going to believe your story about not knowing anything about the meltdown with this e-mail message out there. You had better recall it before someone sees it! Here's how to recall a message:

3 Select Actions → Recall This Message from the menu.

The Recall This Message dialog box appears, as shown in Figure 8-2. When you recall a message, you have two choices:

- Delete unread copies of the message
- Replace unread copies of the message with a new message

We will use the "Delete unread copies of the message" option for this lesson.

≑ NOTE ≑ *Remember that you can't recall messages that have already been read and that Outlook will notify the recipient of any recalled messages.*

4 Click OK and close the Message window.

Now, you need to send out the request to recall the message.

5 Click the Send/Receive button on the toolbar.

Outlook attempts to recall the message and tells you if it was successful or not.

QUICK REFERENCE

TO RECALL A MESSAGE:

1. CLICK THE MAIL BUTTON IN THE NAVIGATION PANE.

2. CLICK THE SENT ITEMS FOLDER IN THE ALL MAIL FOLDERS AREA.

3. DOUBLE-CLICK THE MESSAGE THAT YOU WANT TO RECALL.

4. SELECT ACTIONS → RECALL THIS MESSAGE FROM THE MENU.

NOTE THAT OUTLOOK CAN'T RECALL MESSAGES THAT HAVE ALREADY BEEN READ.

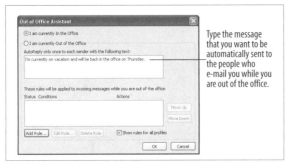

Figure 8-3. The Out of Office Assistant dialog box.

4 Click OK.

So how do you turn off the Out of Office Assistant? The next time you start Microsoft Outlook, a dialog box will appear, asking if you want to turn the Out of Office Assistant off. Click Yes to deactivate the Out of Office Assistant.

So you're finally taking that well-deserved vacation to Mexico. Congratulations! Before you leave, you should set up the Out of Office Assistant to notify other people that you will be out of the office for the next few days. When other users send you e-mail messages, they will automatically receive the Out of Office message that you specify.

≀ NOTE ≀ *The Out of Office Assistant is another Outlook feature that works only in a workgroup environment. If you use Outlook in an Internet-only environment, you're out of luck—there is no Out of Office Assistant.*

In this lesson, you will learn how to set up the Out of Office Assistant.

1 Select Tools → Out Of Office Assistant **from the menu.**

The Out Of Office Assistant dialog box appears, as shown in Figure 8-3.

2 Select the I am currently Out of the Office **option.**

Now you have to specify the message that people will automatically receive when they send you e-mail messages while you are in Mexico.

3 Click in the AutoReply only once to each sender with the following text **box and type your message.**

For example, you might type something like "I am on a short vacation from February 1 to March 30. If you have any questions about the new network server, please contact my assistant Bob at extension 3081." When you're finished, move on to the next step.

QUICK REFERENCE

TO USE THE OUT OF OFFICE ASSISTANT:

1. SELECT TOOLS → OUT OF OFFICE ASSISTANT FROM THE MENU.

2. SELECT THE I AM CURRENTLY OUT OF THE OFFICE OPTION.

3. CLICK IN THE AUTOREPLY ONLY ONCE TO EACH SENDER WITH THE FOLLOWING TEXT BOX AND TYPE YOUR MESSAGE.

4. CLICK OK.

TO TURN THE OUT OF OFFICE ASSISTANT OFF:

• THE NEXT TIME YOU START MICROSOFT OUTLOOK, YOU WILL BE ASKED IF YOU WANT TO TURN OFF THE OUT OF OFFICE ASSISTANT. SIMPLY CLICK YES.

Using Stationery

Figure 8-4. Stationery lets you give your messages a customized background.

Figure 8-5. The Select a Stationery dialog box.

You can jazz up your e-mail messages by writing them on stationery, much like a wedding or party invitation. Stationery can emphasize the importance of the message or grab the reader's interest by providing visual stimulation. From autumn leaves to quilted patterns, Outlook comes with a variety of stationery backgrounds that reflect the spirit of your message.

In this lesson, you will learn how to create a new message using Outlook's stationery.

1 Make sure you're in the Inbox folder and select Actions → New Mail Message Using → More Stationery from the menu.

The Select a Stationery dialog box appears, as shown in Figure 8-5. Outlook comes with a wide assortment of stationery, from no-nonsense corporate backgrounds to whimsical and playful ones. When you select a stationery option from the list, Outlook displays a sample of that background. If you don't like any of the stationery options, you can click the Get More Stationery button to download more stationery from Microsoft's web site.

> **NOTE** *You can only use stationery if your e-mail messages are in Microsoft Outlook Rich Text or HTML format. To see and/or change your message format, select Tools → Options from the menu and click the Mail Format tab.*

2 Browse through the list of stationery options until you find one you like and click OK.

A new Untitled – Message form appears with the selected stationery. Because you should already know how to create and send an e-mail message by now, you can close the new message without sending it.

3 Close the Untitled – Message window without saving your changes.

It is usually considered unprofessional to use stationery in the business world, so be discrete about where and when you use it. It would be a bad idea to send an e-mail to the president of a company using the same teddy bear stationery you use to correspond with your friends.

QUICK REFERENCE

TO USE STATIONERY:

1. SELECT ACTIONS → NEW MAIL MESSAGE USING → MORE STATIONERY FROM THE MENU.

2. BROWSE THROUGH THE LIST OF STATIONERY UNTIL YOU FIND ONE THAT YOU LIKE AND CLICK OK.

Creating a Signature

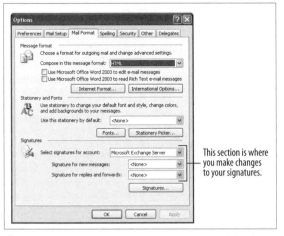

Figure 8-6. The Mail Format tab in the Options dialog box is where you go to add, edit, and select an e-mail signature.

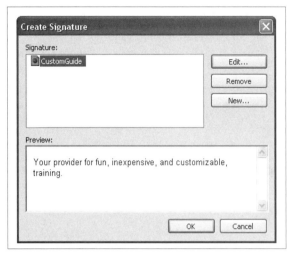

Figure 8-7. You can save more than one signature and manage them in the Create Signature dialog box.

Figure 8-8. The Edit Signature dialog box.

When you write a letter, you usually end it by closing with something that looks like this:

Sincerely yours,

John Hancock
American Patriot and Statesman

Similarly, you can give your e-mail messages a personal touch by ending them with your own, unique signature. In the e-mail world, a *signature* is a text message or file that you use in the closing of an e-mail message. Your online signature can include such things as:

- Your name, title, and organization
- Your phone and fax number
- Your address
- A link to your web page
- Your organization's mission statement, a witty one-liner, or a favorite quote

In this lesson, you will learn how to create a signature that you can add to the bottom of your e-mail messages.

1 Select Tools → Options from the menu.

The Options dialog box appears, as shown in Figure 8-6. To be perfectly honest, Outlook's Options dialog box is really confusing.

The Mail Format tab is where you go to change the appearance of your messages—and to add or edit a signature.

2 Click the Mail Format tab.

The contents of the Mail Format tab appear. The Signature section is where you go to add and edit signatures. You can also specify the default signature here.

3 Click the Signatures button.

The Create Signature dialog box appears, as shown in Figure 8-7. You can create and use more than one signature. For example, you might want to use one signature for your professional correspondence and another for personal correspondence. The Signature text box lists the signatures that are available for use. The Preview text box displays a preview of the selected signature. If you haven't created any signatures, nothing will appear in the Signature dialog box. Here's how to create a new signature:

4 Click the New button.

The Create New Signature dialog box is where you give your signature a name.

5 Type Practice in the text box.

You almost certainly will never need to use the other options listed here, which are used to create a signature from an existing file or template.

6 Verify that the Start with a blank signature option is selected and click Next.

The Edit Signature dialog box appears, as shown in Figure 8-8. This is where you enter the text you want to appear in your signature.

7 Type your name, address, and phone number in the text box.

If your message format supports it, you can click the Font button to change the font size, style, or color. When you've finished creating your signature, you have to close all those dialog boxes.

8 Click Finish. Click OK.

The Edit Signature and Create Signature dialog boxes close.

9 Click OK.

We're ready to add this signature to our next e-mail. We'll cover that in the next lesson.

Some people like to add quotes, words of wisdom, or jokes to their e-mails. See the following list for some examples.

• I would like to help you out. Which way did you come in?

• Work fascinates me. I could sit and watch it for hours.

• Always borrow money from a pessimist. They don't expect to be paid back.

• Computers can never replace human stupidity.

• Hey! Who took the cork off my lunch??!

• If a parsley farmer gets sued, do they garnish his wages?

• "The trouble with the rat-race is that even if you win, you're still a rat." —Lily Tomlin

• I cna ytpe 300 wrods pre mniuet!!!

• A good scapegoat is nearly as welcome as a solution to the problem.

QUICK REFERENCE

TO CREATE A SIGNATURE:

1. SELECT TOOLS → OPTIONS FROM THE MENU.

2. CLICK THE MAIL FORMAT TAB.

3. CLICK THE SIGNATURES BUTTON.

4. CLICK THE NEW BUTTON.

5. TYPE THE NAME OF YOUR NEW SIGNATURE FILE IN THE TEXT BOX.

6. VERIFY THE START WITH A BLANK SIGNATURE OPTION IS SELECTED AND CLICK NEXT.

7. TYPE YOUR SIGNATURE IN THE TEXT BOX.

8. CLICK FINISH, OK, OK.

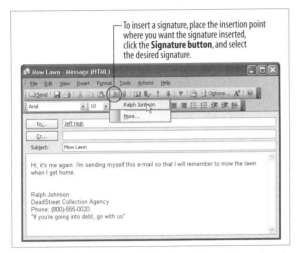

To insert a signature, place the insertion point where you want the signature inserted, click the **Signature button**, and select the desired signature.

Figure 8-9. The Signature button lets you select from a list of available signatures.

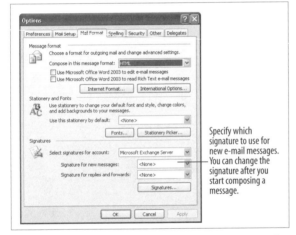

Specify which signature to use for new e-mail messages. You can change the signature after you start composing a message.

Figure 8-10. You can automatically include your signature for all new e-mail messages using the Options dialog box.

In this lesson, you will learn how to use the signature that you created in the previous lesson. You can setup Outlook so that it automatically adds your signature to the end of all of your new e-mail messages. You can also manually insert a signature from the list. You'll learn how to do both in this lesson.

1 Click the New Mail Message button on the toolbar.

First, we'll compose an e-mail message to ourselves.

2 Create the following e-mail message:

To: (Enter your own e-mail address here.)
Subject: Mow Lawn
Body: Hi, it's me again. I'm sending myself this e-mail so that I will remember to mow the lawn when I get home.

Let's add the Practice signature to the bottom of this message. It's a good idea to leave some space between your message and your signature.

3 Press Enter.

This is where you want your signature to appear. Here's how to insert a signature:

4 Click the Signature button on the toolbar (see Figure 8-9), and select the Practice signature.

> **TIP** Another way to insert a signature is to select Insert → Signature and then select the desired signature from the menu.

Outlook inserts the Practice signature you created in the previous lesson.

> **NOTE** If the Signature button doesn't appear on your toolbar, select Tools → Options from the menu, click the Mail Format tab, uncheck the "Use Microsoft Office Word 2003 to edit e-mail messages" checkbox, and click OK. Then, start this lesson over from Step 1.

You don't actually need to send this message.

5 Close the Message window without saving any of your changes.

You can also tell Outlook to automatically insert a signature at the end of all of your new e-mail messages. Here's how to set up a default signature:

6 Select Tools → Options from the menu.

The Options dialog box appears. Once again, the Mail Format tab is where you go to change the appearance of your messages and to specify your signature options.

7 Click the Mail Format **tab.**

The contents of the Mail Format tab appear, as shown in Figure 8-10. All you have to do is select the signature that you want to appear at the bottom of your e-mails.

8 Click the Signature for new messages **list arrow and select the** Practice **signature. Click** OK **when you're finished.**

Let's create a new message to see how the automatic signature feature works.

9 Click the New Mail Message button **on the toolbar.**

Poof! A new message form appears complete with the Practice signature at the end of the page.

10 Close the Message window without saving any of your changes.

It's easy to delete a signature that you no longer use. Here's how:

11 Select Tools → Options **from the menu and click the** Mail Format **tab.**

You need to click the Signatures button to select the signature you want to delete.

12 Click the Signatures button.

The Signature dialog box appears. All that you have to do to delete a signature is select the signature that you want to erase and click the Remove button.

13 Select the Practice **signature from the list, click the** Remove button**, and click** Yes **to confirm the deletion.**

The signature is deleted.

14 Click OK, OK **to close all open dialog boxes.**

QUICK REFERENCE

TO INSERT A SIGNATURE:

- CLICK THE SIGNATURE BUTTON ON THE TOOLBAR AND SELECT THE SIGNATURE.

OR...

- SELECT INSERT → SIGNATURE AND SELECT THE DESIRED SIGNATURE FROM THE MENU.

TO AUTOMATICALLY INSERT A SIGNATURE:

1. SELECT TOOLS → OPTIONS FROM THE MENU.
2. CLICK THE MAIL FORMAT TAB.
3. CLICK THE SIGNATURE FOR NEW MESSAGES LIST ARROW AND SELECT THE DESIRED SIGNATURE.
4. CLICK OK WHEN YOU'RE FINISHED.

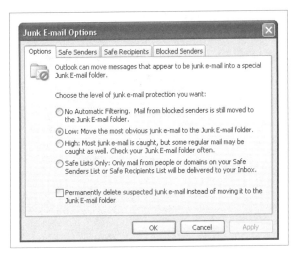

Figure 8-11. The Junk E-mail Options dialog box.

DON'T LET BAD CREDIT HOLD U BACK!

Make MONEY on the Internet with our (almost) FREE software!

tHoUsAnDz of XXX pHoToZ and vIdEoZ – FREE!!!

Leran to ytpe at 300 wrods pre mniuet!!!

Isn't it nice when you open your Inbox and find important e-mail messages like these waiting for you? Probably not. Unsolicited junk mail, known as spam, is easily the most annoying aspect of e-mail, and it's increasing at an alarming rate. In 2001, spam accounted for 8% of all e-mail messages. By the end of 2003, it was more than 50%!

Previous versions of Outlook included a junk e-mail filter that was almost worthless in the fight against spam. Microsoft has fixed this problem in 2003 with a dramatically improved filter. Outside tests have shown that Outlook catches more than 95% of all spam at its High setting. Sometimes, a legitimate message can be mistakenly classified as spam—but don't worry, you can still view all of the messages that Outlook tags as spam. By default, Outlook will move suspected spam messages to a special junk e-mail folder.

> ⦂ NOTE ⦂ *The exact details of how Outlook 2003's junk e-mail filter identifies spam are considered a trade secret. Microsoft doesn't want the bad guys to know how to get around the new filters.*

Here's how to use Outlook's junk e-mail features:

1 Select Tools → Options from the menu.

The Options dialog box appears.

2 Click the Junk E-mail button in the Preferences tab.

The Junk E-mail Options dialog box appears, as shown in Figure 8-11. Now, all that you have to do is select the level of junk e-mail protection that you want. There are several choices. Each has its own advantages and disadvantages:

- **No Automatic Filtering:** Turns off Outlook junk e-mail filters, although e-mail from your blocked senders list is still blocked.

- **Low:** Obvious junk e-mail messages are caught, but a lot of spam will still find its way into your Inbox at this level. This is the default setting.

- **High:** Most (around 95%) spam is blocked, but so are some legitimate messages. You will definitely want to monitor the Junk E-mail folder carefully if you choose this setting.

- **Safe Lists only:** The highest level of security—only people and domains that are in your Safe Senders List or Safe Recipients List will be able to send you e-mail messages. Don't select this option unless you really have a compelling need to do so. Companies merge, people move, and e-mail addresses change. You will stop receiving e-mail from these people when that happens if you use this setting.

3 Select the level of Junk E-mail protection that you want.

You can also specify that Outlook automatically and permanently deletes suspected junk e-mail messages instead of moving them to the Junk E-mail folder. Most of the time this is not a good idea—especially if you select the High setting—because some legitimate messages will inevitably be automatically deleted.

4 Although it is NOT RECOMMENDED, you can click the Permanently delete suspected Junk E-mail instead of moving it to the Junk E-mail folder checkbox.

5 Click OK, OK to close all open dialog boxes.

Your Junk E-mail settings are now saved.

That's it! Outlook will start protecting your Inbox from spam, according to your settings. If you choose one of the two more aggressive spam protection settings, you will probably want to do some fine-tuning to correct any false positives (legitimate e-mails that are flagged as spam) and to block junk e-mail senders who still make it through the filters.

Outlook 2003's new junk e-mail filters are a great tool in the fight against spam, but the best way to avoid spam is not getting on spam mailing lists in the first place. The following list offers some tips for avoiding spam altogether.

- **Use a disposable e-mail address.** Using your real, primary e-mail address anywhere on the Web—on forums, guest books, or simply for your contact information on a web page is a sure way to get added to a spam list. Try using a disposable e-mail address. Set up a free e-mail account with Hotmail, or any other provider, and use that account to post to the Web and make online purchases. Give out your real e-mail address only to the people you want to have it. That way, you can change your disposable e-mail account when your Inbox is full of spam. If you're a domain owner, you can easily change e-mail addresses whenever you want. Another solution is at *http://www.emailias.com*. This is a disposable e-mail service that forwards e-mail from a disposable account to your real e-mail account.

- **Watch those checkboxes!** When you sign up for something on the Web, there is often a innocent-looking checkbox at the end of the form that says, "YES, contact me about products I might be interested in." Translation: "YES, please send me lots and lots of delicious spam!"

- **Use AntiSpam software.** Office 2003's spam filters are good, but there are third-party commercial products available that are even more effective at fighting spam. McAfee SpamKiller, Norton Anti-Spam, and SpamNet (our favorite) are just a few programs that you can use to reduce the amount of spam that you get.

QUICK REFERENCE

TO ACTIVATE AND/OR CONFIGURE OUTLOOK'S JUNK MAIL FILTERS:

1. SELECT TOOLS → OPTIONS FROM THE MENU.

2. CLICK THE JUNK E-MAIL BUTTON IN THE PREFERENCES TAB.

3. SELECT THE LEVEL OF JUNK E-MAIL PROTECTION YOU WANT.

4. ALTHOUGH IT IS NOT RECOMMENDED, YOU CAN CHECK THE PERMANENTLY DELETE SUSPECTED JUNK E-MAIL INSTEAD OF MOVING IT TO THE JUNK E-MAIL FOLDER CHECKBOX.

Figure 8-12. You can add a known junk e-mail sender to your Blocked Senders list.

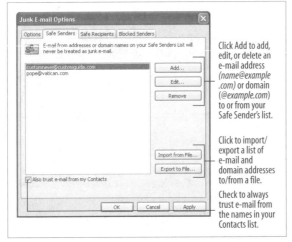

Figure 8-13. The Safe Senders tab of the Junk E-mail Options dialog box.

Outlook 2003's junk e-mail filters aren't 100% effective in stopping spam. They require some fine-tuning in order to correct any false positives (legitimate e-mails that are flagged as spam) and to block junk e-mail senders who still make it through the filters. You can tweak Outlook's Junk E-mail filters by managing three different lists:

- **Safe Senders** includes e-mail addresses that you always want Outlook to recognize as legitimate e-mail messages. This list can include individual e-mail addresses (*peskysalesman@junkmail.com*) or entire domains (*@junkmail.com*).

- **Safe Recipients** works almost the same as the Safe Senders list. Add names to this list that you want to receive e-mail messages from but that *are not addressed*

specifically to you. For example, if you wanted to receive CustomGuide's monthly newsletter, Custom-News, you would add *subscribe@customnews.com*. This way, you will receive the newsletter regardless of who sends it.

- **Blocked Senders** are the *bad guys*: people and domains that you want Outlook to identify as spam, no matter how legitimate the message. This is very useful for dealing with pesky newsletters and marketers who don't respond to your unsubscribe requests.

Let's take a closer look at how to use these three lists.

1 Click the Mail button in the Navigation Pane.

When a junk e-mail message evades Outlook's junk e-mail filters, you can add the sender of an unsolicited e-mail message to Outlook's Blocked Senders list. Doing this will prevent you from getting any more junk mail from the sender.

Here's how to add an e-mail address to your Blocked Senders list:

2 Find and right-click any message from the sender you want to block and select Junk E-mail → Add Sender to Blocked Senders list from the shortcut menu, as shown in Figure 8-12.

Outlook adds the sender to your Junk E-mail list. Outlook will automatically delete any future messages from this sender, provided you have your junk e-mail filters turned on. The procedures for adding senders to the Safe Senders and Safe Recipients lists are almost the same. Right-click a message from the sender that you want to add, select Junk-Email from the shortcut menu, and select the list to which you want to add the sender.

You can easily view and edit these lists at any time. Here's how:

3 Select Tools → Options from the menu.

The Options dialog box appears.

4 Click the Junk E-mail button on the Preferences tab.

The Junk E-mail Options dialog box appears.

6 Click OK, OK to close all open dialog boxes.

As time passses and you add more names to your Blocked Senders list, you'll find that Outlook's anti-spam features become more and more effective at eliminating junk e-mail.

shown in
lete the e-
want Out-
sages.

nts and the
ok and work
rs tab.

QUICK REFERENCE

SENDERS

HE SENDER
ENDER TO
RTCUT MENU.

E

O THE
L → ADD
FROM THE

CKED

THE SENDER
SENDER TO
E SHORTCUT

TO VIEW/EDIT ANY SENDER LIST:

1. SELECT TOOLS → OPTIONS FROM THE MENU.

2. CLICK THE JUNK E-MAIL BUTTON IN THE PREFERENCES TAB.

3. CLICK THE TAB FOR THE DESIRED SENDERS LIST AND MAKE THE DESIRED CHANGES.

POWELL'S TECHNICAL BOOKSTORE
33 N.W. PARK AVENUE
PORTLAND, OR 97209
503/228-3906   FAX 503/228-0505
HTTP://WWW.POWELLS.COM

QTY	PRODUCT	DEPT	PRICE
1	OUTLOOK 2003 PER5786979		29.95
1	SKELETAL SYSTEM Q272704		3.95
21319	TOTAL SALE		$33.90
2	DEBIT		$33.90

CARD NUMBER ************7124   XX/XX
SUPPAIAH/KANAPATHY

00004 06-000 RON 2/08/07 7:16 PM

RETURNS POLICY ON BACK OF RECEIPT.
NON-BOOK ITEMS MUST BE RETURNED
UNOPENED.
THANK YOU FOR SHOPPING AT
POWELL'S TECHNICAL BOOKS!

Formatting Fonts

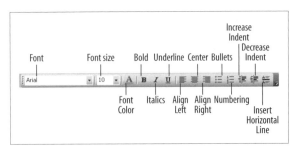

Figure 8-14. The Formatting toolbar.

Figure 8-15. A document with Bold and Italics formatting.

In this lesson, you'll learn how to change the font in your messages. You can change the font style (typeface), size, and color. Emphasize text by making it darker and heavier (bold), slanted (italics), or underlined.

> **NOTE** *You can't use font formatting if your e-mail messages are in Plain Text format. To see and/or change your message format, select Tools → Options from the main menu and click the Mail Format tab.*

1 **Click the** New Mail Message button **on the toolbar.**

You can't format fonts unless your message is formatted in HTML, Microsoft Outlook Rich Text, or Word format. Move on to the next step to verify that your message format supports font and paragraph formatting.

2 **Select** Format → HTML **from the menu.**

HTML (HyperText Markup Language) is a language used to create web pages. It supports both font and paragraph formatting.

Let's write our message!

3 **Create the following e-mail message:**

To: (Enter your own e-mail address here.)
Subject: Canada Tour Package
Body: Thank you for your interest in our Canadian tour package. I am attaching some information that I believe you will find useful. Please note that this promotion is only available until July 31.Please contact me if you have any questions.

4 **Then, press** Enter **twice.**

You are going to add your name to the message here, but first, you want to use a different font to make it stand out.

5 **Click the** Font **list arrow on the Formatting toolbar.**

A list appears with all of the fonts that are available on your computer, listed in alphabetical order. Because there isn't enough room to display all of the font types at once, you may have to scroll up or down the list until you find the font type that you want.

6 **Scroll down the Font list until you see the** Verdana **font and select it.**

Anything you type from this point forward will appear in the selected Verdana font.

You can also change the size of a font. Font size is measured in *points*: the bigger the point number, the larger the size of the font. 10 point and 12 point are the most commonly used font sizes. Changing the font size is similar to changing font types.

7 **Click the** Font Size **list arrow on the Formatting toolbar.**

A list of font sizes appears.

8 **Select** 14 **from the list. Type** Jeff Nelson.

The name Jeff Nelson appears in the Arial 14-point font. You can also select text and change it to a new font.

You can also make the text in your message stand out by making it appear in bold, italic, or underline.

9 Select the Canadian tour package text from the first paragraph and click the Italic button on the Formatting toolbar.

The selected text appears in Italics. Next, let's try applying bold formatting to some text.

10 Select the July 31 text and click the Bold button on the Formatting toolbar.

The selected date appears in boldface formatting.

So far, you've been using the Formatting toolbar to change the type, size, and style of fonts. Another method of adjusting the type and size of fonts is to use the Font dialog box, which you can open using the menu.

11 Select Format → Font from the menu.

The Font dialog box appears. Notice there are options for changing the font type and size, as well as other formatting options. After you've surveyed the Font dialog box, you can close it without making any changes by clicking the Cancel button.

12 Click Cancel to close the Font dialog box without making any changes.

13 Close the message window without saving your changes.

QUICK REFERENCE

TO CHANGE FONT SIZE:

- SELECT THE POINT SIZE FROM THE FONT SIZE LIST ON THE FORMATTING TOOLBAR.

TO CHANGE FONT TYPE:

- SELECT THE FONT FROM THE FONT LIST ON THE FORMATTING TOOLBAR.

TO FORMAT TEXT WITH BOLD, ITALICS, OR UNDERLINING:

- CLICK THE BOLD, ITALICS, OR UNDERLINE BUTTON ON THE FORMATTING TOOLBAR.

OR...

- PRESS THE CTRL KEY, AND THEN PRESS B FOR BOLD, I FOR ITALICS, AND U FOR UNDERLINING.

The formatting toolbar is available for HTML and Rich Text messages.

The formatting toolbar is not available for messages in Plain Text format.

Figure 8-16. Font and paragraph formatting are not available for messages in Plain Text format.

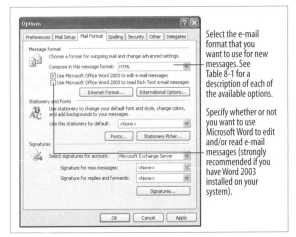

Select the e-mail format that you want to use for new messages. See Table 8-1 for a description of each of the available options.

Specify whether or not you want to use Microsoft Word to edit and/or read e-mail messages (strongly recommended if you have Word 2003 installed on your system).

Figure 8-17. You can change the default message format by selecting Tools → Options from the menu, clicking the Mail Format tab, and selecting the message format.

People in different countries speak different languages, so it makes sense that e-mail programs use and understand different types of message formats. And, just like some people can speak more than one language, many e-mail programs—including Microsoft Outlook—can read and write in different message formats. Microsoft Outlook is actually somewhat of a linguistic expert and can create messages in three different formats, as shown in Table 8-1.

So, which of the formats should you use? That's a decision you'll have to make, and it will depend on which formatting features are important to you and to whom you send your e-mail messages.

If you have Office 2003, you can (and probably should) use Microsoft Word to compose and read your e-mail messages. Microsoft Word has many helpful features that

Outlook doesn't, such as on-the-fly spelling and grammar checking, AutoCorrect and AutoFormat options, and access to your AutoText entries.

Here's how to specify the default message format and e-mail editor:

1 Select Tools → Options from the menu and click the Mail Format tab.

The Options dialog box appears, as shown in Figure 8-17. Here's how to change Outlook's default message format:

2 Click the Compose in this message format list arrow.

This list contains the formats that you can use to create your new messages. Table 8-1 gives a detailed description of each of these messages, including the formatting features and the pros and cons of using them. For now, you can leave the message format as it is.

Next, let's see how to tell Outlook that you want to use Word 2003 to read and/or write e-mail messages.

3 If desired, check and/or uncheck either of the two Microsoft Word options according to your preferences.

That's all there is to it!

4 Close the Options dialog box.

Table 8-1. Available message formats

Format	Description
HTML	HTML (Hypertext Markup Language) is the same language that is used to create web pages. HTML gives you many formatting options and is compatible with most e-mail programs. **Formatting Options Available:** Text and paragraph formatting, numbering, bullets, alignment, horizontal lines, backgrounds, HTML styles, and web pages. **Pros:** Compatible with most e-mail programs. **Cons:** Older e-mail programs may not recognize HTML formatted messages, and there are some minor privacy and security issues.
Rich Text	Rich Text is a good in-between message format that has a moderate amount of text formatting and is compatible with virtually all e-mail programs. **Formatting Options Available:** Text formatting, alignment, and bullets. **Pros:** Compatible with most e-mail programs. **Cons:** Older e-mail programs may not recognize these messages.
Plain Text	Plain Text is the most compatible message format and can be understood by all e-mail programs—even older ones. Because Plain Text messages have no formatting, the Formatting toolbar is disabled when you're working with them. **Formatting Options Available:** None. **Pros:** Universally understood by all e-mail programs. **Cons:** No formatting options.

QUICK REFERENCE

TO CHANGE THE MESSAGE FORMAT:

1. SELECT TOOLS → OPTIONS FROM THE MENU AND CLICK THE MAIL FORMAT TAB.

2. CLICK THE COMPOSE IN THIS MESSAGE FORMAT LIST ARROW AND SELECT THE DESIRED MESSAGE FORMAT.

3. CLICK OK.

TO ENABLE/DISABLE MICROSOFT WORD TO READ AND/OR WRITE E-MAILS IN OUTLOOK:

1. SELECT TOOLS → OPTIONS FROM THE MENU AND CLICK THE MAIL FORMAT TAB.

2. CHECK OR UNCHECK EITHER OF THE TWO MICROSOFT WORD CHECKBOXES ACCORDING TO YOUR PERSONAL PREFERENCES.

3. CLICK OK.

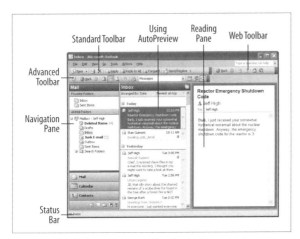

Figure 8-18. Different options for viewing your Mail window.

Outlook offers various options for viewing your Mail window. These views enable you to see any or all of the following: the toolbars, a preview of your messages, the Status Bar, the Reading Pane, and the Navigation Pane. Being able to show or hide these elements of your screen allows you to play with your workspace and arrange it to suit your needs.

In this lesson, we will explore the options available in the View menu of the Mail window.

1 Click the Mail button in the Navigation Pane.

The Inbox appears, as shown in Figure 8-18. Let's say that you're going to stay in the Mail window for a while. You want to maximize your workspace, so we're going to hide the Navigation Pane.

2 Select View → Navigation Pane from the menu.

The Navigation Pane is hidden. Generally, you want to have the Navigation Pane visible, so let's show it again.

3 Select View → Navigation Pane from the menu.

The Navigation Pane reappears.

When you are busy, you don't want to waste your time muddling through unimportant e-mails, such as forwards, but it's hard to know what the e-mail is about without opening it. Outlook offers a solution with the AutoPreview view.

4 Select View → AutoPreview from the menu.

AutoPreview view displays messages in a list and shows the first three lines of each unread message to give you a hint as to which messages you want to read.

5 Select View → AutoPreview from the menu.

Your Inbox is once again displayed in its normal mode.

Use the same procedure to hide or display the Status Bar and toolbars as you did for the Navigation Pane. To see how they appear in the window, refer to Figure 8-18, or go ahead and try it out!

Sometimes, you have a lot of important e-mails in your Inbox that you don't want to delete. This can clutter your Inbox. We're going to learn how to expand and collapse the e-mail groups in your Inbox.

6 Select View → Expand/Collapse Groups → Expand All Groups from the menu.

All of the groups are maximized. If you have an excess of e-mails in your Inbox, you have a lot of information displayed on your screen. Let's condense the Today Group.

7 Click the Today group heading and select View → Expand/Collapse Groups → Collapse This Group from the menu.

> **TIP** Another way to expand or collapse groups is to click the small + or − button that appears next to the Date heading in the Inbox.

Today's e-mails are hidden from view so that only the Today heading is shown. Go ahead and try the other available options in the Expand/Collapse Groups submenu.

The Reading Pane displays the contents of the currently selected message. In previous versions of Outlook, it was called the *Preview Pane* and was located at the bottom of the screen. Microsoft decided to make better use of the larger monitors of the 21st century by moving the Reading Pane to the right side of the screen in Outlook 2003. You can still move the Reading Pane back to its former position at the bottom of the screen, however. Here's how:

8 Select View → Reading Pane → Bottom from the menu.

The Reading Pane moves to the bottom of the screen. Let's move the Reading Pane back to where it belongs.

9 Select View → Reading Pane → Right from the menu.

The Reading Pane moves back to the right of the screen.

Table 8-2 describes the commands in the Mail window's View menu.

Table 8-2. Options in the Mail window View menu

View	Displays
Arrange By	Contains options for organizing your e-mails (see Lesson 8.12 for details).
Navigation Pane	Check or uncheck this option in order to show or hide the Navigation Pane.
Reading Pane	Contains three options in its submenu: Right (display the Pane on the right-hand side of the Mail window), Bottom (display the Pane on the bottom of the Mail window), and Off (hide the Pane).
AutoPreview	Displays your messages in a list and shows the first three lines of each unread message to give you a hint as to which messages you want to read.
Expand/Collapse Groups	Contains five options in its submenu: Collapse or Expand This Group (minimize or maximize a selected group in the Inbox), Collapse or Expand All Groups (minimize or maximize all of the groups in the Inbox), and Always Show Unread and Flagged Messages (when checked, all important and new messages are shown in the window).
Toolbars	There are three toolbars that can be viewed in the Mail window: the Standard toolbar, the Advanced toolbar, and the Web toolbar.
Status Bar	Show or hide the status bar by selecting or deselecting it in the menu.
Reminders Window	Shows the currently active reminder dialog boxes.
Refresh	Refreshes the displayed messages.

QUICK REFERENCE

ACCESS THE MAIL WINDOW VIEWING OPTIONS:

- SELECT VIEW FROM THE MENU BAR AND SELECT THE VIEWING OPTIONS FROM THE MENU.

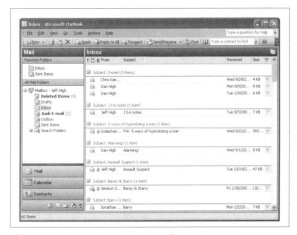

Figure 8-19. Subject View groups messages by their topic.

Figure 8-20. Message Timeline View displays a graph of all of your messages according to when they arrived.

Outlook's Views are very useful for organizing your messages in different ways. You can arrange your mail so that it is organized by date, e-mail account, subject, and so on. Refer to Tables 8-3 and 8-4 for a complete description of all the available Inbox views.

In this lesson, you will learn how to utilize Outlook's message views to help you sort and organize your messages.

We'll start with the actual e-mails that you want to appear in your Inbox.

1 **Select** View → Arrange By → Current View → Last Seven Days **from the menu.**

Only the e-mails that you have received within the last seven days are shown in your Inbox.

Refer to Table 8-3 and go ahead and try some of the other Current View options. Pretty cool, huh? Before we move on to some more detailed viewing options, let's make sure that all of our e-mails are shown in the window.

2 **Select** View → Arrange By → Current View → Messages **from the menu.**

All of the e-mails in your Inbox are displayed. Let's move on.

3 **Select** View → Arrange By → Subject **from the menu.**

Subject view groups messages by their respective topics, as shown in Figure 8-19. Refer to Table 8-4 and try out some other views.

⋮ NOTE ⋮ *When you use the Message Timeline view, as shown in Figure 8-20, many of the Arrange By submenu options disappear. This is due to the fact that a timeline has its own organizational structure. This is the only Current View option that does not allow you to manipulate how the messages are arranged.*

That's all there is to changing the Inbox views. Play around with them until you find a workable organization style for yourself. Inbox views are all about personal preference.

Table 8-3. Current View submenu options

View	Description
Messages	Displays all messages.
Messages With Auto-Preview	Displays all messages and a preview.

Table 8-3. Current View submenu options (Continued)

View	Description
Last Seven Days	Displays all messages received within the last seven days.
Unread Messages in this Folder	Displays all messages that have not yet been read.
Message Timeline	Displays messages in a timeline format.

Table 8-4. Arrange By submenu options

Arrange By	Description
Date	Arranges messages by the dates they were received.
Conversation	Arranges messages by the topic of conversation.
From	Arranges messages by the sender.
To	Arranges messages by the receiver.
Folder	Arranges messages by the folders in which they are stored.
Size	Arranges messages by size.
Subject	Arranges messages by topic.
Type	Arranges messages by type.
Flag	Arranges messages by whether or not they have a flag attached.
Attachments	Arranges messages by whether or not they have an attachment.
E-mail Account	Arranges messages by the e-mail accounts from which they came.
Importance	Arranges messages by importance.
Categories	Arranges messages in categories that you determine.

QUICK REFERENCE

TO CHANGE THE CURRENT VIEW:
- SELECT VIEW → ARRANGE BY → CURRENT VIEW FROM THE MENU AND SELECT A VIEW OPTION.

TO CHANGE E-MAIL ARRANGEMENT:
- SELECT VIEW → ARRANGE BY FROM THE MENU AND SELECT AN ARRANGEMENT OPTION.

Changing E-mail Options

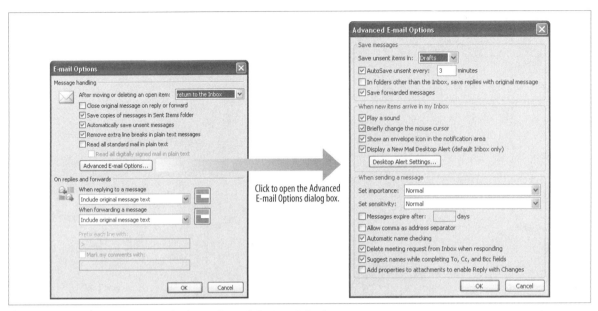

Click to open the Advanced E-mail Options dialog box.

Figure 8-21. The E-mail Options and Advanced E-mail Options dialog boxes.

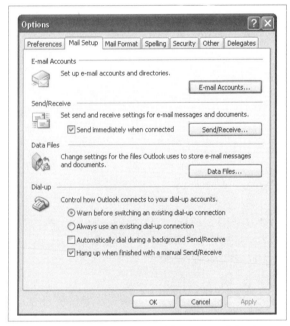

Figure 8-22. The Mail Setup tab of the Options dialog box.

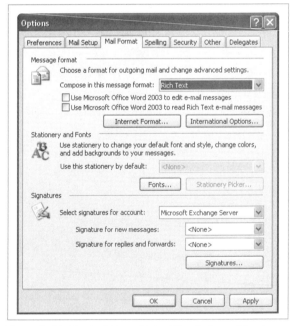

Figure 8-23. The Mail Format tab of the Options dialog box.

People have different tastes and preferences. Some people like Outlook to automatically check for new messages every five minutes, while some are content with having it check for new messages every half an hour. Some people like Outlook to automatically check their e-mails for spelling errors before they are sent, while other people find the spellchecker to be a nuisance. To accommodate these different tastes and preferences, Outlook has more settings than you can shake a stick at.

You could write a separate lesson for each of Outlook's e-mail settings, but the purpose of this lesson is to highlight some of the more important settings. Let's get started!

1 Select Tools → Options from the menu.

The Options window appears. The Options dialog box is the gateway for getting to all of Outlook's options.

2 Click the E-mail Options button in the Preferences tab.

The E-mail Options dialog box appears, as shown in Figure 8-21. Here you can specify how Outlook handles your E-mail messages. For example, you can specify whether or not you want to be notified whenever a new message arrives.

3 Click the Advanced E-mail Options button.

The Advanced E-mail window, which contains more advanced e-mail settings, appears.

4 Close both the Advanced E-mail dialog box and the E-mail Options dialog box.

You should be back to the Options dialog box. The two other places you can go to find e-mail settings are tabs found in the Options dialog box.

5 Click the Mail Setup tab.

The Mail Setup tab appears, as shown in Figure 8-22. Here, you can specify when Outlook sends and receives messages. If you use a modem to connect to the Internet, you will also find the Dial-up section here useful. Let's keep moving.

6 Click the Mail Format tab.

The Mail Format tab is the last stop on our e-mail options tour. The Mail Format tab, as shown in Figure 8-23, lets you modify the look of your messages. For example, you can specify the message format (HTML, plain text, etc.) font used, and create or modify your signatures.

7 Close the Options dialog box.

Table 8-5 lists places where you can change your Outlook e-mail options.

Table 8-5. Places to go to change Outlook's e-mail options

Location	Description
E-mail Options dialog box	Contains settings to specify how Outlook handles messages, such as if outgoing messages are saved in the Sent folder and if Outlook automatically saves unfinished messages as drafts. You can also specify the format for replies and forwards here.
	To Get There: Select Tools → Options from the menu and click the E-mail Options button on the Preferences tab.
Advanced E-mail Options dialog box	Shows more advanced message handling options, such as where Outlook saves unfinished messages and the default importance and sensitivity of new messages.
	To Get There: Select Tools → Options from the menu. Click the E-mail Options button on the Preferences tab and the Advanced Options button.
Mail Setup tab	Contains settings to specify when Outlook sends and receives messages and dial-up settings if you need to connect to the Internet to use Outlook.
	To Get There: Select Tools → Options from the menu and click the Mail Setup tab.
Mail Format tab	Contains settings to change the appearance of your messages, such as the message format (HTML, plain text, etc.), font used, and signature used.
	To Get There: Select Tools → Options from the menu and click the Mail Format tab.

QUICK REFERENCE

TO CHANGE E-MAIL HANDLING OPTIONS:

• SELECT TOOLS → OPTIONS FROM THE MENU AND CLICK THE E-MAIL OPTIONS BUTTON.

TO CHANGE ADVANCED E-MAIL OPTIONS:

• SELECT TOOLS → OPTIONS FROM THE MENU, CLICK THE E-MAIL OPTIONS BUTTON, AND CLICK THE ADVANCED E-MAIL OPTIONS BUTTON.

TO CHANGE E-MAIL DELIVERY OPTIONS:

• SELECT TOOLS → OPTIONS FROM THE MENU AND CLICK THE MAIL SETUP TAB.

TO CHANGE E-MAIL FORMATTING OPTIONS:

• SELECT TOOLS → OPTIONS FROM THE MENU AND CLICK THE MAIL FORMAT TAB.

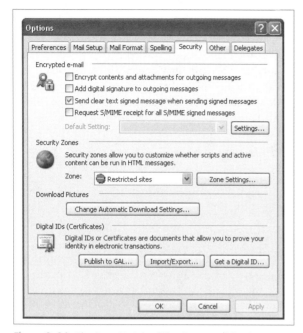

Figure 8-24. The Security tab of the Options dialog box.

Figure 8-25. The Automatic Picture Download Settings dialog box.

The Internet has become a dangerous place. Each time you connect to the Internet, you run the risk, however slight, of allowing malicious users to steal sensitive information from your computer. The computer industry has responded to these growing threats, and hundreds of security products—firewalls, spam-blockers, and anti-virus software—are available to keep your computer and privacy secure from outside threats.

After being embarrassed by several high-profile viruses that specifically targeted Outlook, Microsoft has greatly increased Outlook's security settings. There are many very different types of security threats on the Internet, as described in Table 8-6. In response to these threats, Microsoft Outlook offers many different security features.

There are two important—and controversial—security features in Outlook that you should be aware of, as they will probably affect your e-mail messages at one point or another:

- **Attachment Blocking:** Outlook blocks access to several different types of attachments. All executable files (*.exe*, *.com*, and *.bat*) are blocked and so are files that contain macros or scripts, such as Microsoft Access database files. You can still send these kinds of files as attachments with a little work: either rename the file extension (i.e., rename "program.exe" to "program.ex") or zip the file you want to attach. This setting can only be changed by rooting around in the Windows registry. This is something that's best left to a network administrator.

- **External File and Picture Blocking:** HTML-based e-mail messages often contain links to external pictures that are downloaded from the Internet (e-mail newsletters especially contain lots of pictures). Technically speaking, the sender of these messages can tell when you've opened the e-mail, since they can see if and when you've downloaded the images in their message. This may not seem like much of a security concern, but it lets Spammers know if you've opened their junk e-mail messages. If a Spammer sees that they have found a legitimate e-mail account, they may send you more spam, or worse, sell your e-mail address to other Spammers. While this feature does help protect your privacy, it can also be annoying—especially if you receive and depend on a lot of HTML-based e-mails. It's easy to disable this feature, however. We'll see how in this lesson.

Here's how to view and change Outlook's security settings:

1 Select Tools → Options **from the menu and click the** Security **tab.**

The Security tab of the Options dialog box appears, as shown in Figure 8-24. There are a lot of security settings listed here. Most of them are best left alone, unless you understand them. You can, however, change whether or not Outlook downloads external pictures in HTML messages. Here's how:

2 **Click the** Change Automatic Download Settings button.

The Automatic Picture Download Settings dialog box appears, as shown in Figure 8-25. Here's where you can specify whether or not you want Outlook to download and display pictures in HTML-based e-mail messages.

3 **Make any desired changes and click** OK, OK.

Table 8-6. Common threats to your Inbox

Threat	Description
Attachment viruses	Attachment viruses are still the most common types of viruses. As its name implies, an attachment virus is attached to an e-mail message, which the sender tries to get the recipient to open. The Melissa virus was a highly publicized attachment virus that sent itself to all of the names in a victim's address book. Many of these recipients opened these e-mail attachments because they knew the sender.
Script-based viruses	Script-based viruses exploit security flaws in Microsoft Outlook and Windows that allow malicious code to be embedded in a message and automatically executed when the message is opened.
Web bugs	A web bug is a link to external graphics in an HTML e-mail message. Web bugs allow the message sender to see when a user has opened a message. Spammers love to add web bugs to their e-mail messages to find out which e-mail accounts are legitimate and active.
Spam	More of an annoyance than a threat, spam is electronic, unsolicited e-mail. Spam wastes bandwidth, storage space, and most of all, your time!

QUICK REFERENCE

TO ALLOW/DISALLOW HTML PICTURES IN E-MAIL:

1. SELECT TOOLS → OPTIONS FROM THE MENU AND CLICK THE SECURITY TAB.

2. CLICK THE CHANGE AUTOMATIC DOWNLOAD SETTINGS BUTTON.

3. MAKE ANY DESIRED CHANGES AND CLICK OK, OK

Lesson Summary

Saving Unfinished Messages (Drafts)

To Save a Draft: Click the Save button on the toolbar, or press Ctrl + S. You can also save a draft by closing the new message window and clicking Yes when prompted to save your changes.

To View the Drafts Folder: Click the Drafts folder in the All Mail Folders area of the Navigation Pane.

Recalling a Message

Click the Mail button in the Navigation Pane. Click the Sent Items folder in the All Mail Folders Area of the Navigation Pane. Double-click the message you want to recall and select Actions → Recall This Message from the menu.

Using the Out of Office Assistant

To Use the Out of Office Assistant: Select Tools → Out Of Office Assistant from the menu. Select the I am currently Out of the Office option. Then, click in the AutoReply only once to each sender with the following text box and type your message. Click OK.

To Turn the Out of Office Assistant Off: The next time you start Microsoft Outlook, you will be asked if you want to turn off the Out of Office Assistant. Simply click Yes.

Using Stationery

To Use Stationery: Select Actions → New Mail Message Using → More Stationery from the menu. Browse through the list of stationery until you find one that you like and click OK.

Creating a Signature

To Create a Signature: Select Tools → Options from the menu, click the Mail Format tab, and click the Signatures button. Click the New button and type the name of your new signature file in the text box. Verify the Start with a blank Signature option is checked and click Next. Type your signature in the text box, and then click Finish, OK, OK.

Inserting a Signature

To Insert a Signature: Click the Signature button on the toolbar and select the signature, or select Insert → Signature and select the desired signature from the menu.

To Automatically Insert a Signature: Select Tools → Options from the menu and click the Mail Format tab. Click the Signature for new messages list arrow and select the desired signature. Click OK when you're finished.

Dealing with Junk E-Mail

To Activate and/or Configure Outlook's Junk E-mail Filters: Select Tools → Options from the menu and click the Junk E-mail button in the Preferences tab. Select the level of Junk E-mail protection you want. Although it is NOT RECOMMENDED, you can check the Permanently delete suspected Junk E-mail instead of moving it to the Junk E-mail folder checkbox.

Adding Names to the Blocked and Safe Senders Lists

To Add a Sender to the Safe Senders List: Right-click any message from the sender and select Junk E-mail → Add Sender to Safe Senders list from the shortcut menu. Select the level of junk e-mail protection you want.

To Add a Recipient to the Safe Recipients List: Right-click any message from the recipient and select Junk E-mail → Add Recipient to Safe Recipients list from the shortcut menu.

To Add a Sender to the Blocked Senders List: Right-click any message from the sender and select Junk E-mail → Add Sender to Blocked Senders list from the shortcut menu.

To View/Edit any Sender List: Select Tools → Options from the menu and click the Junk E-mail button in the Preferences tab. Click the tab for the desired senders list and make the desired changes.

Formatting Fonts

To Change Font Size: Select the point size from the Font Size list on the Formatting toolbar.

To Change Font Type: Select the font from the Font list on the Formatting toolbar.

To Format Text with Bold, Italics, or Underlining: Click the Bold, Italics, or Underline button on the Formatting toolbar. Or, press the Ctrl key and: B for Bold, I for Italics, and U for Underlining.

Changing the Message Format and Using Word

To Change the Message Format: Select Tools → Options from the menu and click the Mail Format tab. Click the Compose in this message format list arrow and select the desired message format. Click OK.

To Enable/Disable Microsoft Word to Read and/or Write E-mails in Outlook: Select Tools → Options from the menu and click the Mail Format tab. Check or uncheck either of the two Microsoft Word checkboxes according to your personal preferences and click OK.

Viewing the Mail Window

Access the Mail Window Viewing Options: Select View from the menu bar and select the viewing options from the menu.

Changing Views

To Change the Current View: Select View → Arrange By → Current View from the menu and select a view option.

To Change E-mail Arrangement: Select View → Arrange By from the menu and select an arrangement option.

Changing E-mail Options

To Change E-mail Handling Options: Select Tools → Options from the menu and click the E-mail Options button on the Preferences tab.

To Change Advanced E-mail Options: Select Tools → Options from the menu, click the E-mail Options button, and click the Advanced E-mail Options button.

To Change E-mail Delivery Options: Select Tools → Options from the menu and click the Mail Setup tab.

To Change E-mail Formatting Options: Select Tools → Options from the menu and click the Mail Format tab.

Changing Outlook's Security Settings

To Do Allow/Disallow HTML Pictures in E-mail: Select Tools → Options from the menu and click the Security tab, then click the Change Automatic Download Settings button. Make any desired changes and click OK, OK.

Quiz

1. You're busy composing an e-mail message to the bank explaining why you can't pay your mortgage this month when there's a knock at the door. It's the digital high-definition television you ordered! Since Outlook can't save your unfinished e-mail, you will have to write it again later. (True or False?)

2. You've just sent your boss an e-mail telling him what you *really* think of him, when you receive an e-mail informing you that you've been promoted. Which of the following actions can you take? (Select all that apply.)

   A. Find the sent message in the Sent Items folder, select Actions → Recall This Message from the menu, and delete the message.

   B. Find the sent message in the Sent Items folder, select Actions → Recall This Message from the menu, and replace the message with one thanking your boss for the promotion.

   C. Find the sent message in the Sent Items folder and delete it—it will be deleted from your boss's Inbox as well.

   D. Start cleaning out your desk.

3. Outlook can recall any type of message, and it does so without telling the e-mail recipient anything. (True or False?)

4. Which of the following statements are NOT true? (Select all that apply.)

   A. If you aren't going to be able to check your e-mail for several days, you can use the Out of Office Assistant to notify people that you aren't available.

   B. You can use stationery with any type or format of e-mail message.

   C. In Outlook, a signature is a digitally encrypted code used for security purposes.

   D. You can configure Outlook so that the signature you select appears at the bottom of all new e-mail messages.

5. Outlook does not support font formatting in HTML based e-mail messages. (True or False?)

6. Outlook's e-mail options are user-friendly and intuitive. (True or False?)

Homework

1. Start Microsoft Outlook and click the Inbox folder in the Navigation Pane.

2. Create a signature. Select Tools → Options from the menu, click the Mail Format tab, and click the Signatures button. Click the New button and create the following signature:

   Name: Homework Signature
   Signature: (Enter your name)

3. Close all open dialog boxes.

4. Change the e-mail message format. Select Tools → Options from the menu and click the Mail Format tab. Select HTML from the list and click OK.

5. Create an e-mail message using stationery. Select Actions → New Mail Message Using and select the stationery of your choice.

6. Create an e-mail message using the following information:

   To: (Use your e-mail address)
   Subject: Great Job!
   Body: Hi (enter your name)! It's me, (enter your name). I just wanted to tell you that you're doing a great job learning about Outlook. Keep it up! Sincerely,

7. Insert the Homework Signature at the end of the message.

8. Select and boldface the word "great."

9. Click the Send button to send the message.

Quiz Answers

1. False. Simply click the Save button on the toolbar to save your unfinished e-mail message so that you can come back to it later.

2. A, B, and possibly D. Just remember you can't recall a message that has already been opened!

3. False. Unfortunately, Outlook will notify the e-mail recipient that you have recalled or replaced an e-mail message. But, they won't know what the e-mail said.

4. B and C. B: You can't use stationery in Plain Text–formatted messages. C: In Outlook (and all e-mail programs) a signature is similar to what you put at the end of a letter, and it usually contains your name, title, and possibly your address and phone number.

5. False. Only Plain Text–formatted e-mail messages don't support font formats.

6. False. NASA's mission control panel is probably less confusing than Outlook's e-mail options.

CHAPTER 9
ORGANIZING AND FINDING INFORMATION

CHAPTER OBJECTIVES:

Work with Outlook Data files: Lessons 9.1 and 9.21

Search for information using Find and Advanced Find: Lessons 9.2 and 9.3

Learn how to use the Folder List to organize information: Lesson 9.4

Create a folder: Lesson 9.5

Rename, copy, move, and delete a folder: Lesson 9.6

Use, create, modify, and delete a Search folder: Lessons 9.7 and 9.8

Select multiple items: Lesson 9.9

Flag and categorize Outlook items: Lessons 9.10 and 9.11

Create rules to automatically manage your e-mail messages: Lessons 9.12 through 9.14

Use a grouped view to organize similar Outlook information: Lesson 9.15

Filter and sort e-mail messages: Lessons 9.16 and 9.18

Color-code e-mail messages: Lesson 9.17

Create a custom view to display information: Lessons 9.19 and 9.20

CHAPTER TASK: LEARN TO ORGANIZE OUTLOOK INFORMATION

Prerequisites

- Understand how to use menus, toolbars, dialog boxes, and shortcut keystrokes.

- Understand how to use the Navigation Pane and navigate within Outlook.

- Understand how to compose, send, and receive e-mail.

- Have a basic knowledge of all Outlook tools.

When you work at your desk for a while, your papers and files can tend to pile up and become messy. The same thing happens after you've worked with Outlook for a while—your e-mails, tasks, and appointments start becoming disorganized and harder to find. In this chapter, you'll learn how to take control and organize your Outlook information. You'll learn more about the Folder List and how you can use it to help manage your data. You'll learn how to categorize, group, and flag Outlook items to make them easier to find and work with. Finally, you'll learn how to create rules to automatically manage your e-mails. Because there are so many ways to organize and manage information in Microsoft Outlook, this is one of the longest chapters in the book. We had better get started.

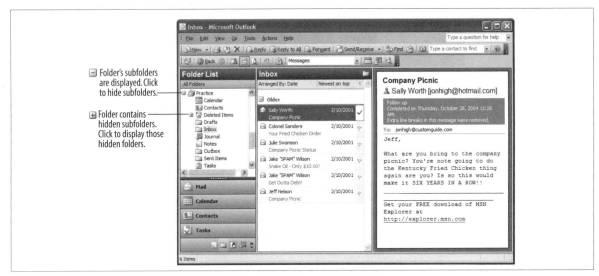

Figure 9-1. You can choose to hide or show subfolders.

Microsoft Outlook is different from other Microsoft Office applications in that you don't need to open or create a new file in order to start using it. Although you may never need to do it, Outlook can open and save files. Outlook files are called Outlook Data files, have a *.PST* extension, and can store any kind of Outlook item—e-mails, appointments, contacts, and so on. If you want to get technical about it, Outlook actually *does* open and save a file named *OUTLOOK.PST* each time you use it.

So why would you ever want to save or open an Outlook Data file? Here are a couple of reasons:

- To back up your Outlook information. (There is an archive command that backs up your Outlook information to an external Outlook Data file—more on that later.)

- To exchange or transfer information. For example, you could save your office computer's Outlook Contacts list as an Outlook Data file and then transfer it to your home computer.

- To provide a set of examples for an Outlook class or tutorial.

Guess what? Since this entire chapter is about organizing information in Outlook, we need some canned examples to work with—and in this lesson you will open an Outlook Data file that contains sample items that you will use throughout the chapter.

1 **Select** File → Open → Outlook Data File **from the menu.**

The Open Outlook Data File dialog box appears. Now you need to find the Outlook Data file you want to open.

2 **Navigate to the folder where your practice files are located.**

Use the "Look in" list and Up One Level button to navigate to the various drives and folders on your computer.

3 **Find and double-click the** Practice **file in the Practice folder.**

Outlook opens the Practice file. You need to display the Folder List in order to see its contents.

4 **Click the** Folder List button **in the Navigation Pane.**

The Folder List displays its contents in a hierarchical view. A plus symbol (+) or a minus symbol (-) beside a folder means it contains several subfolders. You can display the hidden folders within a folder by clicking the plus sign (+) beside the folder.

5 Click the plus symbol (+) beside the Practice folder.

The Practice folder expands and displays all the folders within it. The plus symbol (+) changes to a minus symbol (-), indicating the folder is expanded and is displaying its contents.

6 Click the Inbox folder located under the Practice folder.

The contents of the Inbox folder appear in the main Outlook window.

Make sure you click the Inbox folder located under the Practice folder and not the Inbox folder located under the Mailbox folder.

You can collapse or hide folders to reduce the amount of information that is in the Folder List. To collapse a folder, click the minus sign (-) beside the folder.

7 Click the minus symbol (-) beside the Practice folder.

The Practice folder collapses, and all its subfolders are hidden from view. The minus symbol (-) changes to a plus symbol (+), indicating that all the subfolders in the Practice folder are hidden from view.

Move on to the next step and expand the Practice folder once again.

8 Click the plus symbol (+) beside the Practice folder.

The Practice folder expands and displays all the folders within it.

When you're done using an Outlook Data file you can close it by right-clicking the folder and selecting Close from the shortcut menu. Don't close the Practice folder yet—we have a lot more work to do with it!

QUICK REFERENCE

TO OPEN AN OUTLOOK DATA FILE:

1. SELECT FILE → OPEN → OUTLOOK DATA FILE FROM THE MENU.

2. NAVIGATE TO THE FOLDER THAT CONTAINS THE .PST FILE.

3. DOUBLE-CLICK THE .PST FILE.

TO CLOSE AN OUTLOOK DATA FILE:

1. OPEN THE FOLDER LIST BY CLICKING THE FOLDER LIST BUTTON IN THE NAVIGATION PANE.

2. RIGHT-CLICK THE OUTLOOK DATA FILE YOU WANT TO CLOSE AND SELECT CLOSE FROM THE SHORTCUT MENU.

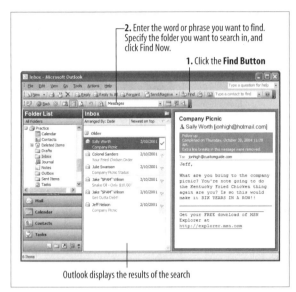

2. Enter the word or phrase you want to find. Specify the folder you want to search in, and click Find Now.

1. Click the **Find Button**

Outlook displays the results of the search

Figure 9-2. Clicking the Find button on the toolbar to search for information in Outlook.

The longer you use Outlook, the more cluttered your folders become and the more difficult it becomes to find a specific e-mail message, appointment, or contact. Luckily, Outlook comes with a great Find feature that sifts through the current folder and retrieves items that contain a specified word or phrase. Find searches your messages' From fields, Subject fields, and even text! Even if you can only remember a little bit about an e-mail message, Find can probably retrieve it.

In this lesson, you will learn how to use Outlook's Find feature to search for e-mail messages in your Inbox.

1 Make sure that you have the Practice folder open and the Folder List displayed.

To search for something, simply click the folder you want to search, click the Find button on the toolbar, and enter the text you're looking for.

2 Click the Inbox folder located under the Practice folder.

Make sure you click the Inbox folder located under the Practice folder and not the Inbox folder located under the Mailbox folder.

3 Click the Find button on the toolbar.

Other ways to use Find are to select Tools → Find → Find from the menu or to press Ctrl + E.

The Find Bar appears at the top of the message window.

Type the word or phrase you're looking for in the "Look for" box.

4 Type picnic in the Look for box.

Before you perform the search, there's one more helpful tool you should use when searching.

5 Click the Options button and make sure the Search all text in each message box is checked.

The "Search all text in each message" box ensures that Outlook looks in the actual text of the messages for the specified word or phrase.

Notice that there is also a "Save Search as Search Folder" option in the menu. We'll talk more about that later in the chapter.

Finally, you're ready to perform the search.

6 Click Find Now.

Outlook searches through the Inbox for messages that contain the word "picnic" and displays the results in the Inbox, as shown in Figure 9-2. Notice that each message has "picnic" in the subject field, except the Colonel Sanders message. This message is included in the search because it has "picnic" in the actual text of the message.

By default, Outlook searches in the current folder when performing a search. But if you want, you can look in other folders using the Search In button.

7 Click the Search In button.

A menu appears with four different e-mail folders: Inbox, All Mail Folders, Mail I Received, and Mail I Sent. You can select one of these folders to perform a search.

You can also choose which folders you want to search in Outlook.

8 Select Choose Folders from the Search In button list.

The Select Folder(s) dialog box appears. To perform a search in multiple Outlook folders at the same time, click the checkbox next to each folder. Click the "Search subfolders" checkbox at the bottom of the dialog box to include subfolders in the search. This feature is especially useful when trying to find items that are related by topic, like e-mail messages and calendar appointments.

You don't need to search in any of these folders, so close the dialog box.

9 Click the Cancel button.

Now let's close the Find Bar.

10 Click the Find Bar Close button.

Find is straightforward and easy-to-use, but it does have some serious limitations:

- It searches only for information based on a specified word or phrase—you can't use it to search for items by the date they were created or by their flag or category type.
- It searches only through the fields listed in Table 9-1.

Even with these limitations, Find is what you'll use 95% of the time to look for information in Outlook. When you need to perform a more powerful search, you'll want to use the Advanced Find feature—the topic of the next lesson.

Table 9-1. Fields Find searches

Folder	Fields searched
Calendar	Subject, Location, and Attendees
Contacts	Name, Company, Addresses, and Category
Inbox	From and Subject
Journal	Subject, Body, Entry Type, Contact, and Company
Notes	Subject
Tasks	Subject, Company, People Involved, and Category

QUICK REFERENCE

TO SEARCH IN THE CURRENT FOLDER:

1. VIEW THE FOLDER YOU WANT TO SEARCH.

2. CLICK THE FIND BUTTON ON THE TOOLBAR.

    OR...

    SELECT TOOLS → FIND → FIND FROM THE MENU.

    OR...

    PRESS CTRL + E.

3. ENTER THE TEXT YOU WANT TO SEARCH FOR IN THE LOOK FOR BOX.

    (OPTIONAL) CLICK THE OPTIONS BUTTON AND SELECT THE SEARCH ALL TEXT IN EACH MESSAGE BOX TO SEARCH THROUGH ALL THE TEXT OF YOUR MESSAGES.

4. CLICK FIND NOW.

TO SEARCH IN OTHER FOLDERS:

1. CLICK SEARCH IN AND SELECT AN E-MAIL FOLDER.

    OR...

    SELECT CHOOSE FOLDERS, CHECK ALL THE FOLDERS YOU WANT TO SEARCH IN, AND CLICK OK.

2. CLICK THE FIND BUTTON ON THE TOOLBAR.

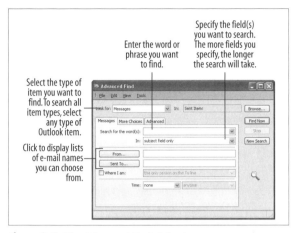

Select the type of item you want to find. To search all item types, select any type of Outlook item.

Click to display lists of e-mail names you can choose from.

Enter the word or phrase you want to find.

Specify the field(s) you want to search. The more fields you specify, the longer the search will take.

Figure 9-3. The Advanced Find dialog box.

Most of the time, you will be able to find what you're looking for using the Find feature's "quick and simple" search of the current folder. However, you may sometimes need to perform an advanced search, which allows you to find items using a variety of options. For example, say your company is being sued for stealing its major competitor's muffin recipe. You could perform an advanced search to find all Outlook items—e-mails, appointments, tasks, and so on—that contain the word "muffin" and then turn over the results to the company's lawyers.

Advanced Find is more difficult to use than Find, but it does have its advantages:

- It can search through all of Outlook's folders at once. For example, Advanced Find could retrieve appointments, e-mails, and tasks that contain the word "squash."
- It can search for items based on their category, flag type, or importance level.
- It can look for a word or phrase in all fields, not just the most common fields, as the Find feature does.

Here's how to perform an advanced search:

1 Click the Find button on the toolbar.

The Find Bar appears at the top of the message window.

2 Click the Options button list arrow in the Find Bar and select Advanced Find.

Other ways to perform an Advanced Find are to select Tools → Find → Advanced Find *from the menu, or press* Ctrl + Shift + F.

The Advanced Find dialog box appears, as shown in Figure 9-3. You can use the Advanced Find dialog box to search all of your Outlook folders for a word or phrase. You can also search for e-mail messages to and/or from a particular person, read or unread e-mail messages, and many, many more criterions.

Notice the Advanced Find dialog box has several tabs. Here's what each one does:

- **Messages:** Lets you search for a word or phrase, specify which fields to search, and specify who the message(s) might have come from or been sent to.
- **More Choices:** Lets you specify the category of the item(s) you want to find. You can also specify to find only read or unread messages, items with or without attachments, or items whose importance is high, normal, or low.
- **Advanced:** Lets you find items by specifying advanced search criteria, such as specific fields to search.

OK—let's look for something!

3 Click the Look For list arrow and select Any type of Outlook item.

This will search all Outlook items for the text you specify.

4 Click in the Search for the word(s) box and type picnic.

Let's start our search.

5 Click the Find Now button.

Outlook searches through the Inbox for messages that contain the word "picnic" and displays the results at the bottom of the Advanced Find dialog box.

6 Close the Advanced Find dialog box.

Now all you have to do is close the Find Bar.

7 Click the Close button on the Find Bar.

Advanced Find can also search for items by their importance level, category, flagged status, and more. In fact, there are so many Advanced Find options that you could write a short book about all of them. The purpose of this lesson isn't to go over each and every Advanced Find option, but to give you an introduction to the Advance Find feature. Most of the Advanced Find options are pretty much self-explanatory, and you won't need a reference guide in order to use them.

QUICK REFERENCE

TO USE ADVANCED FIND:

1. CLICK THE FIND BUTTON ON THE TOOLBAR, CLICK THE OPTIONS BUTTON LIST ARROW ON THE FIND BAR AND SELECT ADVANCED FIND.

   OR...

   SELECT TOOLS → FIND → ADVANCED FIND FROM THE MENU.

   OR...

   PRESS CTRL + SHIFT + F.

2. SPECIFY YOUR SEARCH OPTIONS IN THE ADVANCED FIND DIALOG BOX.

3. CLICK THE FIND NOW BUTTON.

4. CLOSE THE ADVANCED FIND DIALOG BOX WHEN YOU'RE FINISHED.

Using Folders to Organize Information

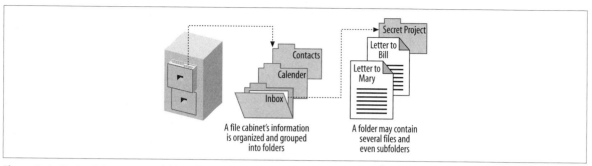

Figure 9-4. Storing information in a file cabinet.

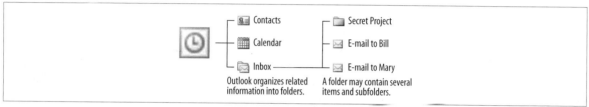

Figure 9-5. Storing Information in Outlook.

While a filing cabinet is used to organize information into related folders, Windows uses folders to organize your files and programs. You can copy, move, and delete files to and from the folders on your hard drive. Similar to Windows, Outlook has its own set of folders for storing the items you create in various modules: appointments, contacts, e-mail messages, and so on. Each tool in Outlook stores its information in its own folder, which you can view in the Navigation Pane.

Just like the folders in a filing cabinet or in Windows, sometimes you may find that one of your Outlook folders is getting too big to manage and you will need to organize and move its information into several new folders or subfolders. For example, you could create a "Personal" folder to store your personal e-mail.

Many people don't use the Folder List because the Navigation Pane includes the folder choices that are most fre-quently used. If you don't receive and/or send much e-mail, you probably don't need to work with the Folder List, either. On the other hand, if you're having difficulty sorting through the deluge of e-mail you seem to receive on a daily basis, you will definitely want to review the next few lessons, which explain how you can use folders to organize your Outlook information.

Take a look at Figures 9-4 and 9-5 to see how similar storing information in a filing cabinet is to storing information in Outlook.

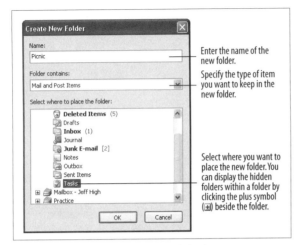

Enter the name of the new folder.

Specify the type of item you want to keep in the new folder.

Select where you want to place the new folder. You can display the hidden folders within a folder by clicking the plus symbol (⊞) beside the folder.

Figure 9-6. The Create New Folder dialog box.

Outlook normally saves all your incoming e-mail messages in the Inbox folder, but sooner or later you may need to expand your horizons and create your own folders to help you organize your e-mail messages and other Outlook items more effectively. This lesson will show you how to create a new folder for storing and organizing your e-mail messages.

1 Click the 📧 New ▾ Mail button in the Navigation Pane.

It's easier to work with a folder if you can see it!

2 Click the ▾ New Mail Message button list arrow on the toolbar and select Folder.

 Other ways to create a new folder are to select File → New → Folder from the menu or to press Ctrl + Shift + E.

The Create New Folder dialog box appears, as shown in Figure 9-6. You have to specify three things:

- The name of the new folder
- The type of item you want to keep in the new folder
- Where you want to place the new folder

3 Click in the Name box and type Picnic.

Next, we need to specify what we want to keep in the new folder.

4 Make sure Mail and Post Items appears in the "Folder contains" list.

Finally, you need to specify where you want to keep the new folder. In this lesson, let's place the new Picnic folder in the Practice folder's Task folder.

5 Click the Tasks folder located under the Practice folder.

OK—you're ready to create your new Picnic folder.

6 Click OK.

Outlook creates the new Picnic folder under the Tasks folder.

QUICK REFERENCE

TO CREATE A NEW FOLDER:

1. CLICK THE NEW MAIL MESSAGE BUTTON LIST ARROW ON THE TOOLBAR AND SELECT FOLDER.

2. SPECIFY THE FOLDER'S NAME, TYPE, AND LOCATION.

3. CLICK OK.

Renaming, Copying, Moving, and Deleting a Folder

Figure 9-7. To move a folder, drag it to a new location.

You can move folders in the Folder List by dragging and dropping them to the desired location.

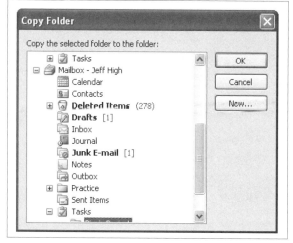

Figure 9-8. The Copy Folder dialog box.

You probably don't reorganize the folders in your file cabinet very often—and you probably won't need to move or copy your Outlook folders very often, either. When you find you *do* need to move or copy a folder, however, you can do so by using one of two simple methods:

• Dragging and dropping

• Using the toolbar or menu

You'll learn how to copy and move folders using both methods in this lesson. You'll also learn how to rename and delete a folder.

1 Click the Folder List button in the Navigation Pane.

The Folder List displays all the folders in Outlook.

You can also move, copy, and rename folders in the Mail pane.

2 Right-click the Picnic folder you created in the previous lesson, and select Rename "Picnic" from the shortcut menu.

Now you can rename the Picnic folder.

3 Type Picnic Project and press Enter.

The folder is renamed.

There are several ways to move and/or copy a folder. One of the most common methods is dragging and dropping.

4 Click and drag the Picnic Project folder to the Inbox folder (located under the Practice folder) as shown in Figure 9-7.

You can copy a folder and its contents by holding down the Ctrl key as you drag the folder.

You're probably already beginning to suspect that there are several methods for doing exactly the same thing in Outlook. Another popular way of moving or copying folders is to use the shortcut menu.

5 Right-click the Picnic Project folder and select Copy "Picnic Project" from the shortcut menu.

The Copy Folder dialog box appears, as shown in Figure 9-8. All you have to do here is specify where you want to copy the folder.

6 Click the Notes folder located under the Practice folder.

This will copy the Picnic Project folder to the Notes folder.

7 Click OK.

Outlook copies the Picnic Project folder to the Notes folder, although you will have to expand the Notes folder to see it.

8 In the Folders List, click the plus symbol (+) beside the Notes folder.

There's the copied Picnic Project folder. The following steps explain how to delete a folder.

9 Click the Picnic Project folder to select it, and then press the Delete key.

A dialog box may appear, asking you to confirm the folder deletion.

10 Click Yes to delete the folder.

The Picnic Project folder and all its contents are deleted and disappear from the window. Outlook places any deleted files or folders in the Deleted Items folder in case you change your mind later on and decide you want to restore the folder.

⁞ NOTE ⁞ *Deleting a folder can be dangerous. Before you do so, make sure it doesn't contain any important information. If you don't know what the contents of a folder are, you shouldn't delete it.*

Whoops! We're going to need the Picnic Project file for an upcoming lesson. Let's restore the deleted folder.

11 Click the plus symbol (+) beside the Deleted Items folder.

There's the deleted Picnic Project folder. Here's how to restore it:

12 Right-click the Picnic Project folder and select Move "Picnic Project" from the shortcut menu.

13 Click the Inbox folder and click OK.

Ta-da! The Picnic Project folder returns to its original location in the Inbox folder.

There's no better way to organize Outlook than by creating and using your own folders to categorize information—especially if you receive several dozen e-mails every day.

QUICK REFERENCE

TO RENAME A FOLDER:

- RIGHT-CLICK THE FOLDER, SELECT RENAME FROM THE SHORTCUT MENU, AND ENTER THE NEW NAME.

TO DELETE A FOLDER:

- SELECT THE FOLDER YOU WANT TO DELETE, PRESS DELETE, AND CLICK YES TO CONFIRM THE DELETION.

TO MOVE A FOLDER:

- CLICK AND DRAG THE FOLDER TO THE DESIRED LOCATION.

NOTE THAT THESE PROCEDURES ARE POSSIBLE IN THE MAIL PANE AND FOLDERS LIST.

Figure 9-9. Search Folders display messages that match specific criteria.

Search Folders are valuable e-mail management tools. They are unlike the other folders in Outlook, such as the Inbox folder that stores all incoming e-mail messages. Search Folders are virtual folders that do not actually contain messages; they are more like views of e-mails that match specific criteria. When you open a Search Folder, the messages you see are stored in other Outlook folders. Because you don't have to constantly move and copy items to other folders in Outlook, Search Folders are easy to use and are more effective for sorting and organizing than standard folders.

Search Folders are great for organizing huge amounts of e-mail messages, such as job applications.

There are three Search Folders that are created by default in Outlook:

• **For Follow Up:** All messages with flags appear here.
• **Large Mail:** E-mail items larger than 100 KB appear here.
• **Unread Mail:** All messages that haven't been read appear here.

You can modify these Search Folders, and even create new ones that follow your own search criteria. This lesson will teach you how to use, create, and modify Search Folders.

1 Click the Mail button in the Navigation Pane.

By default, two Search Folders appear in the Favorite Folders section at the top of the Mail Navigation Pane: Unread Mail and For Follow Up. To see all the Search Folders in Outlook, expand the Search Folder.

2 Click the ⊞ Search Folders expand button under the Mailbox folder in the Navigation Pane.

The folder expands to show the three default Search Folders. Click a Search Folder to view the messages that match its criteria.

3 Click the Unread Mail folder.

All your unread messages appear (if you have any). The messages aren't actually located in the Unread Mail folder, they are stored in your Inbox. The Unread Mail folder is just an easy way to view and go through all your new mail at once. This is especially useful if you have rules that send incoming messages to several different folders.

Now that you have a brief understanding of how Search Folders work, we'll create a new Search Folder using our own criteria.

4 Scroll down the Navigation Pane and select the Practice folder.

Normally you would create a Search Folder with the others in the Mailbox folder, but for the sake of this lesson, we will be using the Practice folder.

5 Select File → New → Search Folder from the menu.

Other ways to create a search folder are to press Ctrl + Shift + P, or, after performing a Find, click the Options button on the Find Bar and select Save Search as Search Folder.

The New Search Folder dialog box appears.

6 Scroll down the dialog box and select Create a custom Search Folder. Click the Choose button.

The Custom Search Folder dialog box appears. This is where you will name the Search Folder, set its criteria, and choose which folders you want the Search Folder to search.

7 Type Picnic messages **in the Name box. Click the Criteria button.**

The Search Folder Criteria dialog box appears. There are three tabs in this dialog box:

- **Messages:** Apply basic criteria to the Search Folder, like searching for words in messages; finding messages sent from an individual(s) or messages you have sent to an individual(s); and searching for messages by when they were sent, received, or created; and so on.

- **More Choices:** Apply more complex criteria, such as finding items under a certain category, items that are read, items with attachments, flagged items, or items of a certain size.

- **Advanced:** Apply advanced criteria with fields to meet specific conditions. This tab is a bit overwhelming if you don't know which fields you want to search by ahead of time, but is very useful if you have a specific need.

We don't need to get too fancy with the criteria for this Search Folder, so the Messages tab will work for now.

8 **In the Messages tab, type** picnic **in the "Search for the word(s)" box. Click the** In **list arrow and select** subject field and message body **from the list. Click** OK.

The Search Folder will compile all the messages that contain the word "picnic" in the subject or message.

After naming the Search Folder and setting the search criteria, the last thing to do is choose which mail folders in which you want to search.

9 **Click the** Browse button.

A list of all the mail folders you can search in appears.

10 **Check the** Inbox **checkbox and click** OK.

Now that you have named the Search Folder, set its criteria, and specified where to look, let's see how it works.

11 **Click** OK, OK **to close the dialog boxes.**

The Picnic messages Search Folder appears, containing all messages that have the word "picnic" in the subject or message field, as shown in Figure 9-9.

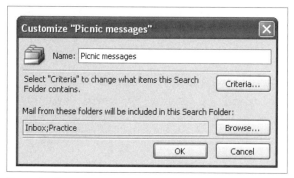

Figure 9-10. The Customize Search Folder dialog box.

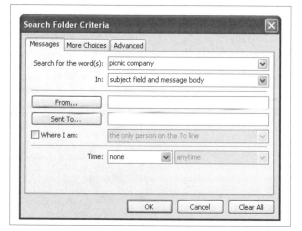

Figure 9-11. The Search Folder Criteria dialog box.

You don't always have to create a new Search Folder. Save time by modifying an existing Search Folder's criteria instead. And if you find that the criteria for an existing Search Folder is no longer needed, you can delete it since it does not actually store items.

1 **Right-click the** Picnic messages **Search Folder and select** Customize this Search Folder **from the shortcut menu.**

The Customize "Picnic messages" dialog box appears, as shown in Figure 9-10. You can modify the Search Folder's name, criteria, or search folders. Let's modify criteria.

2 **Click the** Criteria button**. Add the word** company **to the "Search for the word(s)" box and click** OK **(see Figure 9-11).**

Now the Picnic messages Search Folder will find messages that have the words "picnic" and "company" in the subject or message field.

3 **Click** OK**.**

Notice that the Colonel Sanders messages are no longer included in the Search Folder because they do not have the word "company" in the subject or message.

When you're finished with a Search Folder, go ahead and delete it.

4 **Right-click the** Picnic messages **Search Folder and select** Delete "Picnic messages" **from the shortcut menu.**

Remember that Search Folders do not actually store information, so the items within the folder will not be deleted from their original location.

> ⁝ NOTE ⁝ **If you delete a Search Folder, the files it contains will not be deleted from the Outlook folder in which they are stored.**

5 **Click** Yes **to confirm the deletion.**

QUICK REFERENCE

TO MODIFY A SEARCH FOLDER:

1. RIGHT-CLICK THE SEARCH FOLDER AND SELECT CUSTOMIZE THIS SEARCH FOLDER FROM THE SHORTCUT MENU.

2. MODIFY THE SEARCH FOLDER NAME, CRITERIA, OR SEARCH FOLDERS IN THE CUSTOMIZE DIALOG BOX.

TO DELETE A SEARCH FOLDER:

- RIGHT-CLICK THE SEARCH FOLDER AND SELECT DELETE "SEARCH FOLDER NAME" FROM THE MENU. CLICK YES TO CONFIRM THE DELETION.

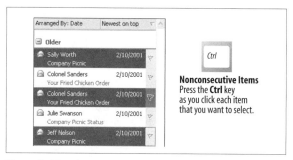

Figure 9-12. Selecting several random items.

Figure 9-13. Selecting a group of consecutive items.

When you select multiple Outlook items, you can move, copy, or delete a whole bunch of items at once instead of individually. For example, you could select all your e-mail messages pertaining to a particular project and move them to a Project folder instead of having to move each e-mail message individually. In this lesson, you will learn how to select multiple Outlook items so that you can move, copy, or delete a group of items at the same time.

1 Make sure the Folder List is displayed.

To display the Folder List, click the Folders List button in the Navigation Pane.

2 Click the Inbox folder located under the Practice folder.

The Inbox contains several messages that pertain to a company picnic. You can select random, or nonadjacent, items by holding down the Ctrl key and then clicking each item you want to select.

3 Hold down the Ctrl key as you click each e-mail message that contains the word "Picnic" in the Subject field, as shown in Figure 9-12.

Now you can move, copy, or delete the selected items all at once.

4 Click and drag the selected messages to the Picnic Project folder in the Folder List.

If you can't find the Picnic Project folder, click the plus sign (+) next to the Inbox folder.

If the items you want to select are adjacent to one another, you can click the first item you want to select, hold down the Shift key, and then click the last item of the group you want to select.

5 Click the first e-mail message, hold down the Shift key, and click the last message.

You've selected the first e-mail message, the last e-mail message, and all the messages in between them (see Figure 9-13).

6 Click anywhere outside the selected messages to deselect them.

Move on to the next step and close the Folder List.

7 Click the Mail button in the Navigation Pane.

The Folder List is closed and the Mail pane opens.

QUICK REFERENCE

TO SELECT SEVERAL CONSECUTIVE ITEMS:

- CLICK THE FIRST ITEM YOU WANT TO SELECT, PRESS AND HOLD DOWN THE SHIFT KEY, AND CLICK THE LAST ITEM YOU WANT TO SELECT.

TO SELECT SEVERAL NONCONSECUTIVE ITEMS:

- PRESS THE CTRL KEY AS YOU CLICK EACH ITEM THAT YOU WANT TO SELECT.

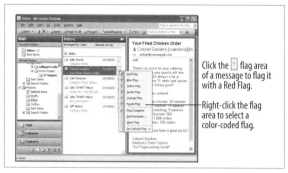

Figure 9-14. You can choose different flag colors, add reminders, clear the flag, and more by right-clicking the flag area.

Click the ▽ flag area of a message to flag it with a Red Flag.

Right-click the flag area to select a color-coded flag.

Figure 9-15. The For Follow Up folder displays all the items you have flagged.

Click the For Follow Up folder to review all your flagged items.

Flagging is an easy way to remind yourself to follow up on an important e-mail message, contact, or task. When you flag an item, a small ▼ icon appears next to the item. You can select one of six color-coded flags and add a reminder date, so that Outlook reminds you to follow up with an item when the specified date arrives. Flags are also very useful when used with Outlook's various views. For example, you can filter out only those e-mail messages, contacts, or tasks that are flagged.

Microsoft has dramatically improved the flag feature in Outlook 2003. You can now flag items with a single click. Outlook 2003 also does a better job of organizing your flagged messages so they're easier to follow up on.

1 Click the Mail button in the Navigation Pane and click the Inbox folder under the Practice folder.

The contents of the Inbox appear. Whether you're working with a message, task, or contact, the procedure for flagging items is the same.

2 Click the Flag area of any unflagged message to flag it.

A red flag appears next to the message. You can also select from six different-colored flags, as shown in Figure 9-14, by right-clicking the Flag area of any message.

Microsoft has made it much easier to follow up with flagged items. Simply click the For Follow Up folder to display all of your flagged messages.

3 Click the For Follow Up folder under the Practice folder.

Outlook displays all messages you have flagged for follow-up, similar to Figure 9-15. Once you have completed a flagged item, simply click the Flag area of the flagged message to mark it as complete.

≡ NOTE ≡ *Normally you would click the For Follow Up folder that appears in the Favorite Folders area of the Navigation Pane. For the sake of this lesson, however, you must select the For Follow Up folder located in the Practice folder.*

4 Click the Flag area of any flagged message to mark it as complete.

You can also clear a flagged message, add a reminder to it, or change its color-coding. Simply right-click the Flag area of any message and select the desired option.

5 Right-click the Flag area of a message.

A shortcut menu appears, as shown in Figure 9-14. We'll leave this message as it is, however.

6 Press Esc to close the shortcut menu without saving any changes.

QUICK REFERENCE

TO FLAG AN ITEM FOR FOLLOW UP:

• CLICK THE FLAG AREA OF THE MESSAGE.

OR...

• RIGHT-CLICK THE FLAG AREA OF THE MESSAGE AND SELECT THE DESIRED FLAG FROM THE SHORTCUT MENU.

TO MARK A FLAGGED MESSAGE AS COMPLETE:

• CLICK THE FLAG AREA OF ANY FLAGGED MESSAGE.

TO CLEAR A FLAG:

• RIGHT-CLICK THE FLAG AREA OF THE MESSAGE AND SELECT CLEAR FLAG FROM THE SHORTCUT MENU.

TO ADD A FLAG REMINDER:

• RIGHT-CLICK THE FLAG AREA OF THE MESSAGE AND SELECT ADD REMINDER FROM THE SHORTCUT MENU. THEN FILL OUT THE DIALOG BOX ACCORDING TO YOUR SPECIFICATIONS.

TO VIEW ALL FLAGGED MESSAGES:

• CLICK THE FOR FOLLOW UP FOLDER IN THE NAVIGATION PANE.

Using Categories

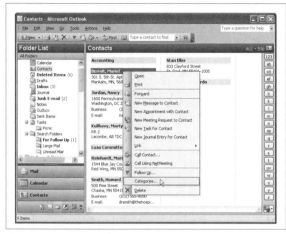

Figure 9-16. To assign one or more categories to any Outlook item, right-click the item and select Categories from the shortcut menu.

Figure 9-17. The Categories dialog box.

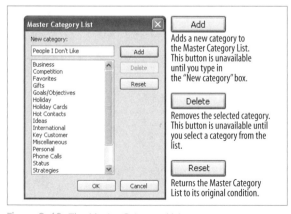

Figure 9-18. The Master Category List.

Since the information stored in Outlook can range from the phone number of your Aunt Mildred to the phone number of Microsoft's CEO, you need a way to keep track of what is what—which is exactly the purpose of Outlook's categories. Categories allow you to organize your Outlook items into specific groups, which, in turn, makes information easier to manage. For example, you might categorize your contacts into business and personal categories. That way, you can only view a specific group of contacts at a time.

1 Click the Folder List button in the Navigation Pane to display the Folder List.

The Folder List appears. In this lesson, we will use the Contacts list located in the Practice Folder.

2 Click the Contacts folder located under the Practice folder.

This folder contains both business and personal contacts—but it's impossible to tell which is which. Here's how to assign a category to a contact:

3 Right-click the Berndt, Murial contact and select Categories from the shortcut menu, as shown in Figure 9-16.

The Categories dialog box appears, as shown in Figure 9-17. There are over 20 pre-made categories to choose from.

4 Find and check the Personal box.

You can also classify items with more than one category. For example, you could categorize a contact as "Business" and as "Key Customer."

5 Find and check the Gifts box.

If you can't find a suitable category, you can easily add your own.

6 Click the Master Category List button.

The Master Category List dialog box appears, as shown in Figure 9-18. To add a new category, simply enter it in the New Category box and click Add.

7 Click Cancel to close the Master Category List dialog box.

We've finished assigning appropriate categories to the Berndt, Murial contact, so we can close the Categories dialog box.

8 Click OK.

You may want to categorize several items at once. To categorize multiple items, simply select the items you want to categorize using the multiple selection technique you learned earlier, and then categorize the items. Let's try it!

9 Click the Eller, Stan contact, hold down the Shift key, and click the Stephano, Bernardo contact.

You've selected the first contact, the last contact, and all the contacts in between the two. Now you can categorize all the selected contacts at once.

10 Right-click any selected contact and select Categories from the shortcut menu.

The Categories dialog box appears.

11 Find and check the Business box.

Outlook assigns the Business category to all the selected contacts.

12 Click OK.

Outlook's categories are to Contacts and Tasks what folders are to e-mail. By categorizing your contacts, you can keep both your personal and business contacts in the same place—but keep them separate at the same time. Likewise, you can use categories to manage several different types of tasks—for example, you could categorize tasks by project.

QUICK REFERENCE

TO ASSIGN ONE OR MORE CATEGORIES TO AN ITEM:

1. RIGHT-CLICK THE ITEM AND SELECT CATEGORIES FROM THE SHORTCUT MENU.

2. CHECK THE CATEGORY YOU WANT TO ASSIGN TO THE ITEM. YOU MAY ASSIGN MORE THAN ONE CATEGORY TO AN ITEM.

3. CLICK OK.

TO ASSIGN ONE OR MORE CATEGORIES TO MULTIPLE ITEMS:

1. SELECT THE ITEMS YOU WANT TO ASSIGN TO THE SAME CATEGORY.

2. RIGHT-CLICK ONE OF THE SELECTED ITEMS AND SELECT CATEGORIES FROM THE SHORTCUT MENU.

3. CHECK THE CATEGORY YOU WANT TO ASSIGN TO THE ITEMS. YOU MAY ASSIGN MORE THAN ONE CATEGORY TO THE ITEMS.

4. CLICK OK.

Creating a Rule by Example

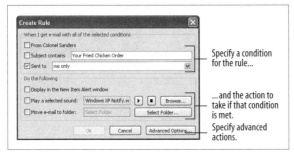

Figure 9-19. The Create Rule dialog box.

Specify a condition for the rule...

...and the action to take if that condition is met.

Specify advanced actions.

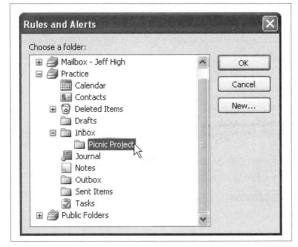

Figure 9-20. The Rules and Alerts dialog box.

A *rule* is a very powerful tool that helps you manage your e-mail messages by automatically performing specific actions. When you create a rule, Outlook applies the rule when messages arrive in your Inbox or when you send a message. For example, you can use rules to automatically to do any of the following:

- Forward all messages sent by Jim Brown to your manager, as soon as they arrive in your Inbox.
- Move all incoming messages that have the word "Picnic" in the Subject box to a Picnic folder.
- Color-code all messages with a high importance level.

You get the idea. You're probably thinking you'll need a degree in computer programming to use such powerful features, right? Wrong! There are two simple ways to create a rule:

- **By Example:** You can create a rule based on an e-mail message. Simply select the message that contains the sender, subject, or recipient you want to use in the rule, and then click the Rule button on the toolbar. (This feature is new in 2003!)

- **Using the Rules Wizard:** You can create a rule from scratch using the Rules Wizard, which walks through the process of creating a rule, step by step.

Both methods are equally simple. We'll focus on how to create a rule by example in this lesson and cover the Rules Wizard in another lesson.

Here's how to create a rule by example:

1 Make sure that you have the Practice folder open and the Folder List displayed.

If you just finished the previous lesson, you shouldn't have to worry about this step.

2 Click the Inbox folder located under the Practice folder.

Make sure you click the Inbox folder located under the Practice folder and not the Inbox folder located under the Mailbox folder.

First, find the message you want to use to create your rule.

3 Select the Your Fried Chicken Order message and click the Create Rule button on the toolbar.

> **TIP** Another way to create a rule by example is to right-click the message you want to base the rule on, and then select Create Rule from the shortcut menu.

The Create Rule dialog box appears, as shown in Figure 9-19. Next, you need to specify a condition for the rule.

4 Check the From Colonel Sanders checkbox.

This will apply the rule to all e-mail messages from Colonel Sanders.

Next, tell Outlook what you want to do when it receives an e-mail message from Colonel Sanders. For this exercise, we'll tell Outlook to move messages from Colonel Sanders to a Picnic folder.

5 Click the Select Folder button.

The Rules and Alerts dialog box appears, as shown in Figure 9-20. Now you have to specify where Outlook should move the e-mail.

6 Scroll down the folder list until you find the Practice folder. **Expand this folder by clicking its** expand button **(the plus symbol).**

Outlook expands the folder and displays all its sub-folders.

7 Expand the Inbox folder by clicking its expand button. **Select the** Picnic Project folder **and click** OK.

This will move all e-mail messages from Colonel Sanders to the Picnic Project folder.

8 Click OK.

Outlook confirms the creation of the new rule. If you want, you can apply the rule to the messages that are already in your Inbox. For example, you could move all your existing messages from Colonel Sanders to the Picnic Project folder. For this exercise, however, we only want to apply the rule to new, incoming e-mail messages.

9 Click OK.

That's all there is to creating a rule by example! The new rule will check all incoming e-mail messages and move them to the Picnic Project folder if they are from Colonel Sanders.

QUICK REFERENCE

TO CREATE A RULE BY EXAMPLE:

1. SELECT THE MESSAGE YOU WANT TO USE TO BASE THE RULE ON AND CLICK THE CREATE RULE BUTTON ON THE TOOLBAR.

   OR...

   RIGHT-CLICK THE MESSAGE YOU WANT TO BASE THE RULE ON AND SELECT CREATE RULE FROM THE SHORTCUT MENU.

2. SELECT A CONDITION FOR THE RULE (FROM, SUBJECT, OR SENT TO).

3. SPECIFY THE ACTION YOU WANT TO TAKE IF THE CONDITION IS MET AND CLICK OK.

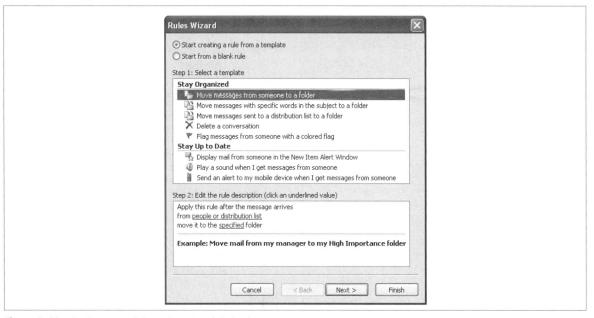

Figure 9-21. The Rules and Alerts dialog box.

Figure 9-22. The first step of the Rules Wizard dialog box.

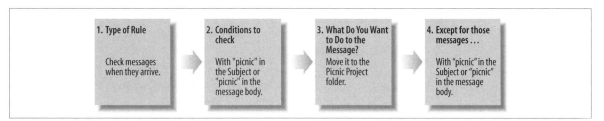

1. Type of Rule

Check messages when they arrive.

2. Conditions to check

With "picnic" in the Subject or "picnic" in the message body.

3. What Do You Want to Do to the Message?

Move it to the Picnic Project folder.

4. Except for those messages . . .

With "picnic" in the Subject or "picnic" in the message body.

Figure 9-23. An example of a rule created with the Rules Wizard.

Creating a rule with the Rules Wizard isn't quite as easy as creating a rule by example, but it's still quite easy to set up and use. This is the topic of this lesson.

1 **Click the** Mail button **in the Navigation Pane.**

Here's how to create a rule using the Rules Wizard.

2 Select Tools → Rules and Alerts **from the menu.**

The Rules and Alerts dialog box appears, as shown in Figure 9-21. This is where you can add new rules and manage existing rules.

3 **Click the** New Rule button.

The first window of the Rules Wizard appears, as shown in Figure 9-22. You have two options for creating a rule:

- **Start from a template:** Lets you create a rule by selecting common rule templates.
- **Start from a blank rule:** Lets you create a rule from scratch. This option is a little more complicated but is much more flexible.

4 **Select the** Start from a blank rule **option.**

Now you have to specify whether or not you want the rule to check incoming or outgoing messages. We'll use the default "Check messages when they arrive" option.

5 **Click** Next.

Next, you need to tell the Rules Wizard what conditions to look for. For example, you might tell the Rules Wizard to look for messages that come from your manager. For this lesson, we want to look for the word "picnic" in any incoming e-mails.

6 **Find and click the** with specific words in the subject **option.**

Now you need to specify the specific word(s) that Outlook should look for in the "Edit the rule description" section at the bottom of the dialog box.

7 **Click the** specific words **link in the rule description section.**

A dialog box appears and prompts you to enter a word or phrase to search for.

8 **Type** picnic, **click** Add, **and then click** OK.

The word "picnic" appears in the rule description section. Some rules have only one set of information to consider; others have two or more. We want to add another condition to our rule—one that checks the message body for the word picnic as well.

9 **Find and click the** with specific words in the body **option.**

The new condition is added to the rule description section.

10 **Click the** specific words **link in the rule description section.**

Once again, a dialog box appears and prompts you to enter the phrase to search for.

11 **Type** picnic, **click** Add, **and then click** OK.

12 **Click** Next.

Now that you've defined the conditions for your Rule, you need to tell Outlook what action to take when it encounters a message with the word "picnic" in the subject or body. You have lots of options to choose from here—from forwarding the message, to deleting it, to flagging it.

We want our Rule to automatically send any picnic messages to the Picnic Project folder that we created earlier.

13 **Find and click the** move it to the specified folder **option.**

The Rules Wizard adds the "move it to the specified folder" option to the rule description. Now you need to tell Outlook where to move the messages.

14 **Click the** specified **link in the rule description section.**

Out jumps a dialog box with your Folder List. All you have to do here is select the folder where you want to move any picnic messages.

15 **Click the** Picnic Project **folder, located under the Inbox folder in the Practice folder, and then click** OK. **Click** Next.

You're almost finished. The last step of the Rules Wizard is specifying any exceptions to the rule. For example, you might want to exempt messages that come from your manager from the "picnic" rule. We don't need any exceptions to our rule.

16 Click Next.

The last step of the Rules Wizard is giving your new rule a name.

17 Type Picnic and click Finish.

The new Picnic rule appears in the Rules and Alerts dialog box.

18 Click OK to close the Rules and Alerts dialog box.

QUICK REFERENCE

TO CREATE A RULE WITH THE RULES WIZARD:

1. SELECT TOOLS → RULES AND ALERTS FROM THE MENU.

2. CLICK THE NEW RULE BUTTON.

3. SELECT THE START FROM A BLANK RULE OPTION, SELECT THE TYPE OF RULE YOU WANT TO CREATE, AND CLICK NEXT.

4. SELECT THE CONDITION(S) YOU WANT TO CHECK.

5. IF NECESSARY, DEFINE THE CONDITIONS IN THE BOTTOM OF THE DIALOG BOX.

6. REPEAT STEPS 4 AND 5 FOR ANY ADDITIONAL CONDITIONS YOU WANT TO CHECK. CLICK NEXT WHEN YOU'RE FINISHED.

7. SPECIFY WHAT YOU WANT TO DO WITH THE MESSAGES THAT MEET THE SPECIFIED CONDITIONS. IF NECESSARY, DEFINE THE ACTIONS IN THE BOTTOM OF THE DIALOG BOX. CLICK NEXT WHEN YOU'RE FINISHED.

8. SPECIFY ANY EXCEPTIONS TO THE CONDITION(S). IF NECESSARY, DEFINE THE EXCEPTIONS IN THE BOTTOM OF THE DIALOG BOX. CLICK NEXT WHEN YOU'RE FINISHED.

9. ENTER A NAME FOR THE NEW RULE AND CLICK FINISH.

Managing Rules

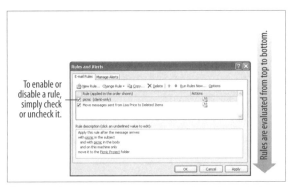

To enable or disable a rule, simply check or uncheck it.

Rules are evaluated from top to bottom.

Figure 9-24. Manage Outlook's rules in the Rules and Alerts dialog box.

If you have to depend on several rules, you'll eventually want to change and delete some of them. Microsoft has made it much easier to manage existing rules in Outlook 2003. You need to open the Rules and Alerts dialog box to manage your existing rules.

1 Select Tools → Rules and Alerts from the menu.

The Rules and Alerts dialog box appears, as shown in Figure 9-24. This is where you can add, delete, and manage Outlook's rules. Let's take a look at how to edit an existing rule.

2 Select any existing rule and click the Change Rule button.

A menu with various editing options appears; if you wanted, you could edit the rule settings, rename the rule, or change the action that is associated with the rule. We'll leave the selected rule alone for this exercise.

3 Click Esc to close the menu without making any changes.

If you don't want Outlook to use a rule you can disable it by unchecking it.

4 Uncheck the Picnic rule.

Here's how to delete a rule:

5 Select the Picnic rule you created in the previous lesson and click the Delete button.

Outlook deletes the Picnic rule. Go ahead and delete any other practice rules you have created.

6 Select the Colonel Sanders rule and click the Delete button.

Outlook deletes the selected rule.

The Rules and Alerts dialog box is pretty straightforward and easy to use, but if anything is unclear, refer to Table 9-2 for a description of its controls.

Table 9-2. The Rules and Alerts dialog box

Button	Description
New Rule...	Creates a new rule.
Change Rule ▾	Modifies the conditions, actions, and exceptions of the selected rule.
Copy...	Copies the selected rule to use as a template for a new rule.
Delete	Deletes the selected rule.
⬆	Move Up: If you have more than one rule this will change the order in which rules are evaluated.
⬇	Move Down: If you have more than one rule this will change the order in which rules are evaluated.
Run Rules Now...	Runs selected rules on the messages already in the Inbox or other folders.
Options	Allows you to import and export your rules. Very useful for backing up your rules and transferring them to another computer.

QUICK REFERENCE

TO EDIT AND MANAGE RULES:

- SELECT TOOLS → RULES AND ALERTS FROM THE MENU.

TO TURN A RULE ON OR OFF:

1. SELECT TOOLS → RULES AND ALERTS FROM THE MENU.

2. CHECK OR UNCHECK THE RULE YOU WANT TO TURN ON OR OFF, RESPECTIVELY.

TO DELETE A RULE:

1. SELECT TOOLS → RULES AND ALERTS FROM THE MENU.

2. SELECT THE RULE YOU WANT TO DELETE AND CLICK THE DELETE BUTTON.

Group By Box
Groups items in the view by the column headings you specify. To group by a column, click and drag the column heading to the Group By Box.

Figure 9-25. The Tasks list grouped by a column.

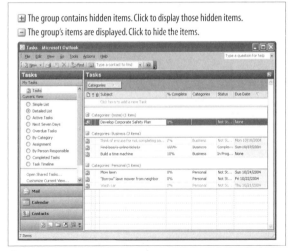

⊞ The group contains hidden items. Click to display those hidden items.
⊟ The group's items are displayed. Click to hide the items.

Figure 9-26. The Tasks list grouped by category.

A *group* is a set of items with something in common, such as e-mail messages from the same sender or tasks with the same due date. When you group items, you organize them in a grouped outline, which you can then expand or collapse to display or hide the items they contain.

You can only group items in a table or timeline view. When you group items by a field that can contain more than one entry—such as the Categories field—items may appear more than once in the table or timeline. For example, if you group by the field Categories and an item has two categories—such as Business and Ideas—the item is listed under both the Business group heading and the Ideas group heading.

Grouping is a lot easier to demonstrate than to explain, so let's start the lesson!

1 Click the Tasks button in the Navigation Pane.

The My Tasks list at the top of the Navigation Pane displays the "Tasks in Practice" list, which is the Tasks List that is located in your Practice folder.

2 Click Tasks in Practice under My Tasks in the Navigation Pane.

This Tasks List contains both personal and business-related tasks—but it's difficult to tell which is which. (OK—maybe it's not that difficult, but let's pretend it is!) You can organize these tasks by grouping them. First, you need to make sure the field you want to use to group the items appears in the column headings. For this lesson, we will group the Tasks List by Category—which doesn't currently appear in the column headings. You can add a field to the column headings by:

- Switching to a view that contains the field you want to use to group information. The Detailed List view usually has most fields in its column headings.

- Manually add the field you want to use to group information. See Lesson 9.19 for more information on how to do this.

In this exercise, we'll switch to the Detailed List view since it contains the required Category field.

3 Click the Detailed List option under Current View in the Navigation Pane.

Outlook displays the Tasks List in Detailed List view and the Category field appears in the column headings.

4 Right-click the column headings and select Group By Box from the shortcut menu.

Other ways to group items are to select View → Arrange By → Show in Groups from the menu, or right-click a column heading and select Group By This Field from the shortcut list.

The Group By Box appears above the column heading. The Group By Box groups items by the column headings you specify.

To group by a column, click and drag the column heading to the Group By box.

5 Click and drag the Categories column heading to the Group By Box, as shown in Figure 9-25.

Notice the "Find method of transportation" task appears in both groups. That's because this task is assigned to both the Business and Personal categories. Figure 9-26 shows an example of tasks listed by category.

Notice the expand and collapse buttons next to each category group. Click the plus symbol (⊞) to view all items in a group. Click the minus symbol (⊟) to collapse all items in a group.

It's easy to ungroup a view. Here's how:

6 Right-click the column headings and select Group By Box from the shortcut menu.

Outlook removes the Group By Box and the tasks remain grouped. That's all there is to grouping information—pretty easy, huh? Before we finish this lesson, we need to switch back to Simple List view.

7 Click the Simple List option under Current View in the Navigation Pane.

Outlook displays the Tasks List in Simple List view.

Most of the time, you'll use Outlook's grouped views to organize information by category, so you'll want to be sure that you're familiar with Outlook's categories and how to use them.

QUICK REFERENCE

TO GROUP ITEMS IN A VIEW:

1. MAKE SURE THE FIELD YOU WANT TO USE TO GROUP THE ITEMS APPEARS AS ONE OF THE COLUMN HEADINGS. IF IT DOESN'T, ADD THE FIELD OR SWITCH TO A VIEW THAT INCLUDES THE FIELD.

2. RIGHT-CLICK THE COLUMN HEADING AND SELECT GROUP BY BOX FROM THE SHORTCUT MENU.

3. CLICK AND DRAG THE COLUMN HEADING YOU WANT TO USE TO GROUP THE ITEMS TO THE GROUP BY BOX.

OR...

SELECT VIEW → ARRANGE BY → SHOW IN GROUPS FROM THE MENU.

OR...

RIGHT-CLICK A COLUMN HEADING AND SELECT GROUP BY THIS FIELD FROM THE SHORTCUT MENU.

TO EXPAND OR COLLAPSE A GROUP:

• CLICK THE GROUP'S PLUS (+) OR MINUS SYMBOL (-).

Filtering Information

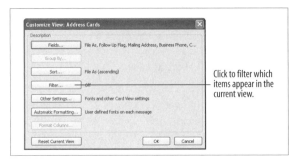

Figure 9-27. The Customize View dialog box.

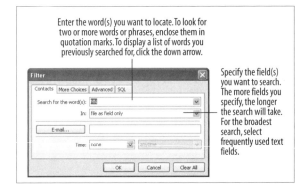

Enter the word(s) you want to locate. To look for two or more words or phrases, enclose them in quotation marks. To display a list of words you previously searched for, click the down arrow.

Specify the field(s) you want to search. The more fields you specify, the longer the search will take. For the broadest search, select frequently used text fields.

Figure 9-28. The Filter dialog box.

Sometimes you may want to see only certain information in an Outlook folder. By applying a filter to a folder or view, you can display only the information that meets your criteria and hide the information that does not. For example, you could filter the Contacts List to display only those clients who live in California.

In this lesson, you'll learn how you can apply a filter to any Outlook folder in order to display only information that meets your criteria.

1 Click the Contacts button **in the Navigation Pane.**

The My Contacts list at the top of the Navigation Pane displays the Contacts in Practice list, the contacts list located in your Practice folder.

2 Click Contacts in Practice **under My Contacts in the Navigation Pane.**

Outlook's filter commands are found in the Customize View dialog box.

3 Scroll down the Navigation Pane and click the Customize Current View **option.**

TIP **Another way to customize a view is to select** View → Arrange By → Current View → Customize Current View **from the menu.**

The Customize View dialog box appears, as shown in Figure 9-27.

4 Click Filter.

The Filter dialog box appears, as shown in Figure 9-28. The controls that appear in the Filter dialog box will change, depending on the type of folder you are viewing.

To create a filter you must first specify the word(s) you want to search for.

5 Type MN **in the** Search for the word(s) **box.**

Next you must specify the field or fields you want to search for in the specified word or phrase.

6 Click the In **list arrow and select** frequently-used text fields.

"Frequently-used text fields" searches the most common text fields for the specified word or phrase. Now we're ready to apply our filter!

7 Click OK **to close the Filter dialog box.**

You're back at the Customize View dialog box.

8 Click OK **to close the Customize View dialog box.**

The Customize View dialog box closes and Outlook applies the filter, displaying only those contacts that contain the word "MN."

It's easy to remove a filter after you've finished using it. Here's how:

9 Select View → Arrange By → Current View → Customize Current View **from the menu.**

The Customize View dialog box appears.

10 Click Filter.

Another way to filter information is to right-click the Contacts list and select Filter from the shortcut menu.

The Filter dialog box appears.

11 Click Clear All.

Outlook clears all information from the Filter dialog box.

12 Click OK to close the Filter dialog box.

Only one more dialog box to close.

13 Click OK to close the Customize View dialog box.

Outlook closes the Customize View dialog box and once again displays all the contacts in the Contacts List.

If you find that you're frequently applying the same filter to a folder, you should create a Custom View that already has a built-in filter. It's much faster to apply a saved filter than it is to create a new one each time. See Lesson 9.20 later in this chapter for more information on how to do this.

QUICK REFERENCE

TO APPLY A FILTER:

1. SELECT VIEW → ARRANGE BY → CURRENT VIEW → CUSTOMIZE CURRENT VIEW FROM THE MENU.

   OR...

   RIGHT-CLICK THE CONTACTS LIST AND SELECT FILTER FROM THE SHORTCUT MENU.

2. CLICK FILTER.

3. SPECIFY THE SEARCH/FILTER OPTIONS IN THE FILTER DIALOG BOX.

4. CLICK OK, OK.

TO REMOVE A FILTER:

1. SELECT VIEW → ARRANGE BY → CURRENT VIEW → CUSTOMIZE CURRENT VIEW FROM THE MENU.

2. CLICK FILTER.

3. CLICK CLEAR ALL.

4. CLICK OK, OK.

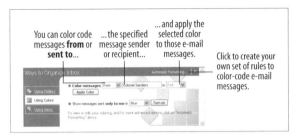

Figure 9-29. The Using Colors tab of the Organize pane.

Figure 9-30. The Automatic Formatting dialog box.

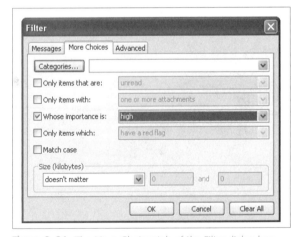

Figure 9-31. The More Choices tab of the Filter dialog box.

If you have to go through a mountain of e-mail messages every day, you might want to consider using Outlook's Automatic Formatting feature to color-code your incoming messages. Automatic Formatting color-codes your messages based on whether or not they were read, their importance level, and so on. For example, you could format any e-mail messages from your boss in red, any unread e-mail messages in blue, and so on. The Automatic Formatting feature has several preset rules you can use to format e-mail messages, or you can create your own.

1 Click the Mail button in the Navigation Pane and click the Inbox folder located under the Practice folder.

Make sure you click the Inbox folder located under the Practice folder and not the Inbox folder located under the Mailbox folder.

2 Select Tools → Organize from the menu.

The Organize pane appears. The Organize pane is an easy way to organize the contents of any folder.

3 Click the Using Colors link in the Organize pane.

The Using Colors tab appears, as shown in Figure 9-29. You can automatically color-code e-mail messages to or from a particular recipient or sender, and you can also create your own color-coding rules by clicking the Automatic Formatting button.

4 Click Automatic Formatting in the upper-right corner of the Organize pane.

The Automatic Formatting dialog box appears, as shown in Figure 9-30. The Automatic Formatting dialog box lists the current automatic formatting rules. If the rule has a check mark in the box next to it, the rule is active. You can also add, modify, and delete automatic formatting rules in the Automatic Formatting dialog box.

⸱ NOTE ⸱ *You will usually want to leave any existing rules alone and keep them checked. For example, the "Unread messages" rule is what automatically formats your new, unread messages in bold—you wouldn't want to mess with that rule, would you?*

The following steps explain how to add a new automatic formatting rule.

5 Click Add.

Strangely, a new dialog box *doesn't* appear—you have to create the new automatic formatting rule straight from the Automatic Formatting dialog box. First, you need to give your new rule a name.

6 Type Urgent in the Name box.

Next, you need to specify how you want the messages that meet the set conditions to be formatted.

7 Click the Font button.

The Font dialog box appears. If you have used other Microsoft Office programs, such as Microsoft Excel, PowerPoint, or Word, you're probably already familiar with the well-known Font dialog box.

8 Click the Color list arrow and select Red.

This will format messages that meet the specified conditions in red. You can also specify additional formatting options, such as the font style and size, but for this lesson we'll just use the red color-coding.

9 Click OK.

The Font dialog box closes and you're back to the Automatic Formatting dialog box.

The last step in creating an automatic formatting rule is to specify the condition you want to check for. Any item in the folder that meets the conditions you specify will be formatted with the settings selected in the Font dialog box.

10 Click the Condition button and click the More Choices tab.

The Filter dialog box appears with the More Choices tab in front, as shown in Figure 9-31. We want to format high-priority e-mail messages in red.

11 Click the Whose importance is box to select it, click the corresponding list arrow, and select high from the list.

You've finished specifying the conditions for your rule, so you can close the dialog box.

12 Click OK.

The Filter dialog box closes, and the new "Urgent" automatic formatting rule appears in the Rules list. You can turn a rule on or off by checking or unchecking it. When you no longer need an automatic formatting rule, you can delete it.

13 Select the Urgent rule from the list and click the Delete button.

Outlook deletes the Urgent automatic formatting rule.

14 Click OK.

The Automatic Formatting dialog box closes and you're back to the Organize pane.

15 Close the Organize pane by clicking its Close button.

QUICK REFERENCE

TO AUTOMATICALLY FORMAT MESSAGES:

1. SELECT TOOLS → ORGANIZE FROM THE MENU.

2. CLICK THE USING COLORS LINK.

3. SPECIFY THE COLOR-CODING OPTIONS YOU WANT TO USE AND CLICK APPLY COLOR.

4. CLOSE THE ORGANIZE PANE.

TO CREATE A NEW FORMATTING RULE:

1. SELECT TOOLS → ORGANIZE FROM THE MENU.

2. CLICK THE USING COLORS LINK.

3. CLICK AUTOMATIC FORMATTING.

4. CLICK ADD.

5. ENTER A NAME FOR THE AUTOMATIC FORMATTING RULE.

6. CLICK THE FONT BUTTON.

7. IN THE FONT DIALOG BOX, SPECIFY HOW YOU WANT THE MESSAGES TO BE FORMATTED AND CLICK OK.

8. CLICK THE CONDITION BUTTON.

9. SELECT THE CONDITION(S) YOU WANT TO CHECK.

10. CLICK OK, OK.

Sorting Information

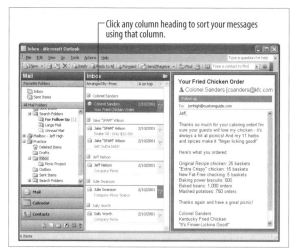

┌ Click any column heading to sort your messages
  using that column.

Figure 9-32. Click on any column heading to sort the view by that field.

If you ever need to find an item, such as a message that's buried deep inside a certain folder, you can quickly sort information in a folder by clicking one of the folder's column headings. For example, clicking the "Newest on top" heading in the Inbox sorts the message list from the newest message to the oldest.

1 Click the Inbox folder located under the Practice folder.

Let's sort the contents of the Inbox by the Subject field.

2 Click the Arranged By: column heading.

A menu appears with various sorting options for the Inbox.

3 Select the Subject option from the menu.

The messages are sorted by their subject. You can also use the column heading on the right to further sort the folder.

4 Click the A on top column heading, as shown in Figure 9-32.

Now the messages are sorted by subject in descending (Z to A) order.

Let's go back to the default sort.

5 Click the Arranged By: column heading and select Date.

This time the messages are sorted chronologically by when they were received.

You can also sort a view by multiple fields: Select View → Current Views → Customize Current View from the menu, click the Sort button, and specify the fields you want to use to sort the view.

Table 9-3 shows some examples of different ways to sort.

Table 9-3. Sort examples

Order	Alphabetic	Numeric	Date
Ascending	A, B, C	1, 2, 3	1/1/99, 1/15/99, 2/1/99
Descending	C, B, A	3, 2, 1,	2/1/99, 1/15/99, 1/1/99

QUICK REFERENCE

TO SORT A VIEW:

- CLICK THE ARRANGED BY: COLUMN HEADING AND SELECT THE OPTION YOU WANT TO USE TO SORT THE FOLDER.

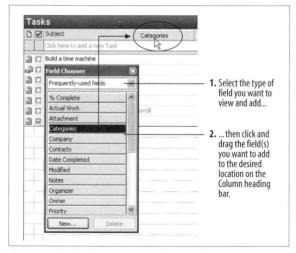

1. Select the type of field you want to view and add...

2. ...then click and drag the field(s) you want to add to the desired location on the Column heading bar.

Figure 9-33. The Field Chooser adds a field to the Tasks List.

The new field appears where you dragged it.

Figure 9-34. The Tasks List with the added Categories field.

When you're viewing information in any of Outlook's tools, you may need to see information in an additional field that isn't normally displayed. For example, the Tasks List's Simple List View displays only the Subject and Due Date fields. If you want to see additional fields, such as the % Complete field, you need to do one of the following:

- Open the item you want to view by double-clicking it. The problem with this approach is that you can view only one item at a time.

- Select a view in the Current View section of the Navigation Pane. The problem with this approach is there may not be a View that includes the field(s) you want to view.

- Add the field to the current view.

This lesson focuses on the last option—adding and removing fields to and from any View.

1 Click the Tasks button in the Navigation Pane and select Tasks in Practice in the Navigation Pane.

2 Make sure you are in Simple List view.

3 Right-click a column heading and select Field Chooser from the shortcut menu.

The Field Chooser appears, as shown in Figure 9-33.

4 Click and drag the Categories field from the Field Chooser onto the column heading bar, as shown in Figures 9-33 and 9-34.

You can also remove any field the same way.

5 Click and drag the Categories field from the column heading bar, then release the mouse button.

You've just removed the Categories field from the Tasks List. Since you're finished using the Field Chooser, you can close it.

6 Close the Field Chooser by clicking its Close button.

QUICK REFERENCE

TO ADD A FIELD:

1. RIGHT-CLICK A COLUMN HEADING AND SELECT FIELD CHOOSER FROM THE SHORTCUT MENU.

2. CLICK AND DRAG THE DESIRED FIELD FROM THE FIELD CHOOSER ONTO THE COLUMN HEADING BAR.

TO REMOVE A FIELD:

- CLICK AND DRAG THE FIELD FROM THE COLUMN HEADING.

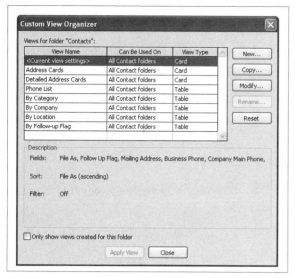

Figure 9-35. The Custom View Organizer dialog box.

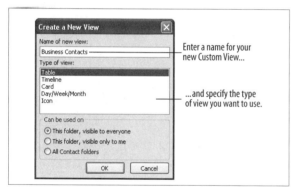

Enter a name for your
new Custom View...

...and specify the type
of view you want to use.

Figure 9-36. The Create a New View dialog box.

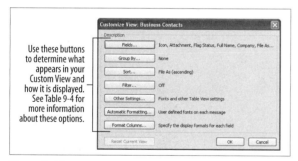

Use these buttons
to determine what
appears in your
Custom View and
how it is displayed.
See Table 9-4 for
more information
about these options.

Figure 9-37. The Customize View dialog box.

Changing fields, sorting options, and filtering a particular folder can get very old, very fast. By creating a *Custom View,* however, you can save the displayed fields, grouping and sorting options, and filter criteria so you don't have to change them manually. This lesson explains how you can create a Custom View to apply to a folder.

1 Click the Contacts button in the Navigation Pane and select Contacts in Practice under My Contacts.

2 Select View → Arrange By → Current View → Define Views from the menu.

The Custom View Organizer dialog box appears, as shown in Figure 9-35. The Custom View Organizer dialog box lets you create, modify, rename, and delete views.

3 Click New.

The Create a New View dialog box appears, as shown in Figure 9-36. Here you need to give your new view a name and determine what type of view it is. You can choose from Table, Timeline, Card, Day/Week/Month, and Icon views.

4 Type Key Customers, ensure Table is selected, and click OK.

The Customize View dialog box appears, as shown in Figure 9-37. This is where you will determine what you want to see in your Custom View, such as the fields and items that are displayed, as well as any sorting, grouping, and formatting options. There are a lot of buttons here—see Table 9-4 to read their descriptions.

5 Click the Filter button.

The Filter dialog box appears. By applying a filter to a Custom View, you can display only the information that meets your criteria. For example, you could filter the Contacts List to display only clients who live in California. Sometimes you may need to view a different tab to specify what you want to filter.

6 Click the More Choices tab.

The More Choices tab appears. This is where you can apply a filter using categories.

7 Click the Categories button.

The Categories dialog box appears. You want your Custom View to display only key customers.

8 Check the Key Customer checkbox and click OK.

The Categories dialog box closes. Now you have to close the Filter dialog box.

9 Click OK to close the Filter dialog box.

The Filter dialog box closes, and you're back to the Customize View dialog box. You could specify additional options for your view at this point by clicking the appropriate buttons, but these are enough options for this exercise.

10 Click OK, then Apply View.

Outlook displays the Contacts List using the new Key Customers view and adds the Key Customers view to the views list.

Move on to the next step and we'll learn how to delete a Custom View.

11 Select View → Arrange By → Current View → Define Views from the menu.

The Custom View Organizer dialog box appears. All you have to do in order to delete a Custom view is the following:

12 Select the Key Customers view from the list, click Delete, and the click OK.

Outlook deletes the Key Customers view.

13 Click Close to close the Custom View Organizer dialog box.

Table 9-4. Customize View dialog box options

View options	Description
Fields	Changes the fields that appear in the current view.
Group By	Changes the groupings in the current view. For example, you can group messages by sender to quickly find all messages from a certain person.
Sort	Changes the sort order in the current view.
Filter	Specifies which items to display in the current view. For example, you can filter to display only messages that were sent yesterday.
Other Settings	Specifies fonts and other settings for the current view.
Automatic Formatting	Specifies the font and colors used on items that meet your criteria.
Format Columns	Specifies how the columns will be formatted and displayed in the view.

QUICK REFERENCE

TO APPLY A CUSTOM VIEW:

• SELECT VIEW → ARRANGE BY → CURRENT VIEW AND SELECT A VIEW FROM THE MENU.

TO CREATE A CUSTOM VIEW:

1. SELECT VIEW → ARRANGE BY → CURRENT VIEW → DEFINE VIEWS FROM THE MENU.

2. CLICK NEW.

3. ENTER A NAME FOR THE VIEW.

4. SELECT THE TYPE OF VIEW YOU WANT TO USE AND CLICK OK.

5. USE THE CUSTOMIZE BUTTONS TO DETERMINE WHAT APPEARS IN YOUR CUSTOM VIEW AND HOW IT IS DISPLAYED. SEE TABLE 9-4 FOR MORE INFORMATION REGARDING THESE OPTIONS.

6. CLICK OK THEN CLICK APPLY VIEW.

TO DELETE A CUSTOM VIEW:

1. SELECT VIEW → ARRANGE BY → CURRENT VIEW → DEFINE VIEWS FROM THE MENU.

2. SELECT THE VIEW YOU WANT TO DELETE, CLICK DELETE, AND THEN CLICK OK.

3. CLICK CLOSE.

Closing an Outlook Data File

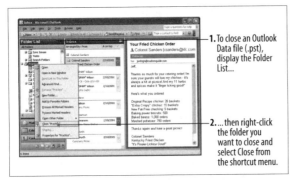

1. To close an Outlook Data file (.pst), display the Folder List...

2. ...then right-click the folder you want to close and select Close from the shortcut menu.

Figure 9-38. Close an Outlook Data file by right-clicking the file and selecting Close from the shortcut menu.

When you open an Outlook Data file (*.pst*), Outlook will continue to open the Outlook Data file each time you start Microsoft Outlook until you close the Outlook Data file. Since we've finished using the Practice Outlook Data file, now is a good time to learn how to close one.

1 Click the  Folder List button in the Navigation Pane.

The Folder List appears. Here's how to close an Outlook Data file:

2 Right-click the Practice folder and select Close "Practice" from the shortcut menu (see Figure 9-38).

Outlook closes the Practice folder (*.pst*) file, and it is no longer displayed in the Folder List.

Since you've finally reached the end of what is definitely the most difficult Outlook chapter, you can close Microsoft Outlook as well.

3 Close Microsoft Outlook.

Congratulations! You've just finished the most difficult chapter in the book—and if you apply what you've learned here, you will finally be able to organize and manage your Outlook information.

QUICK REFERENCE

TO CLOSE AN OUTLOOK DATA FILE:

1. OPEN THE FOLDER LIST BY CLICKING THE FOLDER LIST BUTTON IN THE NAVIGATION PANE.

2. RIGHT-CLICK THE OUTLOOK DATA FILE YOU WANT TO CLOSE AND SELECT CLOSE FROM THE SHORTCUT MENU.

Chapter Nine Review

Working with Outlook Data Files

To Open an Outlook Data File: Select File → Open → Outlook Data File from the menu. Browse to and double-click the *.pst* file.

To Close an Outlook Data File: Open the Folder List by clicking the Folder List button in the Navigation Pane. Right-click the Outlook Data file you want to close and select Close from the shortcut menu.

Finding Information

To Search in the Current Folder: View the folder you want to search. Click the Find button on the toolbar, or select Tools → Find → Find from the menu, or press Ctrl + E. Enter the text you want to search for in the Look for box. (Optional) Click the Options button and select the Search all text in each message box to search through all the text of your messages. Click Find Now.

To Search in Other Folders: Click Search In and select an e-mail folder, or select Choose Folders, check all the folders you want to search in, and click OK. Click the Find button on the toolbar.

Using the Advanced Find Feature

To Use Advanced Find: Click the Find button on the toolbar, click the Options button list arrow on the Find Bar and select Advanced Find, or select Tools → Find → Advanced Find from the menu, or press Ctrl + Shift + F. Specify your search options in the Advanced Find dialog box, and then click the Find Now button. Close the Advanced Find dialog box when you're finished.

Creating a Folder

To Create a New Folder: Click the New Mail Message button list arrow on the toolbar and select Folder. Specify the folder's name, type, and location. Click OK.

Renaming, Copying, Moving, and Deleting a Folder

To Display the Folder List: Open the Folder List by clicking the Folder List button in the Navigation Pane.

To Rename a Folder: Right-click the folder, select Rename from the shortcut menu, and enter the new name.

To Delete a Folder: Select the folder you want to delete, press Delete, and click Yes to confirm the deletion.

To Move a Folder: Click and drag the folder to the desired location.

Note that these procedures are possible in the Mail pane and Folders List.

Using and Creating Search Folders

To Use a Search Folder: Click the Search Folder in the Navigation Pane to view messages that match its criteria.

To Create a Search Folder: Select File → New → Search Folder from the menu, or press Ctrl + Shift + P. Select Create a custom Search Folder. Click the Choose button and type the name of the Search Folder in the Name box. Click the Criteria button, enter criteria for the Search Folder, and click OK. Click the Browse button, check the checkboxes of folders you want to search in, and click OK. Click OK, OK to close the dialog boxes.

Modifying and Deleting Search Folders

To Modify a Search Folder: Right-click the Search Folder and select Customize this Search Folder from the shortcut menu. Modify the Search Folder name, criteria, or search folders in the Customize dialog box.

To Delete a Search Folder: Right-click the Search Folder and select Delete "Search Folder name" from the menu. Click Yes to confirm the deletion.

Selecting Multiple Items

To Select Several Consecutive Items: Click the first item you want to select, press and hold down the Shift key, and click the last item you want to select.

To Select Several Nonconsecutive Items: Press the Ctrl key as you click each item that you want to select.

Flagging Items

To Flag an Item for Follow Up: Click the Flag area of the message or right-click the Flag area of the message and select the desired flag from the shortcut menu.

To Mark a Flagged Message as Complete: Click the Flag area of any flagged message.

To Clear a Flag: Right-click the Flag area of the message and select Clear Flag from the shortcut menu.

To Add a Flag Reminder: Right-click the Flag area of the message and select Add Reminder from the shortcut menu. Then fill out the dialog box to your specifications.

To View all Flagged Messages: Click the For Follow Up folder in the Navigation Pane.

Using Categories

To Assign One or More Categories to an Item: Right-click the item and select Categories from the shortcut menu. Check the category you want to assign to the item (you may assign more than one category to an item). Click OK when you're finished.

To Assign One or More Categories to Multiple Items: Select the items you want to assign to the same category. Right-click one of the selected items and select Categories from the shortcut menu. Check the category you want to assign to the items. You may assign more than one category to the items. Click OK.

Creating a Rule by Example

To Create a Rule by Example: Select a message you want to use to base the rule on and click the Create Rule button on the toolbar, or right-click a message you want to base the rule on and select Create Rule from the shortcut menu. Select a condition for the rule (From, Subject, or Sent To), specify the action you want to take if the condition is met, and click OK.

Creating a Rule with the Rules Wizard

To Create a New Rule: Select Tools → Rules and Alerts from the menu bar. Click the New button, select the Start from a blank rule option, select the type of rule you want to create, and click Next. Select the condition(s) you want to check, and if necessary, define the conditions in the bottom of the dialog box. Repeat these steps for any additional conditions you want to check for. Click Next when you're finished. Specify what you want to do with the messages that meet the specified conditions. If necessary, define the actions in the bottom of the dialog box. Click Next when you're finished. Specify any exceptions to the condition(s). If necessary, define the exceptions in the bottom of the dialog box. Click Next when you're finished. Enter a name for the new rule and click Finish.

Managing Rules

To Edit and Manage Rules: Select Tools → Rules and Alerts from the menu.

To Turn a Rule On or Off: Select Tools → Rules and Alerts from the menu bar and check or uncheck the rule you want to turn on or off.

To Delete a Rule: Select Tools → Rules and Alerts from the menu, select the rule you want to delete and click the Delete button.

Using Grouped Views

To Group Items in a View: Make sure the field you want to use to group the items appears in the Column Headings. If it doesn't, add the field or switch to a View that includes the field. Right-click the column headings and select Group By Box from the shortcut menu. Click and drag the column heading you want to use to group the items to the Group By Box. Or, select View → Arrange By → Show in Groups from the menu. Or, right-click a column heading and select Group By This Field from the shortcut list.

To Expand or Collapse a Group: Click the group's plus ⊞ or minus ⊟ symbol.

Filtering Information

To Apply a Filter: Select View → Arrange By → Current View → Customize Current View from the menu, or right-click the Contacts list and select Filter from the shortcut menu. Click Filter and specify the search/filter options in the Filter dialog box. Click OK, OK.

To Remove a Filter: Select View → Arrange By → Current View → Customize Current View from the menu. Click Filter, then click Clear All. Click OK, OK.

Color-Coding E-mail Messages

To Automatically Format Messages: Select Tools → Organize from the menu and click the Using Colors link. Specify the color-coding options you want to use and click Apply Color. Close the Organize pane when you're finished.

To Create a New Formatting Rule: Select Tools → Organize from the menu and click the Using Colors link. Click Automatic Formatting. Click Add and enter a name for the Automatic Formatting rule. Click the Font button, specify how you want the messages to be formatted in the Font dialog box, and click OK. Click the Condition button, select the condition(s) you want to check, and click OK. Click OK when you're finished.

Sorting Information

Click the Arranged By: column and select the option you want to use to sort the folder.

Adding Fields to a View

To Add a Field: Right-click the column heading and select Field Chooser from the shortcut menu. Click and drag the desired field from the Field Chooser onto the column heading row.

To Remove a Field: Click and drag the field from the column heading row.

Creating a Custom View

To Apply a Custom View: Select View → Arrange By → Current View and select the Custom View from the menu.

To Create a Custom View: Select View → Arrange By → Current View → Define Views from the menu. Click New, enter a name for the View, select the type of view you want to use, and click OK. Use the View Summary buttons to determine what appears in your Custom View and how it is displayed. Click OK, then click Apply View.

To Delete a Custom View: Select View → Arrange By → Current View → Define Views from the menu. Select the view you want to delete, click Delete and OK, then click Close.

Closing an Outlook Data File

To Close an Outlook Data File: Open the Folder List by clicking the Folder List button in the Navigation Pane, right-click the Outlook Data file you want to close, and select Close from the shortcut menu.

Quiz

1. By default, Outlook saves its information in which type of file?
   A. ASCII files (*.txt*)
   B. Outlook Data files (*.pst*)
   C. Microsoft Access Database files (*.mdb*)
   D. Outlook Data files (*.out*)

2. What command is best for searching all Outlook items (e-mails, appointments, tasks, etc.) for the phrase "money laundering"?
   A. Find
   B. Advanced Find
   C. You can't—Outlook can only search the current folder
   D. Search Folders

3. Pressing the Ctrl key as you click multiple items lets you select several consecutive items. (True or False?)

4. Which of the following statements is NOT true?
   A. You can flag important items to remind yourself of them later.
   B. If a view doesn't have a field you want to see, you can add the field using the Field Chooser.
   C. You can click the column headings of a folder to sort its contents.
   D. You can add any Outlook item to one—and only one—category.

5. Which of the following is NOT a rule you could create using the Rules Wizard?
   A. A rule that automatically deletes e-mails with the word "Complaint" in the Subject field.
   B. A rule that automatically responds to messages you receive, notifying the sender that you are out of the office for several days.

C. A rule that automatically moves messages from your spouse to a Spouse folder.

D. A rule that automatically forwards urgent messages to a coworker.

6. In Outlook's *grouped view*, a group is a set of Outlook items with something in common, such as e-mail messages from the same sender or tasks with the same due date. (True or False?)

7. What is a filter?

A. Something that removes coffee grounds from your e-mail messages.

B. Something that screens your incoming e-mail messages for adult content.

C. Something you can apply to a view to see specific information.

D. None of the above.

8. Search Folders store Outlook items. (True or False?)

9. Which of the following are ways to customize a view? (Select all that apply.)

A. Create a grouped view that groups similar Outlook items.

B. Create a filter that displays only those Outlook items that meet the criteria you specify.

C. Color-code e-mail messages based on their importance level, if they have been read or not (e-mail folders only).

D. Add a particular field to the View's column headings.

Homework

1. Start Microsoft Outlook and open the Homework *.pst* (Outlook Data file): Select File → Open → Outlook Data File (.pst) from the menu. Browse to and double-click the Homework *.pst* file.

2. Open the Folders List.

3. Select the Contacts folder under the Homework folder.

4. Assign all contacts from the state of Texas (TX) to the Personal category.

5. Create a filter that displays only contacts from the state of Texas (TX).

6. Perform an advanced search to find all Outlook items that contain the word "ribs".

7. Close the Advanced Find dialog box and the Find pane.

8. Click the Inbox folder in the Navigation Pane.

9. Use the Rules Wizard to create a rule that marks all incoming e-mails with the word "ribs" in the Subject field as urgent. Name the rule "Ribs."

10. Delete the Ribs rule.

11. Close the Homework *.pst* (Outlook Data file).

Quiz Answers

1. B. Outlook normally saves its information in Outlook Data files (*.pst*).

2. B. The Advanced Find command lets you search *all* Outlook items for a word or phrase.

3. False. Pressing the Shift key as you click multiple items lets you select several consecutive items. Pressing the Ctrl key lets you select several nonconsecutive items.

4. D. You can assign more than one category to any Outlook item.

5. B. Although you can't use the Rules Wizard to create a rule that automatically notifies people that you are out of the office, you can do this using the Out of Office Assistant.

6. True. A group is a set of Outlook items with something in common, such as e-mail messages from the same sender or tasks with the same due date.

7. C. A filter is a something you can apply to a view to see specific information.

8. False. Search Folders don't actually store items: they are virtual folders that display Outlook items that match their search criteria.

9. A, B, C, and D. All of these are ways that you can customize an Outlook View.

CHAPTER 10
COLLABORATING WITH OTHER USERS

CHAPTER OBJECTIVES:

Create and respond to a meeting request: Lessons 10.1 through 10.3

Create and work with group schedules: Lesson 10.4

Publish your Calendar on the Internet: Lesson 10.5

Share your Calendar and other Outlook folders: Lesson 10.6

Learn how to open another user's folder: Lessons 10.7 and 10.9

Assign permissions to allow other users to access your Outlook data: Lesson 10.8

Take a vote using e-mail: Lessons 10.10 and 10.11

Assign a task to another Outlook user: Lessons 10.12 and 10.13

Work with public folders: Lessons 10.14 through 10.16

CHAPTER TASK: LEARN TO USE OUTLOOK IN A NETWORK ENVIRONMENT

Prerequisites

- Understand how to use menus, toolbars, dialog boxes, and shortcut keystrokes.
- Understand how to use the Navigation Pane and navigate within Outlook.
- Understand ow to compose, send and receive e-mail.
- A knowledge of the basics of working with all the Outlook tools.

If you use Microsoft Outlook, it's more than likely in a corporate setting on a network that connects hundreds—if not thousands—of computers. In this chapter, you will learn how Outlook lets you work and collaborate with other Outlook users on the network. The folks at Microsoft realized that people often need to work together, so they included a bunch of features in Outlook that help people in large organizations collaborate more effectively. One such feature is the ability to open and modify another user's Outlook information (with their permission of course!). Managers love this feature because they can delegate their Calendar to their assistants and let them manage their busy schedule. Another collaboration feature is the meeting request feature, which lets you easily schedule meetings with other users. Still another collaboration feature is the ability to take a vote via e-mail to get feedback on an important decision.

Microsoft has greatly simplified group collaboration in Outlook 2003 and made it much easier to work with group schedules, share your Calendar, and view another user's Calendar.

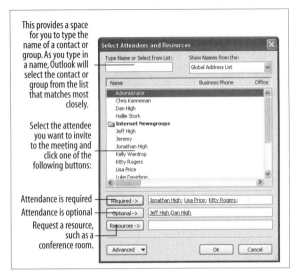

This provides a space for you to type the name of a contact or group. As you type in a name, Outlook will select the contact or group from the list that matches most closely.

Select the attendee you want to invite to the meeting and click one of the following buttons:

Attendance is required

Attendance is optional

Request a resource, such as a conference room.

Figure 10-1. The Select Attendees and Resources dialog box.

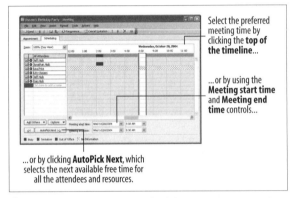

Select the preferred meeting time by clicking the **top of the timeline**...

...or by using the **Meeting start time** and **Meeting end time** controls...

...or by clicking **AutoPick Next**, which selects the next available free time for all the attendees and resources.

Figure 10-2. The Scheduling tab of the Appointment window displays the schedule of a meeting's attendees.

Organizing a meeting with several coworkers is a lot of work. You call the first person and suggest a meeting time, then call a second person, only to find that the second person isn't available when the first one wants to meet. Fortunately, Outlook's Meeting Planner can check everyone's schedule, pick a time, and suggest a meeting time that everyone can live with in a single e-mail message.

In this lesson, you will learn how to plan a meeting with several coworkers and then create and send a meeting request.

1 Switch to the Calendar folder by clicking the Calendar button **in the Navigation Pane.**

Outlook switches to Calendar view.

2 Click the New New Appointment button **list arrow on the toolbar and select** Meeting Request.

Another way to plan a meeting is to select Actions → Plan a Meeting *from the menu.*

First you have to specify who you want to invite to the meeting.

3 Click the To button.

The Select Attendees and Resources dialog box appears, as shown in Figure 10-1. Adding people to a meeting request isn't much different than adding them to an e-mail. There are several invitation options, depending on how important a person's attendance is to the meeting. They are:

- **Required:** People in this list are required to attend the meeting.

- **Optional:** People in this list are not required to attend the meeting.

- **Resources:** This list is for required resources for the meeting, such as a conference room.

4 Click the name of the person you want to invite to the meeting and click either the Required or Optional button, **depending on how important that person's attendance is to the meeting.**

The name you select appears in either the Required or Optional list, depending on which button you click.

5 Repeat Step 4 until you've chosen everyone you want to invite to the meeting. Click OK when you're finished.

The selected names appear in the To box. Next you have to enter some information about the meeting.

6 Enter the Subject and any other information about the meeting, such as its Location and any Notes about the meeting.

Although you can specify the meeting's date and time using the start time and end time controls, it's usually a good idea to check everyone's schedule first.

7 Click the Scheduling tab.

The Scheduling tab, as shown in Figure 10-2, displays the names you selected and their schedule so that you can see when everyone has free time. There are three ways to select your preferred meeting time:

- By clicking the timeline at the top of the Attendee Availability list.

- By entering the meeting start and end time in the boxes at the bottom of the Attendee Availability list.

- By clicking the AutoPick Next button, which selects the next available free time for all the attendees and resources.

8 On the timeline at the top of the Attendee Availability list, click your preferred meeting time.

The time you select appears in the Meeting Start Time box at the bottom of the Attendee Availability list.

You're ready to send your meeting request.

9 Click the Send button on the toolbar.

The meeting request is sent to the people you've invited.

QUICK REFERENCE

TO PLAN A MEETING:

1. CLICK THE CALENDAR BUTTON IN THE NAVIGATION PANE.

2. CLICK THE NEW APPOINTMENT BUTTON LIST ARROW ON THE TOOLBAR AND SELECT MEETING REQUEST.

3. CLICK THE TO BUTTON.

4. CLICK THE NAMES OF THE PEOPLE YOU WANT TO INVITE TO THE MEETING AND CLICK EITHER THE REQUIRED OR OPTIONAL BUTTON.

5. CLICK OK.

6. ENTER A SUBJECT FOR THE MEETING IN THE SUBJECT BOX AND ANY OTHER INFORMATION YOU WANT THE ATTENDEES TO KNOW ABOUT THE MEETING IN THE APPROPRIATE AREAS OF THE FORM.

7. CLICK THE SCHEDULING TAB.

8. SELECT A PREFERRED MEETING TIME.

9. CLICK THE SEND BUTTON ON THE TOOLBAR.

Click one of the buttons on the toolbar to inform the meeting planner of your decision.

Figure 10-3. Receive meeting requests in your e-mail.

When you've been invited to a meeting, you get a special e-mail message with a ▦ icon displayed. When you double-click this message, a meeting request form opens with buttons labeled Accept, Tentative, Decline, Propose New Time, and Calendar. You can click one of these buttons to accept or decline the meeting request and send an e-mail message to the person who organized the meeting, informing that person of your decision. You can even add an explanation in your e-mail message, such as "Sorry, 5:00 AM is just too early for me!"

1 Click the Mail button in the Navigation Pane and click the Send/Receive button on the toolbar.

Meeting requests are easy to identify because of their ▦ icon.

2 Double-click the meeting request message you want to open.

The Meeting Request form appears, similar to the one shown in Figure 10-3. All you have to do here is click one of the following buttons:

- ✓ Accept Outlook adds the meeting to your schedule and sends an e-mail to the meeting organizer, informing her of your decision.

- ? Tentative Outlook adds the meeting to your schedule, marks it as tentative, and sends an e-mail to the meeting organizer, informing her of your decision.

- ✕ Decline Outlook sends an e-mail message to the person who organized the meeting, telling her that you will be unable to attend the meeting.

- Calendar... Outlook displays your calendar so you can see whether you're free to attend the meeting at the suggested time.

3 Enter an explanatory message in the text box and click the appropriate button.

Your response is sent to the Outbox folder and will be sent the next time you click the Send and Receive button.

4 Click the Send/Receive button on the toolbar.

Outlook sends your response to the meeting planner, informing her of your decision.

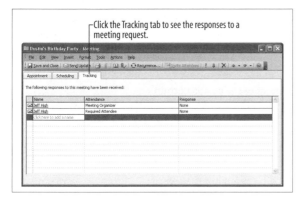

Figure 10-4. The Tracking tab of an appointment displays the current results of a meeting request.

When you organize a meeting with Outlook, you create a small flood of e-mail messages inviting people to attend. They, in turn, respond with another small flood of e-mail messages, either accepting or declining your invitation. Microsoft Outlook keeps track of who said what so that you don't have to. If only it were this easy to plan a wedding!

In this lesson you will learn how to check the status of responses to a meeting request.

1 Click the Calendar button in the Navigation Pane.

The Calendar appears.

2 Find and double-click the appointment you want to check.

The appointment appears in its own form. Here's how to check everyone's responses to your meeting request.

3 Click the Tracking tab.

The Tracking tab appears, as shown in Figure 10-4. The Tracking tab lists the people you invited to the meeting along with their response to your invitation.

⁞ NOTE ⁞ *Everyone who has been invited to a meeting can tell who else was invited by checking the names on the meeting request. However, only the meeting organizer can view who has accepted or declined the meeting request.*

4 Close the Meeting form.

As convenient and powerful as Outlook's meeting request features are, they work only if the attendees receive and then reply to their e-mail. Since some people may be out of the office—and other people are simply just lazy or rude—you will still probably have to make some calls to find out if people can attend your meeting or not.

QUICK REFERENCE

TO CHECK RESPONSES TO A MEETING REQUEST:

1. CLICK THE CALENDAR BUTTON IN THE NAVIGATION PANE.

2. FIND AND DOUBLE-CLICK THE APPOINTMENT YOU WANT TO CHECK.

3. CLICK THE TRACKING TAB.

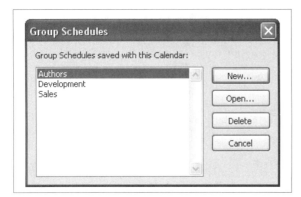

Figure 10-5. The Group Schedules dialog box.

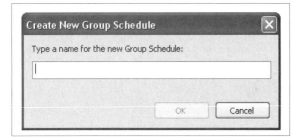

Figure 10-6. The Create New Group Schedule dialog box.

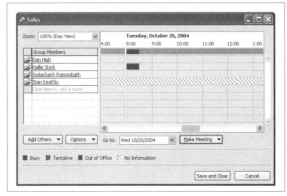

Figure 10-7. The Group Members dialog box displays when everyone in a group is free and/or busy.

No one is an island. Most of us work in some kind of department, and many of us are also members of one or more committees, teams, or boards. It can oftentimes be difficult to keep track of the members of all these different groups—and virtually impossible to stay on top of the individual schedules of those members.

Fortunately, Microsoft realized this so they added some great group scheduling features to Outlook 2003. Outlook 2003 lets you create *groups* to track and manage the members and schedules of all these departments, com-

mittees, and teams. Once you create a group, you can look at your group's schedule to see everyone's agenda and find out who is and who isn't able to attend a meeting.

Here's how to create a group:

1 Click the Calendar button in the Navigation Pane.

Outlook displays your Calendar.

2 Click the 📅 View Group Schedules button on the toolbar.

The Group Schedules dialog box appears. Here you can create, delete, and manage groups whose members and schedules you want to watch. Let's try creating a new group.

3 Click New to create a new group.

The Create New Group Schedule dialog box appears, as shown in Figure 10-6.

4 Enter a name for your group and click OK.

A dialog box for the new group appears. All you have to do now is select the members you want to add to your new group.

5 Click Add Others and select Add from Address Book.

The Select Members dialog box appears.

6 Find and double-click the names of the people you want to add to the group. Click OK when you're finished.

Go ahead and save your new group.

7 Click Save and Close.

Now it's easy for you to view everyone in your group's schedule. Watch…

8 Click the View Group Schedules button on the toolbar.

The Group Schedules dialog box appears, as shown in Figure 10-5.

9 Select the group whose schedule you want to view and click Open.

Outlook displays the schedule for the selected group, as shown in Figure 10-7. Now you can view everyone's agendas and decide when the best time would be to schedule a meeting.

10 Click Save and Close to close the Group Schedules dialog box.

QUICK REFERENCE

TO CREATE A GROUP SCHEDULE:

1. CLICK THE CALENDAR BUTTON IN THE NAVIGATION PANE.

2. CLICK THE VIEW GROUP SCHEDULES BUTTON ON THE TOOLBAR.

3. CLICK NEW TO CREATE A NEW GROUP.

4. ENTER A NAME FOR YOUR GROUP AND CLICK OK.

5. CLICK ADD OTHERS AND SELECT ADD FROM ADDRESS BOOK.

6. FIND AND DOUBLE-CLICK THE NAMES OF THE PEOPLE YOU WANT TO ADD TO THE GROUP. CLICK OK WHEN YOU'RE FINISHED.

7. CLICK SAVE AND CLOSE.

TO VIEW A GROUP SCHEDULE:

• CLICK THE VIEW GROUP SCHEDULES BUTTON ON THE TOOLBAR AND DOUBLE-CLICK THE GROUP WHOSE SCHEDULE YOU WANT TO VIEW.

Set Free/Busy Options and Publishing Your Calendar on the Internet

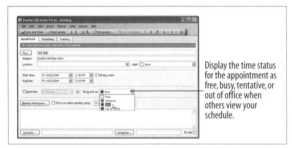

Display the time status for the appointment as free, busy, tentative, or out of office when others view your schedule.

Figure 10-8. In the Appointment form you can choose to show whether your time is free or busy.

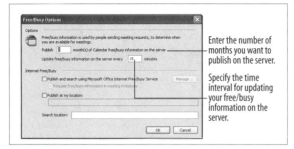

Enter the number of months you want to publish on the server.

Specify the time interval for updating your free/busy information on the server.

Figure 10-9. The Free/Busy Options dialog box.

You must have a schedule before people can view it! This means you should create appointments whenever you will be busy or out of the office. Here are some tips for letting other Outlook users know what your schedule is:

- The "Show time as" list becomes very important if other people view your schedule (see Figure 10-8). The default setting for new appointments is "Busy." However, you can select from any of the options listed in Table 10-1.

- Recurring appointments are also very useful in determining your availability. For example, say you go down to the local health club every day at lunch. You can create a recurring appointment that shows you are unavailable from 12:00 to 1:00 everyday.

- The Free/Busy Options dialog box determines how many months of your schedule other users can view.

You can also publish your Free/Busy information to the Internet if you're not connected to a Microsoft Exchange Server or if you want to let people outside your organization see your schedule. Here's how to publish your schedule to the Internet:

1 Select Tools → Options from the menu and click the Calendar Options button in the Preferences tab.

The Calendar Options dialog box appears.

2 Click the Free/Busy Options button, under the Advanced Options section.

The Free/Busy Options dialog box appears, as shown in Figure 10-9. Now we need to specify how often Outlook will automatically update your Free/Busy information on the Internet.

3 Type the number 20 in the "Update free/busy information on the server every __ minutes" box.

Next we need to specify how many months of your Free/Busy data will be available on the Internet for others to view.

4 Enter the number 3 in the "Publish __ month(s) of Calendar free/busy information on the server" box.

Last, but not least, we have to enter the web address for the location we want our Free/Busy information published to.

5 In the "Publish at my location" box, type the name of the server where your Free/Busy information is stored.

We won't be publishing anything to the Web today, so click Cancel, Cancel, and Cancel to close all open dialog boxes.

Table 10-1 describes the different options listed in the "Show time as" menu in the Appointment form.

Table 10-1. Show time as options

Show time as	Description
Free	Designates that you are available for a meeting.
Tentative	Designates that you have a tentative meeting and may not be available.
Busy	Designates that you are busy and are not available for a meeting.
Out of Office	Designates that you are out of the office and are not available for a meeting.

QUICK REFERENCE

TO PUBLISH YOUR CALENDAR TO THE INTERNET:

1. SELECT TOOLS → OPTIONS FROM THE MENU.

2. CLICK THE CALENDAR OPTIONS BUTTON.

3. CLICK THE FREE/BUSY OPTIONS BUTTON AND ENTER THE SPECIFIED PUBLISHING INFORMATION.

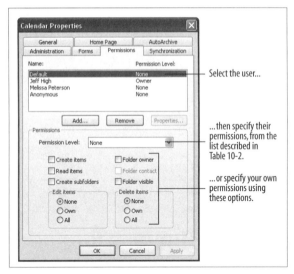

Select the user...

...then specify their permissions, from the list described in Table 10-2.

...or specify your own permissions using these options.

Figure 10-10. The Calendar Properties dialog box.

If you're using Outlook, you probably have a hectic schedule—and so does everyone else at your office. With all these busy schedules, it can be a real problem finding time in the week to get a group of people together for a meeting. Fortunately, Outlook makes it easy to work with all these different schedules. If your organization is using Microsoft Exchange Server, everyone in your organization can share their Calendar, so it's easy to see who's free and when. In fact, you *need* to share your Calendar in order to take advantage of Outlook's automatic scheduling options.

Sharing Calendars was an overly confusing process in previous versions of Outlook—and as a result, many organizations never took advantage of Outlook's group scheduling features. Microsoft has simplified things in Outlook 2003 and made it much easier to share your Calendar.

Although we will be explaining how to share your Calendar folder in this lesson, you can use the same procedure to share *any* Outlook folder, such as your Contacts or Tasks list, Journal, or Notes.

1 Click the Calendar button in the Navigation Pane.

Here's how to share your Calendar:

2 Click Share My Calendar in the Navigation Pane.

TIP

Another way to share a folder is to click the Folder List button to display the Folder List, right-click the folder you want to share, and select Sharing from the shortcut menu.

The Permissions tab appears, as shown in Figure 10-10. Next, you need to select the people who will have permission to access your Calendar.

3 Click Add.

The Add Users dialog box appears. You've probably been doing this long enough to know what to do next.

4 Find and double-click the name(s) of the person(s) who will have access to your folders.

Each name that you double-click appears in the Add Users list.

5 Click OK.

The Add Users dialog box closes and the name(s) you selected appear in the Name list.

6 Select a user from the Name list.

You can select multiple names by holding down the Ctrl key as you click each name. Now you can assign permissions to the selected users.

7 With the username(s) still selected, click the Permission Level list arrow.

A list of available user roles appears. Assigning a role gives a specific set of permissions to the person. Table 10-2 describes the available roles and permissions.

8 Select the role you want to assign to the person.

The selected role appears in the Roles box. The checkboxes below are updated to reflect the tasks the user is permitted to perform.

⋮ NOTE ⋮ *You can also create your own custom permissions by checking or unchecking the checkboxes to grant or deny the corresponding permissions.*

9 **Click** OK.

The selected users can now view and, depending on the permissions you set, even modify the appointments in your Calendar.

Table 10-2. Access permission roles

Role	You can...
Owner	Create, read, modify and delete all items and files, and create subfolders. As the folder owner, you can change the permission levels others have for the folder.
Publishing Editor	Create, read, modify, and delete all items and files, and create subfolders.
Editor	Create, read, modify, and delete all items and files.
Publishing Author	Create and read items and files, create subfolders, and modify and delete items and files you create.
Author	Create and read items and files, and modify and delete items and files you create.
Nonediting Author	Create and read items and files and delete items and files you create. You cannot modify items.
Reviewer	Read items and files only.
Contributor	Create items and files only. The contents of the folder do not appear.
None	Not open the folder; you have no permission.

QUICK REFERENCE

TO SHARE YOUR CALENDAR:

1. CLICK THE CALENDAR BUTTON IN THE NAVIGATION PANE.

2. CLICK SHARE MY CALENDAR IN THE NAVIGATION PANE.

3. CLICK ADD.

4. FIND AND DOUBLE-CLICK THE NAME(S) OF THE PERSON(S) YOU WANT TO HAVE ACCESS TO YOUR CALENDAR.

5. CLICK OK.

6. SELECT THE NAME YOU ADDED TO THE NAME LIST AND CLICK THE PERMISSION LEVEL LIST ARROW.

7. SELECT THE ROLE YOU WANT TO ASSIGN TO THE USER.

8. CLICK OK.

TO SHARE ANY FOLDER:

1. CLICK THE FOLDERS LIST BUTTON TO DISPLAY THE FOLDERS LIST.

2. RIGHT-CLICK THE FOLDER YOU WANT TO SHARE AND SELECT SHARING FROM THE SHORTCUT MENU.

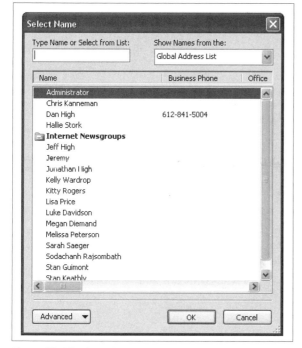

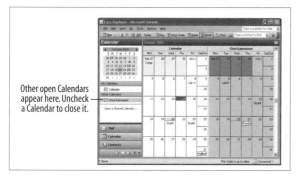

Other open Calendars appear here. Uncheck a Calendar to close it.

If someone has given you the proper permissions, you can open and even modify his Calendar—or any other delegated Outlook folder, such as the Contacts list or the Tasks list. That way, not only can you see what the other person is doing, but also enter an appointment on his behalf. For example, if you worked as a receptionist for a dentist, you could view and enter the dentist's appointments. To do that, you would need to open the dentist's Calendar folder.

You can't open another person's folder unless that person has given you permission first, as described in the previous lesson. Here's how to open another user's Calendar:

1 Click the Calendar button in the Navigation Pane.

Now let's open another user's Calendar.

2 Click Open a Shared Calendar in the Navigation Pane.

 Another way to open a shared folder is to select File → Open → Other User's Folder from the menu.

The Open a Shared Calendar dialog box appears, as shown in Figure 10-11.

3 Click the Name button.

The Select Name dialog box appears, as shown in Figure 10-12. All you have to do is double-click the name of the person whose Calendar or folder you want to open.

4 Find and double-click the name of the person whose Calendar you want to open.

Outlook opens the user's Calendar and displays it next to your Calendar, as shown in Figure 10-13.

Close the Calendar once you're done using it.

5 To close the Calendar, uncheck it in the Other Calendars area of the Navigation Pane.

QUICK REFERENCE

TO OPEN SOMEONE ELSE'S CALENDAR:

1. CLICK THE CALENDAR BUTTON IN THE NAVIGATION PANE.

2. CLICK OPEN A SHARED CALENDAR IN THE NAVIGATION PANE.

3. CLICK THE NAME BUTTON.

4. FIND AND DOUBLE-CLICK THE NAME OF THE PERSON WHOSE CALENDAR YOU WANT TO OPEN.

TO CLOSE A SHARED CALENDAR:

• UNCHECK THE CALENDAR NAME IN THE OTHER CALENDARS AREA OF THE NAVIGATION PANE.

Giving Delegate Permissions

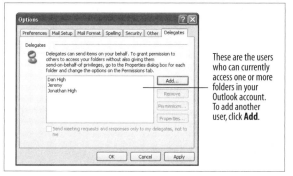

Figure 10-14. The Delegates tab of the Options dialog box.

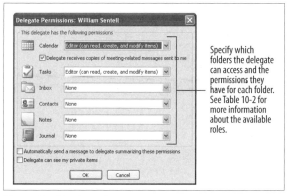

These are the users who can currently access one or more folders in your Outlook account. To add another user, click **Add**.

Specify which folders the delegate can access and the permissions they have for each folder. See Table 10-2 for more information about the available roles.

Figure 10-15. The Delegate Permissions dialog box.

Busy managers often don't have time to micro-manage their schedules and therefore find it difficult to stay on top of things. This is why many managers choose to delegate authority and give the job of managing their calendar, schedule, and even e-mail to an assistant.

When you delegate permissions, you allow the selected individual(s) to send and receive items on your behalf. The most common reason for doing this is to help manage someone else's schedule for them, although if you're incredibly busy (and trusting), you can also let the selected individual(s) manage your Inbox, Tasks list, Contacts list, Notes, and Journal.

You can assign different permissions to different delegates. For example, you could give your assistant permission to view, create, and modify items in both your Calendar and Inbox, while giving another coworker permission to view your Calendar—but not to add or modify any appointments.

In this lesson, you will learn how to delegate permissions to your Outlook folders.

1 Select Tools → Options **from the menu and click the** Delegates **tab.**

The Options dialog box appears with the Delegates tab in front, as shown in Figure 10-14.

Next, you need to select the delegate(s) who will have permission to look at the Outlook folders you pick.

2 Click Add.

The Add Users dialog box appears.

3 Double-click the name of each delegate you want to add.

The name(s) you select appear in the Add Users list. When you've finished adding your delegate(s), move on to the next step.

4 Click OK.

The Delegate Permissions dialog box appears, as shown in Figure 10-15. Here you can choose exactly which permissions you want to give your delegate(s).

5 Make the desired changes in the Delegate Permissions dialog box.

If you don't make any changes at all in the Delegate Permissions dialog box, your delegate(s) will be granted Editor status in your Calendar and Task List. This means that they can read, create, modify, and delete all items in the selected folders.

6 Click OK.

The Delegate Permissions dialog box closes and the names you selected appear in the Options dialog box.

7 Click OK.

The Options dialog box closes.

Remember that when you give someone permission to a particular folder, they can see *everything* in it—including your appointments with your probation officer—so you'll want to be cautious about using Outlook to manage your personal information.

QUICK REFERENCE

TO SET DELEGATE PERMISSIONS:

1. SELECT TOOLS → OPTIONS FROM THE MENU AND CLICK THE DELEGATES TAB.

2. CLICK ADD.

3. DOUBLE-CLICK THE NAME OF EACH DELEGATE YOU WANT TO ADD.

4. CLICK OK.

5. MAKE THE DESIRED CHANGES IN THE DELEGATE PERMISSIONS DIALOG BOX.

6. CLICK OK, OK.

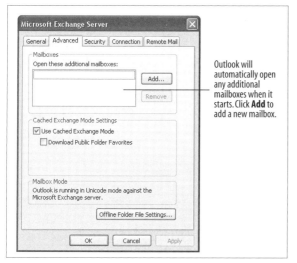

Figure 10-16. The Microsoft Exchange Server dialog box.

Outlook will automatically open any additional mailboxes when it starts. Click Add to add a new mailbox.

Figure 10-17. The Add Mailbox dialog box.

Specify the name of the user whose mailbox you want to open automatically whenever Outlook starts.

If another user has given you access to their Outlook folders and you need to get into these folders frequently, you may want to have them appear in your folder list, where they can be accessed quickly. For example, if you manage your boss's schedule and he has given you permission to view his entire Outlook account, you can set up an Outlook copy so that both your folders and your boss's folders appear in your Outlook folder list.

1 Make sure you have permission to view the person's entire Outlook account, as described in the preceding lesson.

You can't open another user's folder unless they have set the proper permissions. Yes, setting the various permission settings is a pain—but it's better than letting someone snoop around your Outlook information, isn't it?

2 Select Tools → E-Mail Accounts from the menu.

The E-Mail Accounts Wizard appears.

3 Select View or Change Existing E-Mail Accounts and click Next.

A list of all e-mail accounts appears.

4 Select Microsoft Exchange Server and click the Change button.

5 Click the More Settings button and click the Advanced tab.

The Microsoft Exchange Server dialog box appears, as shown in Figure 10-16.

6 Click the Add button. In the Add Mailbox dialog box (as shown in Figure 10-17), type the name of the user whose folders you want to view.

The format of how you enter the name (Last, First, or First, Last) may depend on how your exchange server is set up.

7 Click OK.

If the person you selected didn't give you permission to view his Outlook account, you'll get an error message saying the name you entered couldn't be matched to a name in the address list. If this happens, make sure the person you want to add gave you the proper permissions to his account.

If you would like to view the shared folders of another person, repeat Steps 5–7 for each person you want to add.

8 Click Next. Click Finish.

The E-mail Accounts dialog box closes.

9 Scroll to the end of the All Mail Folders section in the Navigation Pane.

Notice that a new section called Mailbox (followed by the person's name) now appears. This is where the person's Outlook folders are located.

What's nice about setting up access permissions is that people can only open and/or modify the folders you designate. For instance, you can give your administrative assistant permission to automatically open your Calendar folder—but not your Inbox.

QUICK REFERENCE

TO OPEN A SHARED FOLDER AUTOMATICALLY:

1. MAKE SURE YOU HAVE PERMISSION TO VIEW THE PERSON'S ENTIRE OUTLOOK ACCOUNT.

2. SELECT TOOLS → E-MAIL ACCOUNTS FROM THE MENU, SELECT THE VIEW OR CHANGE EXISTING E-MAIL ACCOUNTS OPTION, AND CLICK NEXT.

3. SELECT MICROSOFT EXCHANGE SERVER FROM THE LIST AND CLICK THE CHANGE BUTTON.

4. CLICK THE MORE SETTINGS BUTTON AND THEN CLICK THE ADVANCED TAB.

5. CLICK THE ADD BUTTON AND TYPE IN THE NAME OF THE USER WITH THE SHARED FOLDERS YOU WANT TO VIEW.

6. CLICK OK, NEXT, FINISH.

Taking a Vote

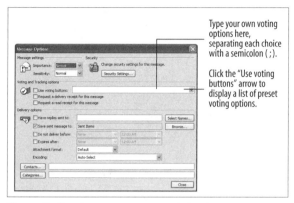

Type your own voting options here, separating each choice with a semicolon (;).

Click the "Use voting buttons" arrow to display a list of preset voting options.

Figure 10-18. The Message Options dialog box.

Getting feedback from other coworkers can be a difficult and time-consuming task. How can you get a coworker to make a decision if you can't find her most of the time? Luckily, Outlook has a powerful survey tool that lets you conduct a vote via e-mail, and then it automatically tabulates the results for you. When you conduct a vote, you add buttons to an e-mail message that you send to a group of people. Recipients of your e-mail can simply click a button to respond and "vote." Their vote is automatically recorded in the copy of your original e-mail message that is stored in your Sent Items folder.

In this lesson, you will learn how to conduct a vote with Outlook.

1 Click the New Mail Message button on the toolbar.

First, we'll compose a new e-mail message to ourselves.

2 Create the following e-mail message:

To: (Enter your own e-mail address here)
Subject: Pizza or Chinese?
Body: Pizza or Chinese?

To add voting buttons to an e-mail message, you need to change the message's options.

3 Click the Options button on the toolbar.

TIP *Another way to change a message's options is to select* View → Options *from the menu.*

The Message Options dialog box appears, as shown in Figure 10-18.

4 Click the Use voting buttons checkbox and then click the Use voting buttons list arrow.

A list of preset voting buttons appears. The preset voting buttons include:

- Approve; Reject
- Yes; No
- Yes; No; Maybe

Not exactly a thorough list, is it? Don't worry—you can also type in your own choices; just make sure to separate your options with a semicolon—for example, Bert; Ernie.

5 In the Use voting buttons box, type Pizza; Chinese.

We're ready to conduct our vote.

6 Click Close.

The Options dialog box closes.

7 Click the Send button on the toolbar.

The message form closes and Outlook sends the survey e-mail to your Inbox.

When your recipients open your message, they can click the button of their choice and then send their decision back to you, where it will be tallied automatically by Outlook. If only the Florida voting canvassing boards had used Outlook during the 2000 presidential elections.

QUICK REFERENCE

TO TAKE A VOTE USING E-MAIL:

1. CLICK THE INBOX FOLDER IN THE NAVIGATION PANE.

2. CLICK THE NEW MAIL MESSAGE BUTTON ON THE TOOLBAR.

3. CREATE THE E-MAIL MESSAGE AND SPECIFY THE RECIPIENTS.

4. CLICK THE OPTIONS BUTTON ON THE TOOLBAR.

5. CHECK THE USE VOTING BUTTONS CHECKBOX.

6. CLICK IN THE USE VOTING BUTTONS BOX AND ENTER THE VOTING OPTIONS, MAKING SURE TO SEPARATE EACH OPTION WITH A SEMICOLON.

7. CLICK CLOSE.

8. CLICK THE SEND BUTTON ON THE TOOLBAR.

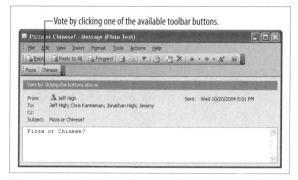

Figure 10-19. Recipients of a vote will receive an e-mail with the available voting choices displayed as toolbar buttons.

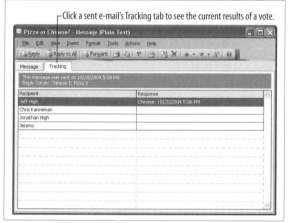

Figure 10-20. You can view the responses of a vote by opening the sent message (in the Sent Items folder) and clicking the Tracking tab.

Election results are coming in! When people respond to a survey e-mail by clicking the button of their choice, their responses are delivered to your Inbox and their answer appears in the Subject field so that you can see their response at a glance. If you are tracking a large number of responses, you can also check your copy of the original message in the Sent Items folder, which tracks all the voting responses.

In this lesson, you will learn how to respond to a survey e-mail and how to review the voting responses from such an e-mail.

1 Click the Send/Receive button on the toolbar.

You should receive at least one message (the "Pizza or Chinese?" message you sent to yourself in the previous lesson).

2 Double-click the Pizza or Chinese? message.

The message opens in its own window, as shown in Figure 10-19. Notice the "Pizza" and "Chinese" buttons that appear immediately below the toolbar. To respond to a survey e-mail, simply click one of the available voting buttons.

3 Click the Chinese button.

Outlook records your vote and sends the results back to the person who created the survey message—in this case, you!

4 Click the Send/Receive button on the toolbar.

You should receive an e-mail message labeled "Chinese: Pizza or Chinese?" This is the result of the voting decision you made in Step 3. If you had chosen pizza, the message would have been labeled "Pizza: Pizza or Chinese?"

If you are only tracking a handful of votes, you can probably tally the results by simply looking at the Subjects in the e-mail responses you receive. If you are tracking a large number of responses, however, you may want to let Outlook tally the results for you. You can get a full tally of your vote by checking the copy of the original message in the Sent Items folder.

5 Click the Sent Items folder in the Navigation Pane

The contents of the Sent Items folder are displayed.

6 Find and double-click the Pizza or Chinese? message.

The original "Pizza or Chinese?" message you sent opens in its own window.

7 Click the Tracking tab.

The Tracking tab shows you a list of the people you've asked to vote and how they voted, as shown in Figure 10-20. The Tracking tab also tallies the voting results in a banner at the top of the page.

8 Close the e-mail message.

Just like meeting requests, Outlook's voting features work only if the recipients receive and then reply to their e-mail.

QUICK REFERENCE

TO RESPOND TO A VOTE:

- OPEN THE E-MAIL AND CLICK THE DESIRED VOTING BUTTON ON THE TOOLBAR.

TO TRACK THE RESULTS OF A VOTE:

1. CLICK THE SENT ITEMS FOLDER IN THE NAVIGATION PANE.

2. DOUBLE-CLICK THE ORIGINAL VOTING MESSAGE.

3. CLICK THE TRACKING TAB TO VIEW THE CURRENT RESULTS OF YOUR VOTE.

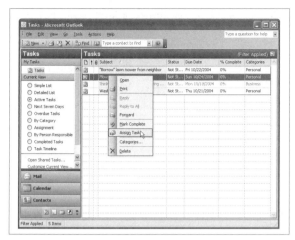

Figure 10-21. Assigning a task to another person.

Enter the name of the person to whom you want to assign the task, just as you would address an e-mail message.

Figure 10-22. Assigning a task to another user is just like sending them an e-mail message.

The folks at Microsoft realize that there's no sense putting off until tomorrow what you can assign to someone else today. That's why Outlook lets you assign tasks to a coworker and keep track of that person's progress on the task. In this lesson, you will learn how to assign a task to another Outlook user.

1 Click the Tasks button in the Navigation Pane.

Outlook switches to Tasks view. First, we need to create a task that we can assign to someone.

2 Click in the Click here to add a new Task box, type Develop Corporate Safety Plan, and press Enter.

Yikes! This task sounds too big for you to handle! Better assign it to someone else.

3 Right-click the Develop Corporate Safety Plan task and select Assign Task from the shortcut menu (see Figure 10-21 for an example).

The Develop Corporate Safety Plan appears in its own window. All you have to do is enter the name of the person to whom you want to assign the task in the To box, the same way you would address an e-mail message.

4 Type the e-mail address of the person to whom you want to assign the task in the To box, as shown in Figure 10-22.

Alternatively, you can click the To button and select the person's name from the Address Book.

There are several additional options that you should be aware of when assigning a task, such as:

* **Status:** Specifies the status of the task. The status is displayed when you send a status report. The Status list options are Not Started, In Progress, Completed, Waiting on Someone Else, and Deferred. See Table 10-3 for a detailed description of each.

* **Keep an updated copy of this Task on my Task List:** Creates a copy of the task in your task list that is updated when the owner makes changes to the task. This option is checked by default—and you should keep it that way.

* **Send me a status report when this Task is complete:** Specifies that a message is sent to you verifying that the task is complete when the recipient finishes it. This option is checked by default—and you should keep it that way.

You can also assign other options to a task.

5 Specify any additional options for the task, such as Due Date, Start Date, and/or Priority.

OK—you're ready to assign the task.

6 Click the Send button on the toolbar.

Outlook places the task in your Outbox and will send the task the next time you click the Send/Receive button on the toolbar.

The task recipient will receive an e-mail message with a task request icon (🔲) displayed. When they double-click the message, they can either accept or decline the task by clicking the appropriate button on the toolbar, and you will be notified of their decision.

Table 10-3 lists the Task status options that are available.

Table 10-3. Task status options

Status	Description
Not Started	The task has not been started yet. Selecting this option resets the % Complete box to 0%.
In Progress	The task is being worked on. Use the % Complete box to specify the percentage of the task that is finished.
Completed	The task is finished. Selecting this option sets the % Complete box to 100%.
Waiting on Someone Else	The task is on hold because someone else isn't doing his job!
Deferred	The task has been assigned to some other poor soul.

QUICK REFERENCE

TO ASSIGN A TASK TO ANOTHER USER:

1. CLICK THE TASKS BUTTON IN THE NAVIGATION PANE.

2. RIGHT-CLICK THE TASK YOU WANT TO ASSIGN AND SELECT ASSIGN TASK FROM THE SHORTCUT MENU.

3. TYPE THE RECIPIENT'S E-MAIL ADDRESS IN THE TO FIELD.

OR...

CLICK THE TO BUTTON TO THE LEFT OF THE TO BOX, CLICK THE NAME OF THE RECIPIENT IN THE NAME LIST, AND THEN CLICK THE TO BUTTON. CLICK OK WHEN YOU'RE FINISHED.

4. CLICK THE SEND BUTTON ON THE TOOLBAR.

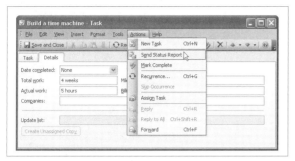

Figure 10-23. You can send a status report that shows the progress on a task to another person.

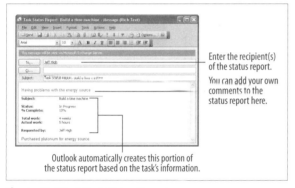

Enter the recipient(s) of the status report.

You can add your own comments to the status report here.

Outlook automatically creates this portion of the status report based on the task's information.

Figure 10-24. A Task Status Report message.

Whenever the recipient of a task modifies the task that he or she has accepted—such as changing the % Complete box—a task message is automatically sent to your Inbox, updating you of the task's progress. You can also keep other people informed about a task's progress by sending them a status report yourself.

In this lesson, you will learn how to manually send a status report to another Outlook user.

1 Click the New Task button on the toolbar.

A new task form appears.

2 Create the following task:

Subject: Build a time machine
Start Date: Use today's date
Due Date: Use the last day of the current month
Status: Not Started

Move on to the next step when you're finished.

3 Click the Save and Close button on the toolbar.

The next day comes and you start working hard on that time machine. Better update the task.

4 Double-click the Build a time machine task.

The "Build a time machine" task appears in its own window.

5 Make the following changes to the task:

Status: In Progress
% Complete: 10%
Notes: Purchased plutonium for energy source.

The Details tab lets you enter even more information about the task.

6 Click the Details tab.

The Details tab appears.

7 Make the following changes to the task:

Total work: 4 weeks
Actual work: 5 hours

You're so proud of your hard work that you decide to send your boss a status report of the task. Here's how:

8 Select Actions → Send Status Report from the menu, as shown in Figure 10-23.

A new e-mail message appears with information about the current task in the body of the message (see Figure 10-24). If you have assigned this task to someone, his name will automatically appear in the To box. You can send anyone a status report—whether he's been assigned the task or not—by entering his name in the To box.

9 Enter your e-mail address in the To box.

Alternatively, you can click the To button and select the person's name from the Address Book. If you want, you can add your own comments to the status report, just like you would add comments to a forward or reply.

10 Click the Send button on the toolbar.

Outlook places the status report in your Outbox and will send it the next time you click the Send/Receive button on the toolbar.

Remember that it's usually unnecessary to send the person who assigned you a task a status report on it, as Outlook will automatically generate and e-mail him a status report whenever you update the task.

QUICK REFERENCE

TO SEND A STATUS REPORT:

1. DOUBLE-CLICK THE TASK FOR WHICH YOU WANT TO CREATE A STATUS REPORT.

2. SELECT ACTIONS → SEND STATUS REPORT FROM THE MENU.

3. TYPE THE RECIPIENT'S ADDRESS IN THE TO FIELD.

OR...

CLICK THE TO BUTTON TO THE LEFT OF THE TO BOX, CLICK THE NAME OF THE RECIPIENT IN THE NAME LIST, AND THEN CLICK THE TO BUTTON. CLICK OK WHEN YOU'RE FINISHED.

4. (OPTIONAL) ENTER YOUR OWN COMMENTS IN THE MESSAGE BODY AREA.

5. CLICK THE SEND BUTTON ON THE TOOLBAR.

Working with Public Folders

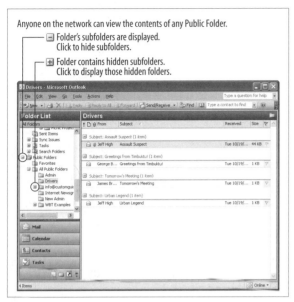

Anyone on the network can view the contents of any Public Folder.

— Folder's subfolders are displayed.
Click to hide subfolders.

— Folder contains hidden subfolders.
Click to display those hidden folders.

Figure 10-25. You can view your organization's public folders by displaying the Folder List.

Another workgroup feature in Outlook is the ability to use public folders. A public folder is an Outlook folder that can be viewed and accessed by many people on the network. Public folders look just like any other folders and may contain a Contact list used by the entire company, or a task list used by an entire department. You can also use public folders to create an online discussion to share ideas on a particular topic or to create a classified ads site for the company. If you think Outlook's public folders sound a lot like a community bulletin board, you've got the right idea.

Public folders are stored on a Microsoft Exchange Server computer. Anyone on the network who uses the mail server can read and post to the server's public folders—but only if they have the proper access permissions.

In this lesson, you will learn how to view a public folder.

1 Open the Folder List by clicking the Folder List button in the Navigation Pane.

The Folder List appears, as shown in Figure 10-25. Remember that the Folder List displays its contents in a *hierarchical* view. A plus symbol (+) or a minus symbol (-) beside a folder means a folder contains several subfolders. Normally, these subfolders are hidden. You can display the hidden subfolders within a folder by clicking the plus sign (+) next to the folder.

2 Click the plus symbol (+) next to Public Folders.

Public Folders expands and displays the subfolders nested within.

⁞ NOTE ⁞ *If you don't see a Public folder, it's proba-bly because your organization doesn't use them—a lot of organizations don't.*

3 Click the name of the public folder you want to view.

The contents of the public folder appear in the main Outlook window.

QUICK REFERENCE

TO OPEN A PUBLIC FOLDER:

1. OPEN THE FOLDER LIST BY CLICKING THE FOLDER LIST BUTTON IN THE NAVIGATION PANE.

2. CLICK THE PLUS SYMBOL NEXT TO PUBLIC FOLDERS.

3. SELECT THE PUBLIC FOLDER YOU WANT TO VIEW.

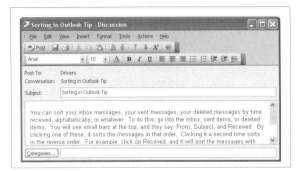

Figure 10-26. You can add a new post to a public folder.

Many public folders are open discussions in which any-one can participate. All the messages can be read by any-body, and anyone can post a reply. For example, if you wanted to start a discussion about your company's lousy food service, you could start a "Yucky Food Service" topic so that other users could share their thoughts and opinions about the subject.

In this lesson, you will learn how to post a new item to a public discussion folder.

1 Click the Folder List button in the Navigation Pane.

The Folder List appears.

2 Click the plus symbol (+) next to Public Folders.

Public Folders expands and displays the subfolders nested within.

3 Click the name of the public folder you want to view.

The contents of the public folder appear in the main Outlook window.

Here's how to post a new item to the discussion folder:

4 Select File → New → Post in this Folder from the menu, or click the New Post in This Folder button on the toolbar.

A new Discussion form appears, ready for you to post your message to the discussion folder.

5 Type your subject and message, as shown in Figure 10-26.

When you're finished, move on to the next step.

6 Click the Post button on the toolbar.

Your message joins the list of items in the public dis-cussion folder.

Before you create a new topic in a public folder, quickly scan the folder to see whether there is already a similar topic to which you can post a reply. We'll learn how to post a reply in the next lesson.

QUICK REFERENCE

TO ADD A NEW ITEM TO A PUBLIC FOLDER:

1. OPEN THE APPROPRIATE PUBLIC FOLDER.

2. SELECT FILE → NEW → POST IN THIS FOLDER FROM THE MENU.

3. TYPE YOUR SUBJECT AND MESSAGE.

4. CLICK THE POST BUTTON ON THE TOOLBAR.

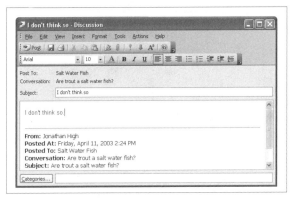

Figure 10-27. Replying to a posting in a public discussion folder.

Not only can you start a new topic—you can also reply to an existing topic. In this lesson, you will learn how to add your thoughts to an existing discussion.

1 Click the Folder List button in the Navigation Pane.

The Folder List appears.

2 Click the plus symbol (+) next to Public Folders.

Public Folders expands and displays the subfolders nested within.

3 Click the name of the public folder you want to view.

The contents of the public folder appear in the main Outlook window.

4 Find and double-click the message you want to reply to.

The message opens in its own window so you can read it. Here's how to reply to a message:

5 Click the  Post Reply button on the toolbar.

The Discussion Reply window appears. The text of the original message appears in your reply, just as it does when you reply to an e-mail.

6 Type your subject and message, as shown in Figure 10-27.

Your reply appears in a different color than the original text. When you're finished, move on to the next step.

7 Click the Post button on the toolbar.

Your reply joins the list of items in the public discussion folder.

When you post a reply, try to be courteous and polite—remember that literally hundreds of people may be able to see what you've written.

> ## QUICK REFERENCE
>
> **REPLYING TO ITEMS IN A PUBLIC FOLDER:**
>
> 1. OPEN THE APPROPRIATE PUBLIC FOLDER.
> 2. FIND AND DOUBLE-CLICK THE MESSAGE TO WHICH YOU WANT TO REPLY.
> 3. CLICK THE POST REPLY BUTTON ON THE TOOLBAR.
> 4. ENTER YOUR RESPONSE TO THE POSTING.
> 5. CLICK THE POST BUTTON ON THE TOOLBAR.

Lesson Summary

Planning a Meeting

To Plan a Meeting: Click the Calendar button in the Navigation Pane. Click the New Appointment button list arrow on the toolbar and select Meeting Request. Click the To button and click the names of the people you want to invite to the meeting, and then click either the Required or Optional button as required, and then click OK. Enter a subject for the meeting in the Subject box and any other information you want the attendees to know about the meeting in the appropriate areas of the form. Click the Scheduling tab and select a preferred meeting time. Click the Send button on the toolbar.

Respond to a Meeting Request

To Respond to a Meeting Request: Double-click the meeting request message you want to open. Click one of the following buttons on the toolbar:

✓ Accept Accept the meeting and add it to your schedule.

? Tentative Tentatively accept the meeting and add it to your calendar.

✗ Decline Decline the meeting.

Calendar... Display your calendar so you can see your schedule.

Outlook will send an e-mail to the person who organized the meeting, informing them of your decision.

Checking Responses to a Meeting Request

To Check Responses to a Meeting Request: Click the Calendar button in the Navigation Pane. Find and double-click the appointment you want to check and click the Tracking tab.

Creating and Working with Group Schedules

To Create a Group Schedule: Click the Calendar button in the Navigation Pane and click the View Group Schedules button on the toolbar. Click New to create a new group, enter a name for your group, and click OK. Click Add Others and select Add from Address Book. Find and double-click the names of the people you want to add to the group. Click OK when you're finished, and then click Save and Close.

To View a Group Schedule: Click the View Group Schedules button on the toolbar and double-click the group whose schedule you want to view.

Publishing Your Calendar on the Internet

To Publish Your Calendar to the Internet: Select Tools → Options from the menu. Click the Calendar Options button and then click the Free/Busy Options button and enter the specified publishing information.

Sharing Your Calendar and Folders

To Share Your Calendar: Click the Calendar button in the Navigation Pane and click Share My Calendar. Click Add, and then find and double-click the name(s) of the person(s) you want to have access to your Calendar. Click OK when you're finished. Select the username(s) you added to the Name list and click the Permission Level list arrow. Select the role you want to assign and click OK.

To Share any Folder: Click the Folders List button to display the Folders List, then right-click the folder you want to share and select Sharing from the shortcut menu.

Opening Someone Else's Calendar

To Open Someone Else's Calendar: Click the Calendar button in the Navigation Pane, and then click Open a Shared Calendar in the Navigation Pane. Click the Name button then find and double-click the name of the person whose Calendar you want to open.

To Close a Shared Calendar: Uncheck the Calendar name in the Other Calendars area of the Navigation Pane.

Giving Delegate Permissions

To Set Delegate Permissions: Select Tools → Options from the menu and click the Delegates tab. Click Add and double-click the name of each delegate you want to add. Click OK. Make the desired changes in the Delegate Permissions dialog box. Click OK, OK.

Open Shared Folders Automatically

To Open a Shared Folder Automatically: First, make sure you have permission to view the person's entire Outlook account. Select Tools → E-Mail Accounts from the menu, select the View or Change Existing E-mail Accounts option, and click Next. Then select Microsoft Exchange Server from the list and click the Change button. Click the More Settings button and then click the Advanced tab. Click the Add button and type in the name of the user with the shared folders you want to view. Click OK, Next, Finish.

Taking a Vote

To Take a Vote Using E-mail: Click the Inbox folder in the Navigation Pane. Click the New Mail Message button on the toolbar, create the e-mail message, and specify the recipients. Click the Options button on the toolbar and check the Use voting buttons checkbox. Click in the Use voting buttons box and enter the voting options, making sure to separate each option with a semicolon (;). When you're finished, click Close and then click the Send button on the toolbar.

Responding To and Tracking Votes

To Respond to a Vote: Open the e-mail and click the desired voting button on the toolbar.

To Track the Results of a Vote: Click the Sent Items folder in the Navigation Pane. Double-click the original voting message. Click the Tracking tab to view the current results of your vote.

Assigning Tasks to Another User

To Assign a Task to Another User: Click the Tasks button in the Navigation Pane. Find and right-click the task you want to assign and select Assign Task from the shortcut menu. Type the recipient's e-mail address in the To field; or click the To button to the left of the To box, click the name of the recipient in the Name list, then click the To

button. Click OK and click the Send button on the toolbar when you're finished.

Sending a Status Report

To Send a Status Report: Find and double-click the task for which you want to create a status report. Select Actions → Send Status Report from the menu. Type the recipient's address in the To field or click the To button to the left of the To box, click the name of the recipient in the Name list, and then click the To button. (Optional) Enter your own comments in the message body area. Click OK and click the Send button on the toolbar when you're finished.

Working with Public Folders

To Open a Public Folder: Open the Folder List by clicking the Folder List button in the Navigation Pane. Click the plus symbol next to 📁 Public Folders and select the public folder you want to view.

Adding a New Item to a Public Folder

To Add a New Item to a Public Folder: Open the appropriate public folder. Select File → New → Post in this Folder from the menu and type your subject and message. When you're finished, click the Post button on the toolbar.

Replying to Items in a Public Discussion Folder

To Reply to Items in a Public Folder: Open the appropriate public folder, find and double-click the message you want to reply to, and click the Post Reply button on the toolbar. Enter your response to the posting and click the Post button on the toolbar.

Quiz

1. Which of the following is NOT an example of one of Outlook's group collaboration features?
   A. Merging several different folders from different Outlook users together into a single, grouped folder
   B. Opening another person's folder
   C. Planning a meeting with other Outlook users
   D. Assigning a task to another user

2. When planning a meeting, if you add a person to the Required list, Outlook automatically assumes they will attend the meeting. (True or False?)

3. Which of the following statements are NOT true? (Select all that apply.)
   A. You can check the status of a meeting request by opening the appointment you want to check and clicking the Scheduling tab.

B. If you use Outlook in a workgroup environment, you should always use the Show Time list when creating appointments to let other users know your availability.

C. By default, anyone on the network can open any of your Outlook folders. You must change Outlook's delegate permissions to disallow other users from snooping around your information in Outlook.

D. The best way to take a vote in Outlook is to create a Public Folder, in which people can post their votes and/or opinions.

4. Your boss is too lazy to manage his own Outlook calendar and wants you to do it. Which of the following tasks do you need to complete in order to open your boss's calendar whenever you start Outlook? (Select all that apply.)

A. Make sure you have permission to access your boss's entire Outlook account.

B. Make sure you have permission to access your boss's calendar folder.

C. Select File → Open → Other User's Folder from the menu, click the Name button, find and double-click your boss's name, click the [▾] Folder arrow, select the name of the folder you want to view, select the Open Automatically option, and click OK.

D. Select Tools → E-Mail Accounts from the menu, select View or Change Existing E-Mail Accounts, and click Next. Select Microsoft Exchange Server from the list and click the Change button. Click the More Settings button and then click the Advanced tab, click the Add button, and type the name of your boss in the following format: Last Name, First Name.

5. To create a vote, you would create an e-mail message, click the Options button on the toolbar, and then specify the voting buttons you want to appear in the e-mail message. (True or False?)

6. When you receive a response from a vote, make sure that you keep track of each vote, as Outlook doesn't have the capability to track the results automatically. (True or False?)

7. You're a high school teacher who has been put in charge of organizing a dance. Feeling under-motivated, you decide to give the various jobs associated with the dance to other teachers. What is the best way of doing this using Outlook?

A. Secretly add the required tasks to other teachers' Tasks Lists by opening their Tasks List folders.

B. Create a fake recurring appointment that shows everyone that you are busy from 6:00 AM to 9:00 PM every day for the next six months and thus couldn't possibly have enough time to work on the various tasks associated with the dance.

C. Use Outlook to plan a meeting with the other teachers where you can talk about the dance and hopefully give the various tasks over to someone else.

D. Add the required tasks for the dance to Outlook's Task List and then assign them to other users.

Homework

1. Start Microsoft Outlook and click the Calendar button in the Navigation Pane.

2. Create an appointment using the following information:

   Subject: Surprise Layoff Meeting
   Start Time: 8:00 AM on Monday of next week
   End Time: 9:00 AM on Monday of next week

3. Open the Surprise Layoff Meeting appointment and click the Scheduling tab.

4. Click the Add Others button. Invite several people of your choice to the Surprise Layoff Meeting.

5. When you have finished creating the Meeting Request, delete it—don't actually send it.

6. Click the Inbox folder in the Navigation Pane and create the following e-mail message:

   To: (Enter your e-mail address)
   Subject: Primary Color Vote
   Message Body: What's your favorite primary color?

7. Click the Options button on the toolbar, check the "Use voting buttons" checkbox, and type "Red; Yellow; Blue" in the "Use voting buttons" box.

8. Send yourself the message. When you receive the Primary Color Vote, click one of the voting buttons.

9. Open the Folders List and click the Sent Items folder.

10. Find and double-click the Primary Color Vote and click the Tracking tab to view the current voting results.

11. If it's possible at your location, try opening another user's Calendar folder.

Quiz Answers

1. A. Merging several different folders together into a single, grouped folder is not one of Outlook's group collaboration features—you can't even do this in Outlook!

2. False. Adding a person to the Required list only lets the person know that their presence is required at the meeting—they can still decline to attend the meeting.

3. D. The best—and really the only—way to take a vote in Outlook is to create an e-mail, click the Options button on the toolbar, and specify the voting options.

4. A, B, and C. You need to complete every one of these steps in order to automatically open your boss's calendar.

5. True. To create a vote, you create an e-mail message, click the Options button on the toolbar, and then specify the voting buttons you want to appear in the e-mail message.

6. False. Outlook tracks the results of a vote in the original e-mail message stored in the Sent Items folder.

7. D. The best way to get out of all that work is to assign some of the tasks to other teachers.

CHAPTER 11
ADVANCED TOPICS

CHAPTER OBJECTIVES:

Add frequently used commands to Outlook's toolbar: Lesson 11.1

Use the Outlook tools together: Lesson 11.2

Send a fax: Lesson 11.3

Archive old Outlook information: Lessons 11.4 through 11.6

Import information into Outlook from an external file: Lesson 11.7

Export Outlook information to a different file format: Lesson 11.8

Automatically start Outlook when you turn on your computer: Lesson 11.9

Access your e-mail from a free e-mail service: Lesson 11.10

CHAPTER TASK: LEARN HOW TO CONFIGURE AND USE OUTLOOK'S MORE ADVANCED FEATURES

Prerequisites

- Understand how to use menus, toolbars, dialog boxes, and shortcut keystrokes.
- Understand how to use the Navigation Pane and navigate within Outlook.
- Understand how to compose, send, and receive e-mail.
- Have a basic knowledge of all of Outlook's tools.

You can customize Outlook in a variety of ways to meet your own individual needs. This chapter explains how you can tailor Outlook to work the way you want. You are already familiar with Outlook's toolbar, and you can use it to access frequently used commands. In this chapter, you will get to add the commands you use the most to the toolbar.

Next, you'll move on to import and export information to and from external files. For example, you can easily export information from Outlook's Contacts List to a Microsoft Excel spreadsheet or a delimited text file. You will also learn how to archive old Outlook information to an external file.

The last topics covered by this chapter concern how to access your Outlook e-mail account from a free, web-based e-mail service, such as Microsoft's Hotmail, and how to configure your computer so that Outlook automatically loads at startup.

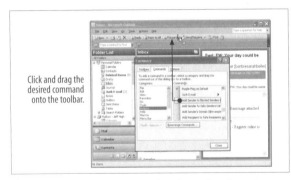

Click and drag the desired command onto the toolbar.

Figure 11-1. Adding a command to the toolbar from the Customize dialog box.

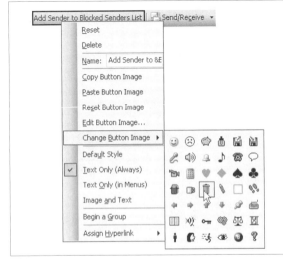

Figure 11-2. Right-click any toolbar button to change the button's text and/or image.

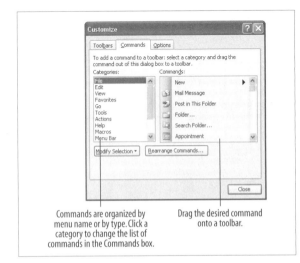

Commands are organized by menu name or by type. Click a category to change the list of commands in the Commands box.

Drag the desired command onto a toolbar.

Figure 11-3. The Customize dialog box.

The purpose of Outlook's toolbars is to provide buttons for the commands you use most frequently. You can modify Outlook's toolbars for the commands you use most often by adding or deleting their buttons. In this lesson, you will modify Outlook's toolbars.

1 Click the Mail button in the Navigation Pane.

Outlook is different from the other Microsoft Office applications in that its toolbar buttons change depending on the current view.

For example, while you're in the Inbox, the toolbar contains buttons for Replying and Forwarding messages. But switch to the Calendar, and these buttons are replaced by Daily, Work Week, Weekly, and Monthly view buttons. Here's how to customize a toolbar.

2 Select Tools → Customize from the menu.

> *TIP*
> *Another way to customize a toolbar is to right-click any toolbar and select Customize from the shortcut menu.*

The Customize dialog box appears. You can select toolbars you want to view or create a new custom toolbar in this dialog box.

3 Click the Commands tab.

The Commands tab appears in front of the Customize dialog box. This is where you select the buttons and commands you want to appear on your toolbar. The commands are organized by categories just like Outlook's menus.

4 In the Categories list, select Actions.

Notice that the Commands list is updated to display all the available commands in the Actions category.

5 In the Commands list, scroll to the Add Sender to Blocked Senders List command and drag it to the toolbar, as shown in Figure 11-1.

The Add Sender to Blocked Senders List button appears in the toolbar. The only problem is that its description takes up too much room.

6 Right-click the Add Sender to Blocked Senders List button on the toolbar.

A shortcut menu for changing the image or text for the selected button appears.

7 In the Name text box, edit the button name to read Add to Blocked Senders.

The name of the button changes on the toolbar.

There are also several dozen preset icons you can use for your toolbar buttons.

8 Right-click on the new button and select Default Style from the shortcut menu.

The Default Style is a plain blue button without any descriptive text. Let's select a more appropriate icon for the Add to Blocked Senders button.

9 Right-click the Add to Blocked Senders button on the toolbar and select Change Button Image → 🗑 , as shown in Figure 11-2.

You're finished creating a button!

10 Click Close to close the Customize dialog box.

You're back at the Inbox. Notice that the Add to Blocked Senders button (🗑) appears on the toolbar. When you no longer need a toolbar button, you can remove it.

11 Select Tools → Customize from the menu.

The Customize dialog box appears, as shown in Figure 11-3. To remove a button, simply drag it off the toolbar.

12 Click and drag the Add to Blocked Senders button (🗑) off the toolbar.

That's all there is to customizing the toolbar!

13 Click Close to close the Customize dialog box.

Adding your frequently used commands to the toolbar is one of the most effective ways to make Microsoft Outlook more enjoyable and faster to use.

QUICK REFERENCE

TO ADD A BUTTON TO A TOOLBAR:

1. SELECT TOOLS → CUSTOMIZE FROM THE MENU.

   OR...

   RIGHT-CLICK ANY TOOLBAR AND SELECT CUSTOMIZE FROM THE SHORTCUT MENU.

2. CLICK THE COMMANDS TAB.

3. SELECT THE COMMAND CATEGORY FROM THE CATEGORIES LIST, THEN FIND THE DESIRED COMMAND IN THE COMMANDS LIST AND DRAG THE COMMAND ONTO THE TOOLBAR.

TO CHANGE A BUTTON'S TEXT OR IMAGE:

1. SELECT TOOLS → CUSTOMIZE FROM THE MENU.

   OR...

   RIGHT-CLICK ANY TOOLBAR AND SELECT CUSTOMIZE FROM THE SHORTCUT MENU.

2. RIGHT-CLICK THE BUTTON AND MODIFY THE TEXT AND/OR IMAGE USING THE SHORTCUT MENU OPTIONS.

Using the Tools Together

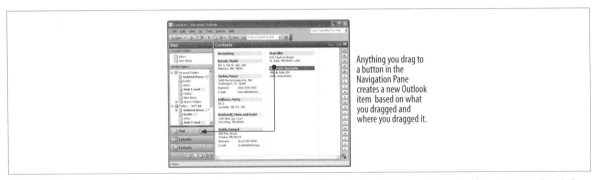

Anything you drag to a button in the Navigation Pane creates a new Outlook item based on what you dragged and where you dragged it.

Figure 11-4. You can send an e-mail message to a contact in your Contact list by clicking and dragging the contact to the Mail button in the Navigation Pane.

One of the easiest ways to use the Outlook tools together is to create a new item by dragging an item onto a button in the Navigation Pane. For example, anything you drag to the Inbox becomes an outgoing e-mail message. Table 11-1 describes this in more detail.

Table 11-1. Using Drag-and-Drop in Microsoft Outlook

Drag this...	Here...	To create...
E-mail message	Calendar	A new appointment with the content of the e-mail message included as the appointment's description.
	Contacts	A new contact that contains the name and e-mail address of the e-mail's sender (**Useful!**).
	Tasks	A new task with the content of the e-mail message included as the task's description.
	Notes	A new note based on the content of the e-mail message.
	Journal	A new journal entry that contains the content of the e-mail message and when it was received.
Appointment	Mail	A new e-mail message with information about the appointment.
	Contacts	A new contact with information about the appointment in the contacts notes (**Seldom Used**).
	Tasks	A new task based on the appointment.
	Notes	A new note based on the content of the appointment.
	Journal	A new journal entry based on the date, time, and description of the appointment.

Table 11-1. Using Drag-and-Drop in Microsoft Outlook (Continued)

Drag this...	Here...	To create...
Contact	Mail	A new e-mail message addressed to the contact (**Useful!**).
	Calendar	A new meeting request with the contact (**Useful!**).
	Tasks	A new task request assigned to the contact (**Useful!**).
	Notes	A new note based on the contact's information (**Seldom Used**).
	Journal	A new journal entry based on the contact's information (**Seldom Used**).
Task	Mail	A new e-mail message with information about the task.
	Calendar	A new appointment based on the task.
	Contacts	A new contact with information about the task in the contacts notes (**Seldom Used**).
	Notes	A new note based on the content of the task.
	Journal	A new journal entry based on the date, time, and description of the appointment.
Note	Mail	A new e-mail message based on the content of the note.
	Calendar	A new appointment based on the content of the note.
	Contacts	A new contact based on the content of the note (**Seldom Used**).
	Tasks	A new task based on the content of the note.
	Journal	A new journal entry based on the content of the note.
Journal Entry	Mail	A new e-mail message with information about the journal entry.
	Calendar	A new appointment with information about the journal entry.
	Contacts	A new contact with information about the journal entry (**Seldom Used**).
	Tasks	A new task with information about the journal entry.
	Notes	A new appointment with the content of the e-mail message included as the appointment's description.

QUICK REFERENCE

TO USE THE OUTLOOK TOOLS TOGETHER:

• DRAG AN ITEM TO A BUTTON IN THE NAVIGATION PANE. SEE TABLE 11-1 FOR MORE INFORMATION.

Sending Faxes

Fill out the recipient information and Subject line.

Select a fax cover sheet, or create your own.

Preview how the fax will look before sending it.

Calculate the cost of the fax before sending it.

Contact your fax provider.

Figure 11-5. The fax message window.

A valuable feature in Outlook 2003 is the ability to send faxes right from the program. Instead of scanning paper copies into a fax machine, Outlook creates (.TIF) image files of the file and cover letter. These image files are then sent to the fax service provider in an e-mail. When the fax message is received, the fax service sends the image files through the telephone wires to the fax machine.

If none of that made sense, all you really need to know is that the new fax feature saves time and a lot of paper, and is incredibly easy to use.

≷ NOTE ≷   *You must have Outlook and Word installed to use the fax service, and Outlook must be open to send your fax. If Outlook is not open and you click Send, the fax will be stored in your Outbox until the next time you open Outlook.*

1 Open the file you want to fax.

If you don't have the file open, you can always attach it, just as you would attach a file to an e-mail message.

2 Select File → New → Fax from the menu.

An e-mail message window opens, as shown in Figure 11-5.

≷ NOTE ≷   *If you do not have a fax service provider installed on your computer, you will be prompted to sign up with a provider over the Internet. It's very easy to do so; just follow the instructions to choose a provider and sign up for the fax service. Many providers offer a free 30-day trial in case you're trying to decide whether or not you want this service.*

Complete the information in the fax message window.

3 Enter the recipient's name and fax number at the top of the window.

You can send the same fax to multiple recipients by clicking the Add More button at the end of the row.

4 Type the fax subject in the Subject line.

Once you have entered the fax message information, fill out the cover letter.

5 Select the Business Fax cover sheet template in the Fax Service task pane.

The template appears. Replace the template text with information that applies to the fax being sent.

≷ NOTE ≷   *The information you include on your cover sheet may require some extra thought if you are sending the fax to multiple recipients.*

Once you've completed the cover letter, check out other options in the Fax Service task pane.

6 Click the Preview button in the Fax Service task pane.

The FaxImage window appears with a preview of the pages in the fax.

You can also get an estimate of how much the fax is going to cost you from your fax service provider.

7 Click the Calculate Cost button in the task pane.

A browser window opens with an estimate of what your provider will charge you for sending the fax.

8 Close the browser window.

Once you're satisfied with how your fax is going to look, you're ready to send it.

9 Click the Send button in the fax message window.

The fax e-mail is sent, and the recipient will receive the fax in no time.

You should also receive an e-mail from your provider, telling you whether or not the fax was successful.

QUICK REFERENCE

TO USE THE FAX SERVICE:

- YOU MUST BE SIGNED UP WITH A FAX SERVICE PROVIDER.

AND...

- YOU MUST HAVE WORD AND OUTLOOK 2003 INSTALLED ON YOUR COMPUTER.

TO SEND A FAX:

1. SELECT FILE → NEW → INTERNET FAX FROM THE MENU.

2. ENTER THE FAX INFORMATION: THE RECIPIENT'S NAME AND FAX NUMBER, AND A SUBJECT.

3. CLICK THE ATTACH BUTTON AND SELECT THE FILE YOU WANT TO FAX.

4. CHOOSE THE TYPE OF COVER SHEET YOU WANT TO USE IN THE FAX SERVICE TASK PANE AND FILL IT OUT.

5. CLICK THE SEND BUTTON.

TO PREVIEW THE FAX:

- CLICK THE PREVIEW BUTTON IN THE FAX SERVICE TASK PANE.

TO CALCULATE COST OF FAX:

- CLICK THE CALCULATE COST BUTTON IN THE FAX SERVICE TASK PANE.

TO FAX MULTIPLE FILES:

- CLICK THE ATTACH BUTTON IN THE FAX MESSAGE WINDOW AND ATTACH EACH FILE YOU WANT TO FAX.

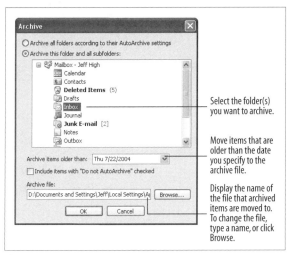

Figure 11-6. The Archive dialog box.

Select the folder(s) you want to archive.

Move items that are older than the date you specify to the archive file.

Display the name of the file that archived items are moved to. To change the file, type a name, or click Browse.

Your Outlook folders become larger as more items are stored in them. As your folders become larger, Outlook becomes slower, and finding items can become increasingly difficult. That is where archiving becomes useful. When you archive Outlook information, you transfer old items to a storage file and then delete it from its original folder in Outlook. There are two ways to archive information in Outlook:

- **Manually:** You can manually transfer old items from a selected folder by selecting File → Archive on the menu.

- **Automatically using AutoArchive:** Once you configure Outlook's AutoArchive feature, Outlook will automatically archive old information. Several Outlook folders are set up with AutoArchive already turned on. These folders and their default aging periods are Calendar (6 months), Tasks (6 months), Journal (6 months), Sent Items (2 months), and Deleted Items (2 months). Inbox, Notes, Contacts, and Drafts do not have AutoArchive activated automatically.

Remember that when you archive information, the original items are copied to the archive file and then removed from the current folder—so be cautious about what you archive.

This lesson explains how to archive Outlook information manually.

1 Select File → Archive from the menu.

The Archive dialog box appears, as shown in Figure 11-6. This is where you determine what you want to archive.

2 Make sure the Archive This Folder and all subfolders option is selected.

Selecting this option tells Outlook to archive the folder(s) you select.

3 Select the folder that you want to archive.

Next, you need to specify how old the items must be before they are archived. If you use e-mail frequently, the Inbox and Sent folders make excellent archive candidates.

4 Click the Archive items older than list arrow and select the date to specify how old items must be in order to be archived.

For example, you could archive any e-mail messages that are older than three months.

5 (Optional) Specify the name and location of the archive file in the Archive File box.

By default, Outlook saves the archive file in a rather obscure location that you will probably have a great deal of trouble finding. You may want to specify a filename and folder that are easier for you to find if you plan on looking at any archived information later.

⸎ NOTE ⸎ *If you decide to specify the name and folder of the archive file, make sure that you use this same file when you archive information in the future. When you archive information, Outlook doesn't overwrite the archive file but appends any new items to it. By using the same archive file, you can keep all your old Outlook information in the same place.*

6 Click OK.

Outlook archives the items in the specified folder that are older than the specified date, saving them in the archive file and then removing them from their original locations.

The most important thing to remember when archiving information is that items that are archived are removed from Outlook, so make sure you don't archive any items that you will need immediately.

QUICK REFERENCE

TO MANUALLY ARCHIVE ITEMS:

1. SELECT FILE → ARCHIVE FROM THE MENU.

2. ENSURE THE ARCHIVE THIS FOLDER AND ALL SUBFOLDERS OPTION IS SELECTED.

3. SELECT THE FOLDER THAT YOU WANT TO ARCHIVE.

4. CLICK THE ARCHIVE ITEMS OLDER THAN LIST ARROW AND SELECT THE DATE TO SPECIFY HOW OLD ITEMS MUST BE IN ORDER TO BE ARCHIVED.

5. (OPTIONAL) SPECIFY THE NAME AND LOCATION OF THE ARCHIVE FILE IN THE ARCHIVE FILE BOX.

6. CLICK OK.

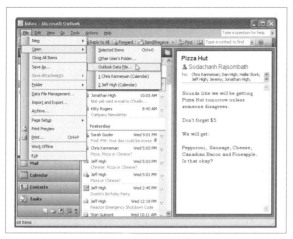

Figure 11-7. You can open an archive file by selecting File →
Open → Outlook Data File (.pst) from the menu.

When you archive information, Outlook removes it from
its folder and saves it in a special archive file. Someday
you may find it necessary to go back and take a look at
the information stored in the archive file.

> *Depending on how Outlook is set up, your
> Archive folders may already appear in the
> Navigation Pane.*

Here's how to retrieve archived items:

1 **Select** File → Open → Outlook Data File **from the
menu, as shown in Figure 11-7.**

The Open Outlook Data File dialog box appears.

Find the archive file you want to open.

2 **Navigate to the folder where your archive file is
located.**

Use the "Look in" list and Up One Level button to
navigate to the various drives and folders on your
computer.

Outlook normally saves its archive file in *Set-
tings\Administrator\Application Data\Microsoft\Out-
look\archive.pst*.

If you're having problems finding the archive file, try
using the Windows Find or Search feature. Simply
click the Start button, select Find or Search, and tell
Windows to search for the file *archive.pst*.

3 **Find and double-click the** archive.pst **file.**

Outlook opens the archive file. You need to display
the Folder List in order to see its contents.

4 **Click the** Folder List button **in the Navigation Pane.**

The Folder List displays its contents in a hierarchical
view. A plus symbol (+) or a minus symbol (-) beside
a folder means it contains several subfolders. You can
display the hidden folders within a folder by clicking
the plus symbol beside the folder.

5 **Click the** plus symbol **(+) next to** Archive Folders.

The Archive folder expands and displays all the folders within it. The plus symbol (+) changes to a minus
symbol (-), indicating the folder is expanded and is
displaying its contents.

6 **Find and click the specific folder you want to view.**

Make sure you click one of the folders located under
the 📁 Archive Folder and not a folder located under
the Mailbox folder. The contents of the specific
archive folder appear in the main Outlook window.

If you want to restore an archived item, simply drag it
to its appropriate folder under the Outlook Today
folder. For example, if you want to restore an old e-
mail message, simply click and drag the e-mail from
the Inbox folder under the Archive Folder to the
Inbox folder under the Outlook Today folder.

When you've finished viewing and/or restoring any
archived items, you can close the archive file. Here's
how:

7 **Right-click the** Archive Folders **and select** Close
"Archive Folders" **from the shortcut menu.**

Outlook closes the Archive Folder.

An e-mail or appointment that seems unimportant to
you now might become very important later on, so you
will want to make sure your Outlook information is
safely archived. When you back up the information on
your computer, make sure that you also make a backup
of Outlook's archive file.

QUICK REFERENCE

TO RETRIEVE INFORMATION FROM AN ARCHIVE FILE:

1. SELECT FILE → OPEN → OUTLOOK DATA FILE FROM THE MENU.

2. BROWSE TO THE FOLDER THAT CONTAINS THE ARCHIVE FILE.

3. DOUBLE-CLICK THE ARCHIVE.PST OR SIMILAR ARCHIVE FILE.

4. OPEN THE FOLDER LIST BY CLICKING THE FOLDER LIST BUTTON.

5. CLICK THE PLUS SYMBOL NEXT TO THE ARCHIVE FOLDER.

6. FIND AND CLICK THE SPECIFIC FOLDER YOU WANT TO VIEW.

7. (OPTIONAL) CLICK AND DRAG THE ITEMS YOU WANT TO RETRIEVE TO THE DESIRED FOLDER.

TO CLOSE AN ARCHIVE FILE:

• RIGHT-CLICK THE ARCHIVE FOLDER AND SELECT CLOSE "ARCHIVE FOLDERS" FROM THE SHORTCUT MENU.

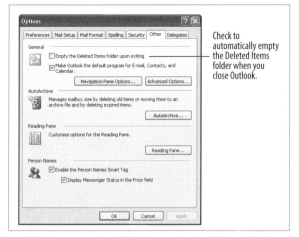

Check to
automatically empty
the Deleted Items
folder when you
close Outlook.

Figure 11-8. The Other tab of the Options dialog box.

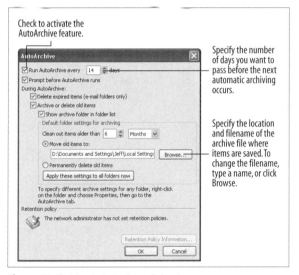

Check to activate the
AutoArchive feature.

Specify the number
of days you want to
pass before the next
automatic archiving
occurs.

Specify the location
and filename of the
archive file where
items are saved. To
change the filename,
type a name, or click
Browse.

Figure 11-9. The AutoArchive dialog box.

If you're a busy person, you may want to have Outlook automatically archive old information for you with its AutoArchive feature. AutoArchive automatically archives your Outlook data every time you use Outlook, based on your settings. For example, you might specify that AutoArchive archives any appointments in your Calendar folder that are more than four months old.

Setting up AutoArchive is a two-step procedure. First, you need to turn on the AutoArchive feature in Outlook's Options dialog box. Then, you must configure the AutoArchive settings for each folder that you want to automatically archive. AutoArchive already has several default settings for the various Outlook folders. These default settings are listed in Table 11-2.

1 Select Tools → Options **from the menu and click the** Other **tab.**

The Other tab appears, as shown in Figure 11-8. There is one item of interest here—the "Empty the Deleted Items folder upon exiting" checkbox. Select this box to automatically delete all of the items in the Deleted Items folder when you exit Outlook.

2 Click the AutoArchive button.

The AutoArchive dialog box appears, as shown in Figure 11-9. Here's how to activate AutoArchive:

3 Click the Run AutoArchive every **checkbox to activate AutoArchive.**

The AutoArchive feature is actually turned on by default to run every 14 days.

You can specify the number of days that pass before the next automatic archiving occurs by entering a new number of days in the text box.

4 (Optional) Enter the number of days you want to pass before the next automatic archiving occurs in the days **box.**

Now the AutoArchive tool will run at the specified time interval. You can also have AutoArchive prompt you before it moves anything to an archive file.

5 (Optional) Make sure the Prompt before AutoArchive runs **checkbox is selected if you want to be notified before AutoArchive archives any items.**

By default, this checkbox is selected so you have the option of running the AutoArchive before it happens.

Finally, you can change the default file where Outlook moves any archived information.

6 (Optional) Click the Browse button **and specify the name and folder where you want to store the archive files in the Find Personal Folders dialog box. Click** Cancel.

That's all there is to turning on the AutoArchive feature.

7 Click OK **to close the AutoArchive dialog box and** OK **to close the Options dialog box.**

AutoArchive will automatically archive information based on the settings listed in Table 11-2. If you want, you can change these settings on a folder-by-folder basis.

8 Open the Folder List and right-click the folder you want to change. Select Properties from the shortcut menu.

The Properties dialog box for the selected folder appears.

9 Click the AutoArchive tab.

The AutoArchive tab for the selected folder appears. This is a simplified version of the AutoArchive dialog box.

10 Specify the desired AutoArchive options for the folder and click OK.

The following table lists how long items will remain in the selected folder before they are archived.

Table 11-2. AutoArchive default settings

Folder	Duration
Calendar	Six months
Deleted Items	Two months
Inbox	Six months
Journal	Six months
Sent Items	Two months
Tasks	Six months
Notes, Contacts, and Drafts	AutoArchive does not normally archive information in these folders.

QUICK REFERENCE

TO ACTIVATE AUTOARCHIVE:

1. SELECT TOOLS → OPTIONS FROM THE MENU AND SELECT THE OTHER TAB.

2. CLICK THE AUTOARCHIVE BUTTON.

3. CLICK THE RUN AUTOARCHIVE EVERY CHECKBOX TO ACTIVATE AUTOARCHIVE.

4. (OPTIONAL) ENTER THE NUMBER OF DAYS YOU WANT TO PASS BEFORE THE NEXT AUTOMATIC ARCHIVING OCCURS IN THE DAYS BOX.

5. (OPTIONAL) SELECT THE PROMPT BEFORE AUTOARCHIVE RUNS CHECKBOX IF YOU WANT TO BE NOTIFIED BEFORE AUTOARCHIVE ARCHIVES ANY ITEMS.

6. (OPTIONAL) CLICK THE BROWSE BUTTON AND SPECIFY THE NAME AND FOLDER WHERE YOU WANT TO STORE THE ARCHIVE FILES IN THE FIND PERSONAL FOLDERS DIALOG BOX.

7. CLICK OK, OK.

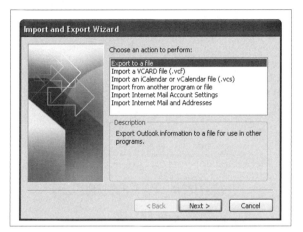

Figure 11-10. The Import and Export Wizard dialog box.

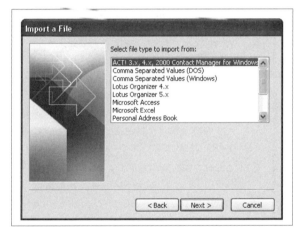

Figure 11-11. Step 2 of the Import Wizard: specifying the type of file you want to import.

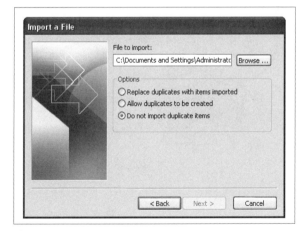

Figure 11-12. Step 3 of the Import Wizard: specifying the location of the file you want to import.

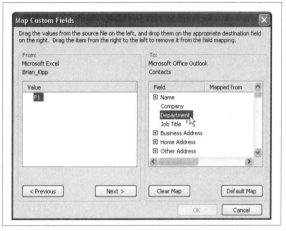

Figure 11-13. You can map the fields of the imported file to the fields in Outlook's Contacts List.

People from different countries speak different languages, just as computer programs save files in different formats. Fortunately, just like some people can speak several languages, Outlook can read and write in other file formats.

Here's how to import an external file into Outlook.

> **⹈ NOTE ⹈** *The file formats that Outlook can import and export depends on which options were selected when you installed Outlook. You can always add more file formats later—just make sure you have your installation CD handy!*

1 Select File → Import and Export **from the menu.**

The Import and Export Wizard dialog box appears, as shown in Figure 11-10.

>
> **TIP**
> *Another way to import an external data file is to right-click any empty area of the Database window and select Import from the shortcut menu.*

2 Select the Import from another program or file **option and click** Next.

The Import a File dialog box appears, as shown in Figure 11-11.

Tell Outlook what type of file you want to import.

3 Select the appropriate file format from the list and click Next.

Another Import a File dialog box appears, as shown in Figure 11-12.

Here you need select the file type you want to import.

4 Click the Browse button, and then find and double-click the file you want to import. Click Next.

Next, you have to tell Outlook where to import the information. Most of the time, this will be the Contacts folder.

5 Select the destination folder (usually Contacts) and click Next.

Confirm the information you want to import and map the fields.

6 Click the Import checkbox for each file item you want to import and click the Map Custom Fields button.

The Map Custom Fields dialog box appears, as shown in Figure 11-13.

Here comes the tricky part. Different programs may give the same fields different names. For example, Outlook has a field called "First Name," but another program may call a similar field "First." When you map a field, you tell Outlook which information goes where. For example, information in the "First" field goes in Outlook's "First Name" field.

7 Drag the values from the source file on the left, and drop them on the appropriate destination field on the right.

When you're finished mapping all the fields, move on to the next step.

‹ NOTE › *Like other Outlook menus, some of the labels on the right side of the Map Custom Fields dialog box have plus signs next to them, indicating that they contain more information that is not currently being shown.*

8 Click OK.

You're back to the Import a File dialog box.

9 Click Finish.

Outlook imports the information from the external file into the folder you specified.

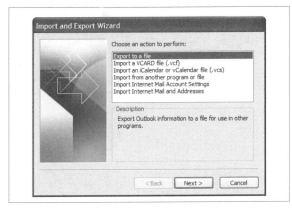

Figure 11-14. The Import and Export Wizard dialog box.

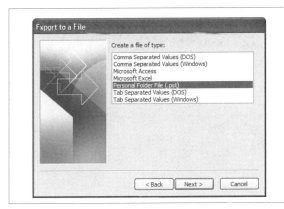

Figure 11-15. Step 2 of the Export Wizard: specifying the type of file you want to export to.

Figure 11-16. Step 3 of the Export Wizard: specifying the folder whose information you want to export.

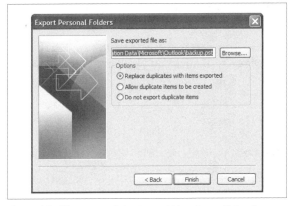

Figure 11-17. Step 4 of the Export Wizard: specifying the name and location of the information you want to export.

When you export Outlook information, you save it in a different format so that it can be understood and opened by different programs. For example, you might export your Contacts list to an Excel worksheet.

In this lesson, you will learn how to export information in an Outlook folder to an external file.

1 Select File → Import and Export **from the menu.**

The Import and Export Wizard dialog box appears, as shown in Figure 11-14.

2 Select the Export to a file **option and click** Next.

The Export to a File dialog box appears, as shown in Figure 11-15. Here is where you tell Outlook the type of file you want to export to.

3 Select the desired file format from the list and click Next.

The third step in the Export Wizard appears, as shown in Figure 11-16. Here you need to select the folder containing the data you want to export.

4 Select the folder containing the data you want to export and click Next.

The final step in the Export Wizard appears, as shown in Figure 11-17. Now you can save the exported information.

5 Specify the name and folder where you want to save the exported information. Click Next.

Remember that you can use the Browse button to navigate to the folder where you want to save the exported file.

6 Click Finish.

Outlook saves the information to the file.

Outlook can read and write to a number of different file formats. Table 11-3 lists the more common file formats that people import and/or export information to and from.

Table 11-3. Exportable file formats and extensions

File Format	Extensions
Personal Folder File	.pst
Text (Comma delimited)	.csv
Text (Tab delimited)	.txt
Microsoft Access	.mdb
Microsoft Excel	.xls, .xlt
Microsoft FoxPro	.dbf

QUICK REFERENCE

TO EXPORT INFORMATION:

1. SELECT FILE → IMPORT AND EXPORT FROM THE MENU.

2. SELECT THE EXPORT TO A FILE OPTION FROM THE LIST AND CLICK NEXT.

3. SELECT THE DESIRED FILE FORMAT FROM THE LIST AND CLICK NEXT.

4. SELECT THE FOLDER CONTAINING THE DATA YOU WANT TO EXPORT AND CLICK NEXT.

5. SPECIFY THE NAME AND FOLDER WHERE YOU WANT TO SAVE THE EXPORTED INFORMATION AND CLICK NEXT. CLICK FINISH TO COMPLETE THE WIZARD.

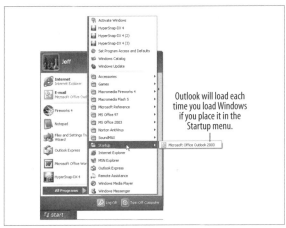

Figure 11-18. Any programs, files, or folders you place in the Startup folder in the All Programs menu will start or open automatically every time you load Windows.

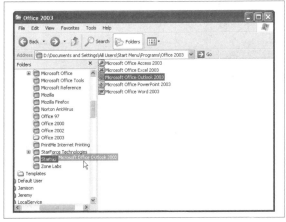

Figure 11-19. Copying an Outlook shortcut to the Startup folder.

Outlook is a program that you usually need to use on a daily basis. Since you will probably use Outlook to receive e-mail messages and remind you about appointments, it's a good idea to keep Outlook up and running all day. If you use Outlook every day, you might want to configure Microsoft Windows so that it automatically starts Outlook whenever you turn on your computer.

This lesson shows you how to launch Outlook automatically when you start Windows and how to stop it from automatically starting. Let's get started!

1 Right-click the Start button and select Open All Users from the shortcut menu.

The Start Menu window appears.

2 Double-click the Programs folder.

The contents of the Programs folder appear in the window.

The Startup folder, which is in the Programs folder, is special. Windows will automatically open anything in the Startup folder every time you turn your computer on.

To copy a shortcut of Outlook to the Startup folder, use the Folders pane.

3 Click the Folders button on the toolbar.

The window splits into two panes, displaying a hierarchical view of the Start menu's contents in the left pane.

Now you can employ the file management tasks you've learned: expand and collapse folders, and move and copy files.

4 If necessary, click the Start menu folder expand button in the left pane of the window to view its subfolders. Again in the left pane, click the Microsoft Office folder.

The contents of the Microsoft Office folder appear in the right pane of the window.

Now copy the Outlook shortcut from the Microsoft Office folder to the Startup folder in the left pane of the window.

5 Press and hold the Ctrl key as you click and drag the Microsoft Office Outlook 2003 shortcut from the the right pane to the Startup folder in the left pane, as shown in Figure 11-19.

> ⋮ NOTE ⋮ *Your copy of Outlook may be located in a subfolder of the Programs folder, making it more challenging to find.*

You've copied the Outlook program shortcut from the Programs folder to the Startup folder. Now Outlook will automatically launch every time you turn on your computer and start Windows.

If you no longer want a program to start automatically, simply delete or move the program's shortcut from the Startup folder.

6 Delete the Microsoft Office Outlook 2003 **shortcut from the Startup folder.**

This lesson is finished.

7 Close the window.

⸖ NOTE ⸖ *Try not to place programs in the Startup folder unless you really do use them every time you start Windows. Having too many programs open at the same time takes up memory and can greatly increase the amount of time it takes for Windows to start.*

QUICK REFERENCE

TO START A PROGRAM AUTOMATICALLY WHEN YOU LOAD WINDOWS:

I. RIGHT-CLICK THE START BUTTON AND SELECT OPEN ALL USERS FROM THE SHORTCUT MENU.

2. ADD THE PROGRAM, FILE, OR FOLDER TO THE STARTUP FOLDER IN THE PROGRAMS FOLDER.

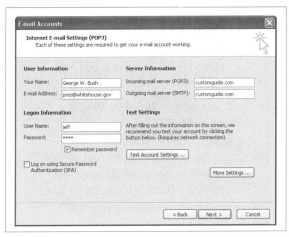

Figure 11-20. Using POP mail.

These days, it seems like everyone has an e-mail account that ends in @hotmail.com, @yahoo.com, or @juno.com. These are web-based e-mail accounts, which let you send, receive, and read your e-mail using any web browser, such as Microsoft Internet Explorer or Netscape Navigator. Most web-based e-mail services can be accessed from anywhere in the world so long as you have a computer with a connection to the Internet. The downside to free e-mail services is that they tend to be slow and have limited storage space for attachments.

While web-based e-mail accounts aren't suitable for corporate e-mail, you can buy a subscription so you can access your corporate e-mail account and view your e-mail from anywhere in the world.

Of course, you will need a web-based e-mail account set up in order to access your corporate e-mail. Once you have an account, see what kind of subscription you need to view POP mail. Then, you will need the following information to access your Outlook e-mail account:

- **Incoming Mail (POP3) Server:** The name of your POP server used for receiving incoming e-mail messages. You can get this information from your Internet service provider or LAN administrator.
- **Account Name:** Specifies your account name. This is the same as the part of your e-mail address to the left of the @ sign.

- **Password:** Your password to access your e-mail account. Since Outlook automatically enters your e-mail account for you, chances are you won't remember your password and will have to either look it up or ask your Internet service provider or LAN administrator for it. And no, your password isn't ******.

Although there are literally hundreds of web-based e-mail services out there, most people seem to use Microsoft's Hotmail or Yahoo. The procedure and cost for configuring these services to access a POP3 e-mail account varies from service to service, but this lesson will give you pointers on how to get started.

1 Get out a pen and piece of paper to write down your e-mail information.

Unless you're a network administrator or a real computer nerd, you probably don't know all your e-mail information.

2 Call your Network Administrator or Internet Service Provider and ask them for the name of your POP3 server, your e-mail account name, and password. Write this information down.

Once you have this information recorded, move on to the next step.

3 Start your web browser and go to the web-based e-mail service you want to use.

For example, if you use Hotmail as your web-based e-mail service, you would type "www.hotmail.com" in the in the Address box.

4 If you're already signed up to use the e-mail service, enter your username and password. If you're not currently signed up to use the e-mail service, find and click the Sign up now or similar link and enter the required information.

5 Find out what kind of membership you need to view POP mail, and how much it costs.

Once you're logged in to your e-mail service and have the ability to use POP mail, you can configure it to access your corporate e-mail account. Here's how:

6 Find and click an Options link or button somewhere on the web page.

The Options page of your free e-mail account lets you configure how your e-mail works, similar to Outlook's E-mail Options dialog box. Somewhere on this page, you will (hopefully) find a link or button that mentions POP Mail. This is where you need to go to configure your free e-mail service to check your corporate e-mail.

7 Find and click any link or button that mentions POP Mail.

Somewhere on this page, you will need to provide your free e-mail service with the name of your POP3 server, your account name, and your password.

8 Enter your POP3 Server name, your account name, and your password in the appropriate boxes.

For an example of a typical POP3 set-up screen, look at Figure 11-20.

Most free e-mail services won't check your POP3 e-mail accounts unless you tell them to by clicking a Check Other Mail or POP Mail link or button.

9 To check your corporate e-mail account, find and click a Check Other Mail, POP Mail, or similar link or button.

If everything is set up properly, your free e-mail service *should* be able to access your corporate e-mail account—and now you can access your e-mail from cyber cafes all over the world!

Configuring a free e-mail service to access your corporate e-mail accounts sounds like a fairly simple process—and it should be—but unfortunately, that's often not the case. Some e-mail servers use a different e-mail format or won't allow unrestricted computers to access them, and thus you won't be able to access them from Hotmail or any other e-mail service.

QUICK REFERENCE

TO ACCESS YOUR E-MAIL ON A FREE E-MAIL SERVICE:

1. CALL YOUR NETWORK ADMINISTRATOR OR INTERNET SERVICE PROVIDER AND ASK THEM FOR THE NAME OF YOUR POP3 SERVER, YOUR E-MAIL ACCOUNT NAME, AND YOUR PASSWORD. THEN WRITE THIS INFORMATION DOWN.

2. START YOUR WEB BROWSER AND GO TO THE WEB-BASED E-MAIL SERVICE YOU WANT TO USE.

3. IF YOU'RE ALREADY SIGNED UP TO USE THE E-MAIL SERVICE, ENTER YOUR USERNAME AND PASSWORD. IF YOU'RE NOT CURRENTLY SIGNED UP TO USE THE E-MAIL SERVICE, FIND AND CLICK THE SIGN UP NOW OR A SIMILAR LINK AND ENTER THE REQUIRED INFORMATION.

4. FIND THE COST AND TYPE OF SUBSCRIPTION THAT SUPPORTS POP MAIL.

5. FIND AND CLICK AN OPTIONS LINK OR BUTTON SOMEWHERE ON THE WEB PAGE.

6. FIND AND CLICK ANY LINK OR BUTTON THAT MENTIONS POP MAIL.

7. ENTER YOUR POP3 SERVER NAME, YOUR ACCOUNT NAME, AND YOUR PASSWORD IN THE APPROPRIATE BOXES.

TO ACCESS YOUR E-MAIL ON A WEB-BASED E-MAIL SERVICE:

• FIND AND CLICK A CHECK OTHER MAIL, POP MAIL, OR SIMILAR LINK OR BUTTON.

Lesson Summary

Customizing Outlook's Toolbar

To Add a Button to a Toolbar: Select Tools → Customize from the menu or right-click any toolbar and select Customize from the shortcut menu. Click the Commands tab and select the command category from the Categories list. Then find the desired command in the Commands list and drag the command onto the toolbar.

To Change a Button's Text or Image: Select Tools → Customize from the menu or right-click any toolbar and select Customize from the shortcut menu. Right-click the button and modify the text and/or image using the shortcut menu options.

Using the Tools Together

Drag an item to the appropriate button in the Navigation Pane. For example, to send an e-mail message to a contact, drag the contact to the Mail button in the Navigation Pane.

Sending Faxes

To Use the Fax Service: You must be signed up with a fax service provider, and you must have Word and Outlook 2003 installed on your computer.

To Send a Fax: Open the file you want to fax and select File → New → Internet Fax from the menu. Enter the fax information: recipient name and fax number, and a subject. Choose the type of cover sheet you want to use in the Fax Service task pane and fill it out. Click the Send button.

To Preview the Fax: Click the Preview button in the Fax Service task pane.

To Calculate Cost of Fax: Click the Calculate Cost button in the Fax Service task pane.

To Fax Multiple Files: Click the Attach button in the fax message window and attach each file you want to fax.

Manually Archiving Information

To Manually Archive Items: Select File → Archive from the menu. Ensure the Archive This Folder and all subfolders option is selected, and then select the folder that you want to archive. Click the Archive items older than

list arrow and select the date to specify how old items must be in order to be archived. (Optional) Specify the name and location of the archive file in the Archive File box. Click OK to archive the folder(s).

Retrieving Archived Items

To Retrieve Information from an Archive File: Select File → Open → Outlook Data File from the menu. Browse to the folder that contains the archive file, and then double-click the archive.pst or similar archive file. Open the Folder list by clicking the Folder List button. Click the plus symbol next to the archive folder, and then find and click the specific folder you want to view. (Optional) Click and drag the items you want to retrieve to the desired folder.

To Close an Archive File: Right-click the archive folder and select Close "Archive Folders" from the shortcut menu.

Using AutoArchive

To Activate AutoArchive: Select Tools → Options from the menu, select the Other tab, and click the AutoArchive button. Check the Run AutoArchive every checkbox to activate AutoArchive.

(Optional) Enter the number of days you want to pass before the next automatic archiving occurs in the days box. (Optional) Select the Prompt before AutoArchive runs checkbox if you want to be notified before AutoArchive archives any items.

(Optional) Click the Browse button and specify the name and folder where you want to store the archive files in the Find Personal Folders dialog box.

When you're finished, click OK, OK.

Importing Information

To Import Information: Select File → Import and Export from the menu. Select the Import from another program or file option and click Next. Select the appropriate file format from the list and click Next. Click the Browse button, then browse to, find, and double-click the file you want to import and click Next. Select the destination folder (usually Contacts) and click Next. Click the

Import checkbox and click the Map Custom Fields button. Drag the values from the source file on the left and drop them on the appropriate destination field on the right. Click OK, and then Finish.

Exporting Information

To Export Information: Select File → Import and Export from the menu. Select the Export to a file option from the list and click Next. Select the desired file format from the list and click Next. Select the folder containing the data you want to export and click Next. Specify the name and folder where you want to save the exported information and click Next. Click Finish to complete the wizard.

Starting Outlook Automatically When Windows Starts

Right-click the Start button and select Open All Users from the shortcut menu. Add the program, file, or folder to the Startup folder in the Programs folder.

Accessing Your Outlook E-mail on an E-mail Service

To Create Access To Your E-mail on a Free E-mail Service: Call your Network Administrator or Internet Service Provider and ask them for the Name of your POP3 server, your e-mail account name, and your password, and then write this information down. Start your web browser and go to the web-based e-mail service you want to use. If you're already signed up to use the e-mail service, enter your username and password. If you're not currently signed up to use the e-mail service, find and click the Sign up now or similar link and enter the required information. Find the cost and type of subscription that supports POP mail. Find and click an Options link or button somewhere on the web page. Find and click any link or button that mentions POP Mail. Enter your POP3 Server name, your account name, and your password in the appropriate boxes.

To Access Your E-mail on a Free E-mail Service: Find and click a Check Other Mail, POP Mail, or similar link or button.

Quiz

1. It seems like you're getting more junk e-mail every day and it's taking too long to wade through all those menus to access the Add Sender to Blocked Senders List command. How can you fix this problem?

   A. Add the Add Sender to Blocked Senders List command to a button on the toolbar.

   B. Create a rule that automatically deletes all your incoming e-mail.

   C. Quit filling out "Send Me More Information" forms on the Internet.

   D. Assign the add to Junk Senders List command to a macro.

2. You've just received an e-mail from someone you want to add to your Contacts list. What's the fastest way to do this?

   A. Click the Contacts button in the Navigation Pane, click the New Contact button on the toolbar, and manually enter the contact.

   B. Select the e-mail and press Ctrl + A.

   C. Drag the e-mail to the Contacts button in the Navigation Pane.

   D. Select the e-mail and click the Add to Contacts button on the toolbar.

3. By default, the AutoArchive feature automatically archives any e-mail messages older than one month. (True or False?)

4. When you archive an Outlook folder, its old information is permanently deleted and cannot be retrieved. (True or False?)

5. You want to transfer your Contact list from work onto your home computer. What's the easiest way of doing this?

   A. Back up everything on your work computer and restore it all on your home computer.

   B. Export the Contacts list to a comma-delimited text file and import it on your home computer.

C. Save the Contacts list to an Outlook Data file, open it on your home computer, open the Folders List, and move the contacts from the Outlook Data file to your Contacts List.

D. Print out a hard copy of the Contacts List, bring it home, put it in your scanner and have Outlook's OCR automatically input all the information for you.

Homework

1. Start Microsoft Outlook and open the Homework *.pst* (Outlook Data) by selecting File → Open → Outlook Data File (*.pst*) from the menu. Browse to and double-click the Homework *.pst* file.

2. Open the Folders List.

3. Select the Contacts folder under the Homework Outlook Data file.

4. Select File → Import and Export from the menu.

5. Export the information in the Homework Outlook Data file's Contact folder to a comma-separated values (Windows) file named "Export."

6. View the current AutoArchive settings.

7. Import information from an Excel spreadsheet into the Homework Outlook Data file's Contact list.

8. Select the Import from another program or file option and click Next.

9. Select Microsoft Excel from the list and click Next.

10. Browse to and double-click the Name List file.

11. Select the Contacts folder under the Homework Outlook Data file.

12. Follow the remaining onscreen instructions to import the Name List file into Outlook.

13. Close the Homework *.pst* (Outlook Data file).

Quiz Answers

1. A. Adding the Add Sender to Blocked Senders List command to the toolbar lets you access it with a single click of the mouse.

2. C. You can add an e-mail sender to your Contacts List by dragging any e-mail from them to the Contacts button in the Navigation Pane.

3. False. If the AutoArchive feature is turned on (which it may not be), Outlook will only automatically archive e-mail messages older than six months.

4. False. You can open any archive file (stored in *.pst* Outlook Data files) in Outlook.

5. C. The fastest and easiest way to transfer information between two different Outlook installations is to save the information to a *.pst* Outlook Data file.

INDEX

Colophon

Our look is the result of reader comments, our own experimentation, and feedback from distribution channels. Distinctive covers complement our distinctive approach to technical topics, breathing personality and life into potentially dry subjects.

Mary Brady was the production editor and the proofreader for *Outlook 2003 Personal Trainer*. Philip Dangler and Claire Cloutier provided quality control. Julie Hawks wrote the index.

The cover image of the comic book hero is an original illustration by Lou Brooks. The art of illustrator Lou Brooks has appeared on the covers of *Time* and *Newsweek* eight times, and his logo design for the game Monopoly is used throughout the world to this day. His work has also appeared in just about every major publication, and it has been animated for MTV, Nickelodeon, and HBO.

Emma Colby designed and produced the cover of this book with Adobe InDesign CS and Photoshop CS. The typefaces used on the cover are Base Twelve, designed by Zuzana Licko and issued by Emigre, Inc., and JY Comic Pro, issued by AGFA Monotype.

Melanie Wang designed the interior layout. Emma Colby designed the CD label. This book was converted by Andrew Savikas and Joe Wizda to FrameMaker 5.5.6 with a format conversion tool created by Erik Ray, Jason McIntosh, Neil Walls, and Mike Sierra that uses Perl and XML technologies. The typefaces are Minion, designed by Robert Slimbach and issued by Adobe Systems; Base Twelve and Base Nine; JY Comic Pro; and TheSansMono Condensed, designed by Luc(as) de Groot and issued by LucasFonts.

The technical illustrations that appear in the book were produced by Robert Romano and Jessamyn Read using Macromedia FreeHand MX and Adobe Photoshop CS.